KAREN KE

THE RESEARCH PAPER WORKBOOK

Longman English and Humanities Series
Series Editor: Lee Jacobus

THE RESEARCH PAPER WORKBOOK

Third Edition

ELLEN STRENSKI
University of California at Los Angeles

MADGE MANFRED
Mohegan Community College

Longman
New York & London

The Research Paper Workbook, Third Edition

Copyright © 1992, 1985, 1981 by Longman Publishing Group.
All rights reserved.
No part of this publication may be reproduced,
stored in a retrieval system, or transmitted
in any form or by any means, electronic, mechanical,
photocopying, recording, or otherwise,
without the prior permission of the publisher.

Longman, 10 Bank Street, White Plains, N.Y. 10606

Associated companies:
Longman Group Ltd., London
Longman Cheshire Pty., Melbourne
Longman Paul Pty., Auckland
Copp Clark Pitman, Toronto

Executive editor: Gordon T. R. Anderson
Assistant editor: David A. E. Fox
Production editor: Ann P. Kearns
Text design: Betty L. Sokol
Cover design: David Levy
Text art: Fine Line, Inc.
Production supervisor: Richard C. Bretan

Excerpts on pages 120 through 123 are from "The Great Climate Debate," by Robert M. White. Copyright © July 1990, by *Scientific American*, Inc. All rights reserved. Reprinted by permission.

0-8013-0815-1

3 4 5 6 7 8 9 10-HA-95949392

To Tren

Contents

PREFACE   xiii

INTRODUCTION   1

Research in Our Daily Lives   1
The Research Paper   2
How This Book Will Help You   3
    Articles: "It's (Yawn!) the Natural Thing to Do,"
      by Barbara Brotman   5
      "Yawning: A Homeostatic Reflex and Its Psychological
      Significance," by Heinz E. Lehmann, M.D.   8
Exercises   9
WORKSHEET 1: Exploring   11

CHAPTER 1   GETTING STARTED   13

Check the Requirements   13
Set Up a Schedule   13
Develop Possible Topics   14
Topics and Questions to Avoid   18
Exercises   19
WORKSHEET 2: Developing Topics   21

CHAPTER 2   LOCATING INFORMATION IN PRINT   23

Where to Begin   23
The Library Reference Section: Your First Step   23
Specific Constraints   23

viii   CONTENTS

    Keeping Track of Sources: Bibliography Cards   24
    Reference Works   26
    Identifying Subject Headings: Your Second Step   33
    Locating Books   34
    Bibliography Card for a Book   36
    Articles in Magazines and Journals   37
    Bibliography Card for an Article   42
    Abstracts   42
    Newspapers and Other Sources   44
    Summary of Information Sources in the Library   45
    Searching Commercial Computer Databases   46
    Assessing Potential Sources   47
    Refining Your Bibliography   48
    A Professional Shortcut (Use Caution)   50

    Exercises   51

    WORKSHEET 3: Using an Encyclopedia   55
    WORKSHEET 4: Translating Card Catalog Information   57
    WORKSHEET 5: Using Periodical Indexes   59
    WORKSHEET 6: Compiling a Preliminary Bibliography   61
    WORKSHEET 7: Annotating Your Bibliography   63

CHAPTER 3   COLLECTING FIRSTHAND INFORMATION   65

    Benefits of Firsthand Information   65
    Telephoning   67
    Writing a Letter   67
    Observing a Public Meeting or Event   69
    Conducting a Personal Interview   69
    Surveying Opinion with a Questionnaire   71

    Exercises   72

    WORKSHEET 8: Getting Firsthand Information   73

CHAPTER 4   CRITICAL READING   75

    Pre-Reading   75
    Active Reading   77
        Article: "To Trust, Perchance to Buy," by Donald J. Moine   79
    Techniques for Reading Difficult Material   83
    Post-Reading   85
    Paraphrasing   86
    Summarizing   88
    Comparing and Contrasting   92

Evaluating 93
Exercises 96

CHAPTER 5 — PLANNING AND PROPOSING A RESEARCH STRATEGY — 107

Aiming at a Thesis of Your Own 108
Writing a Statement of Intent 111
Sample Statement of Intent 112
Writing a Proposal 114
Sample Proposal 115
Exercises 117
WORKSHEET 9: Proposing a Strategy 125

CHAPTER 6 — WRITING PAPERS BASED ON READING — 127

Writing a Summary 127
    Article: "High-Tech House Arrest," by Keenen Peck 133
Sample Summary 140
Writing a Comparison/Contrast Paper 142
Sample Comparison/Contrast Paper 144
Writing an Academic Argument 146
Sample Argumentative Paper 151
Writing a Reaction Paper 154
    Articles: "A Nonbearing Account," by Noel Perrin 161
    "Can We Buy Our Way Out of Overpopulation?"
    by Marilyn Gardner 166
Sample Reaction Paper 168
Exercises 171

CHAPTER 7 — ORGANIZING YOUR RESEARCH — 173

Taking Notes 173
Avoiding Plagiarism 178
Sample Note Cards 179
A Set of Sample Note Cards for One Article 180
    Article: "Whose Life Is It, Anyway?" by Jack Rosenberger 181
Revising Your Note Cards 186
Working toward a Provisional Outline 188
Making the Outline 191
Sample Sentence Outline 192
Sample Topic Outline 192

Exercises   193
WORKSHEET 10: Taking Notes   201
WORKSHEET 11: Provisional Outline   203

CHAPTER 8 DRAFTING AND REVISING YOUR PAPER   205

Drafts   205
Constructing Paragraphs   206
Incorporating and Acknowledging Sources   209
Providing Transitions and Signal Words   215
Preparing an Abstract   218
The Introduction   219
The Conclusion   221
The Title   222
Your Rough Draft   223
Using a Listener   223
Revising   223

Exercises   225

WORKSHEET 12: Peer Evaluation   227
WORKSHEET 13: Self-evaluation of Draft   229

CHAPTER 9 DOCUMENTING YOUR SOURCES   231

The Purpose of Documentation   231
What Needs Documenting?   232
Methods of Documentation: An Overview   233
Comparative Models: Note, MLA, and APA   236
Formatting a Final Draft: Note System   249
Formatting a Final Draft: Parenthesis System, MLA   251
Formatting a Final Draft: Parenthesis System, APA   253
Number System: A Variation of the Parenthesis System   255
Summary of Major Systems of Documentation   257

Exercises   258

WORKSHEET 14: Documentation   261

Final Checklist   263

CHAPTER 10 SAMPLE RESEARCH PAPERS   265

Illustration of the Note System   266
   Sample Paper: "Redress: From the Congressional Floor to the Hearts of the Japanese Americans," by Kevin M. Uriu   266

Illustration of the Parenthesis System (MLA Style)   279
   Sample Paper: "Breakfast Cereal: Fact and Fantasy,"
      by Brandy Graves   279
Illustration of the Parenthesis System (APA Style)   287
   Sample Paper: "Hypnosis: What's in a Name?"
      by Sylvia Jefferson   287

ANTHOLOGY: A Conversation about Our Use and Abuse
of Animals   301

Introduction   301
Contents of the Anthology   303
   "**Why Worry about the Animals?**" by Jean Bethke Elshtain   304
   "**Animal Rights,**" by Molly O'Neill   312
   "**Am I Blue? . . .**" by Alice Walker   316
   "**What's Wrong with Animal Rights?**"
      by Barbara Grizzuti Harrison   320
   "**At Issue: Does Conservation Justify Keeping Animals in Zoos?**"
      Editorial Research Reports   322
   "**The Facts about Animal Research,**" by Robert J. White   324
   "**Better Health Care Doesn't Justify Animal Research,**"
      by Kenneth L. Feder and Michael Alan Park   329

INDEX   331

Preface

This text is designed primarily for students who have had little or no experience in writing a research paper and who may be working in a variety of libraries. Many parts of the book can also be used profitably by students at more advanced levels.

We began by asking: What do students need to know in order to successfully complete a research paper assignment? After a task analysis, we then searched for materials that would appeal to students of differing abilities, ages, and aspirations; created exercises that would allow students to practice the skills in a purposeful sequence; and provided worksheets that would enable the instructor to monitor the students' progress. The text is comprehensive and clear enough so that students can use this book on their own, spending as little time on each section as their previous training requires. However, there is enough material in the book to allow its use as a text for a semester-long sequence of assignments that culminate in a research paper.

The Research Paper Workbook has been extensively tested in the classroom. We are grateful to our students and colleagues for their cooperation and suggestions, which have made this a much better book than we could have created on our own. In particular we want to thank Theresa Ammirati, John Bassinger, Jim Coleman, John Roche, Gabriella Schlesinger, Mike Sullivan, Louise Walkup, Linda Crootof, David Henry, Irving Kirsch, Lisa Lebduska, Walter Nott, Sue Lyons, Rosemary Adams, Kriss Beveridge, and Vicky Wetherell. Inspiration for parts of the text comes from Shelley Phipps, librarian at the University of Arizona. Diane Zwemer and Raymond Soto, librarians at UCLA, and Marc Gittelsohn, librarian at the University of California, San Diego, helped us with material in Chapter 2. Our editor, Lee Jacobus, who encouraged us through the completion of this work, deserves our special thanks. And we very gratefully and fondly dedicate this edition to the memory of Gordon T. R. Anderson, Executive Editor at Longman from 1977 until his untimely death in 1990.

There are a number of changes in this third edition. We have elaborated the documentation chapter, providing a wealth of examples for the MLA, APA, and Chicago note systems. There is also a brief explanation of the number system used in many of the sciences. Apart from updating the technical aspects of writing a research paper, we have significantly expanded the section on critical reading, the mastery of which we believe to be a precondition for successful research. This edition now includes substantial guidance on writing preliminary papers: a proposal, summary, comparison/contrast, argument, and reaction paper. We have also included an anthology of readings, "A Conversation about Our Use and Abuse of Animals," which can be used for class exercises including a short, controlled research paper. These additions reflect the book's comprehensive reach, which includes not just technical details, but the active engagement with texts that all good research demands.

The accompanying *Instructor's Manual* supports in a systematic way instructors and librarians who assist students with research projects. It provides such help as a model syllabus and gives not only the answers to the exercises but the rationale behind them.

Introduction

RESEARCH IN OUR DAILY LIVES

Any alert human being is constantly engaged in research, that is, in finding information about an interesting topic. The subject may be how to tune an engine, choose the right kind of insurance, or travel on a limited budget. Perhaps you want to know the best way to finance a college education. The sources you consult may include manuals, pamphlets, TV programs, or competent friends. Frequently you have to combine information from a couple of sources or decide on the best authority if you receive conflicting directions or opinions. In the process of gathering information and sorting it out, you transform the material; you make it your own in some special way, and you become a source who can share knowledge with others.

In certain situations, it is important to know how to present your findings in a formal way. For example, suppose you learn that developers are proposing to build an industrial park very close to your home. They claim it will lower taxes and increase jobs. But will it? You engage in a bit of research and discover that most employees will be transferred from another plant and that taxes are likely to increase because of greater road use and the demand for additional town services. At this point you can mutter and gripe to your friends and neighbors. However, if you want to have an impact, you must reach a larger audience—and this means writing. It means presenting the facts in a persuasive manner and documenting the sources of your information so that people will trust your data.

Most good writing—whether it is a news or feature story in the daily paper, a televised documentary, or even a novel—has been carefully researched. A skilled writer knows that to get and keep someone's attention the material must have the "ring of truth," which comes from believable details.

THE RESEARCH PAPER

The formal research paper also presents information and aims to convince its readers. However, the academic community is a specialized audience. Professors and researchers at colleges and universities have established certain procedures for conducting their work and reporting it. Research papers must follow these expectations about method and format in order to persuade readers. Primary research involves original experiments, observation or analysis of texts such as historical documents or literary works. A key principle of the method is that knowledge is advanced by asking small, answerable questions—in other words, by narrowing the study to a specific aspect of a broader subject. For example, there is a great deal that is not understood about hypnosis. A psychologist might decide to investigate the specific question of whether a certain technique would increase a person's susceptibility to hypnosis. After reading the research that had already been done in this area, the psychologist would create a hypothesis or informed hunch about what would happen if an experiment was conducted. The conclusions reached after analyzing the results of the experiment would then be stated as a thesis or main idea that the researcher would prove in a written report. Reports on primary research are published in scholarly and professional journals.

At this stage of your career, you are considered an apprentice scholar and will be concerned mostly with secondary research, which means finding out what the recognized authorities on a particular subject have to say about a topic that has caught your interest. Two types of research paper are commonly assigned in college: the *report* and the *thesis*. In a report you must condense, synthesize, and organize information to present an up-to-date account of a topic. For example, you might do a report on the different types of solar heating systems. In a thesis paper you must go beyond summary of the facts and present an analysis of the information and conclusions that you have reached about the topic. For example, in researching solar heating you might draw conclusions about the practicality of solar heating for the middle-income family or the need for tax incentives to encourage installation of solar heating. In effect, a thesis paper is an extended argument to support conclusions that you have reached after an open-minded investigation of your topic. Although we will illustrate the skills involved in writing a report, the emphasis will be on the thesis because it is the more difficult of the two papers to write.

The research paper is often assigned to undergraduates because it serves so many purposes. First, it teaches you to be an independent learner rather than just a passive recipient of information that is given in class. You learn how to locate information in and outside of the library. You learn about the complexity of a subject by going beyond the surface generalizations. As you write your research paper, you practice the ways of thinking and writing that are characteristic of the academic community. Sample research papers are presented, starting on page 263, and previewing them as soon as possible will help to give you an idea of the range of styles and formats.

HOW THIS BOOK WILL HELP YOU

The written paper is only the last step in a process, and it is that process we want to stress in this book. Much of the anxiety associated with the research paper can be alleviated by breaking the task down into manageable steps and building on the skills that you have already developed. The step-by-step system presented in this book was developed to help you overcome the common pitfalls. We cannot guarantee a solution to all the problems you will face, but we do think that this book will improve your outlook and skills.

The first difficulty that students encounter with a research paper is getting started. We will help you plan a schedule, show you a variety of methods for developing topics, and acquaint you with a spectrum of interesting questions. The second hurdle, finding information on your subject, will seem less difficult because we will be helping you to locate information right from the start. Furthermore, the steps required to complete the research paper will be spread over a long enough period of time so that you will be able to request materials if they are not immediately available. To be honest, the difficulty of tracking down materials can be the most frustrating aspect of writing a research paper, but the detective work involved can also be fun.

Taking good notes, then sorting and organizing them, can seem like an overwhelming task, but we will show you how the initial investment of time in setting up an organized system of note-taking will save you many hours when it comes to organizing the materials. In fact, the system described in this book will foster organizational skills from the very beginning.

Documentation and the technical aspects of form cause some students undue panic. Relax! There is no need to memorize all the rules; you will become familiar with the key ingredients as we go along. When the time comes to write your paper, you will be able to consult the appropriate models in the book. If you have access to a computer, there are word processing programs that make the technical aspects of writing a research paper much easier. Basically, there are two formats: <u>one which inserts information within the text of your paper by using parentheses</u>; the other which places separate footnotes either at the bottom of the page or at the back of the paper. Both formats also include a list of the sources that were used in your paper. Every academic discipline uses a version of one of these two formats. The best approach is to learn the two basic formats. As you continue in your studies, you can consult the professional journals in your major. You can then model your papers to follow the documentation style of that discipline.

If you are one of those students who dread papers because you hate to write, all we can say is *you are not alone.* Even professionals admit that getting the words down on paper is difficult. Rarely do the words flow; more often, writing is a matter of discipline, of sitting down and forcing out imperfect ideas that will have to be revised later. What we put on paper strikes us like a candid photo taken at an unflattering moment. The ideas seem so much more impressive in our heads than they do in black and white. Yet, practice in the process of composition can bring satisfaction. This book will give you that practice by breaking the research paper into manageable steps. At each step you will receive advice from your instructor; this will eliminate the feeling that you are floundering. There will be ample time to correct mistakes *before* you hand in the final draft.

Much of your dissatisfaction will fade because our approach assumes that your first efforts will be rough and that your ideas need time to evolve. This is a research paper that cannot be written the night before it is due. The step-by-step approach will foster a natural evolution of your ideas. The paper will grow by stages into a carefully crafted work that you will be proud to hand in.

Too often students regard the research paper as an academic ritual of patching together a bunch of information and dressing it up with footnotes and a bibliography. And perhaps that attitude is justified by the way research papers are sometimes assigned at the beginning of the term and then barely mentioned again until they are due. Our premise is that research springs from a fundamental human curiosity about the world, a desire to learn the hows and whys of what goes on around us. The formal research paper developed as a means of sharing information with others, which is also a common impulse. We hope this book will make sense of the form so that the excitement of learning will not be spoiled by apprehension about technical matters.

To conclude this chapter, here is a feature article that reports on research into a universal human act—yawning. It is a good illustration of the way in which people become involved in research and some of the problems they encounter. The newspaper article is followed by a short selection from the medical journal in which the research was originally reported. Comparing it with the newspaper article will give you a sense of the difference in style and format between material written for a mass audience and research papers written for professional journals.

IT'S (YAWN!) THE NATURAL THING TO DO

Barbara Brotman

This very morning, you probably pandiculated. The back of your jaws began making their intentions clear; your mouth began to gape wide: you took a deep breath; maybe your ears popped; you stretched your whole body; and then you exhaled with a sigh.

You yawned and stretched. Or, from the Latin verb *pandiculari*, to stretch oneself, you pandiculated.

And you weren't alone. Millions of people start their day with a yawn. They often approach the end of their day with a yawn. They liberally sprinkle the times in between with yawns, especially if they happen to attend political rallies or try to read Karl Marx in the original.

Dogs yawn. Cats yawn, a fact which cannot escape you if the cat in question has just quaffed a liver-and-fish-flavored lunch. Crocodiles yawn, and not just to measure the oral fit of a prospective dinner. Turtles and birds yawn. Babies yawn, and they haven't seen nearly enough of the world to be world-weary.

The garden-variety yawn has been described as "halfway between a reflex and an expressive movement." Or as "an indirect vasomotor adjustment furthering the circulation in the lungs and brain."

But the precise reason we yawn is one of life's mysteries, along with the size of the universe and the duration of eternity.

We yawn when we're sleepy; but we stop when we're in bed ready for sleep. We yawn when we're bored or inactive.

We also sometimes yawn when we're sick. Yawning may accompany diabetic coma, kidney disease, asthma, epilepsy, brain tumors, withdrawal from opium dependence, stroke, or large doses of sedatives.

Doctors become alarmed if a patient with a brain hemorrhage starts to yawn; it indicates the patient's brain is dangerously low on oxygen. On the other hand, yawning is a good sign in patients who are convalescing, especially from infectious diseases.

Most people assume yawning is the body's way of taking a good, deep breath to rev up the circulation. They're wrong. In fact, a yawn is followed by a temporary cessation of breathing, called apnea, that undoes any metabolic good the yawn might have done. Besides, if the body wanted to take in lots of oxygen, there's a much more efficient way of doing it—hyperventilation.

Copyright © 1980 Chicago Tribune. Reprinted by permission. All rights reserved.

No, yawning is a physiological mistake, a vestigial reflex that has outlived its original usefulness, according to Dr. Heinz Lehmann, a professor of psychiatry at McGill University in Montreal. He has traced the evolution of the yawn, and he points out that it was an extremely useful mechanism for prehistoric man.

Australopithecus didn't reach for a gin and tonic when he needed a lift, and other drugs were just a gleam beneath Stone Man's beetle brow, so their bodies did what they could. When prehistoric man needed extra energy, his mouth gaped open and his muscles, from the jaw to the throat to the muscles that move the bones of the inner ear, to the diaphragm, all constricted, pressing into the blood vessels of the neck. He yawned and stretched. He pandiculated.

For just a moment, that pressure on the neck's blood vessels prevents some blood from flowing out of the brain back down to the heart. Instead, Lehmann says, blood accumulates in the brain, giving it just a little more oxygen, a little more energy.

And in the old days, when Paleolithic mommies admonished their children to act their age, not their cubic inch brain measurement, that was enough. When the yawn was over, blood coursed even more forcefully through the veins; circulation momentarily improved, and cave man perked right up and clubbed his dinner.

Alas, those days are gone. A momentary soaking in blood may be enough even today to jolt a crocodile's energies, but not your modern dog, cat, or human. Bug-eyed from streams of coffee and heaps of sugar, we modern humans need more than a yawn to help us club our dinner.

"But man has done something very interesting," Lehmann explained, warming to the ground where few medical researchers have trod. "He has taken the reflex and made it into a means of expression."

We yawn now to express ourselves, he said, just as we laugh or cry. We yawn to tell somebody he is a bore—"An unconscious expression of hostility," Lehmann calls it, and we yawn to express fatigue.

We do it for all the world as if our bodies thought yawning would help. It doesn't, of course; our bodies, in this case, are wrong, Lehmann says.

Just as we yawn to wake up, we also yawn to reestablish contact with reality. That's why you see people yawn when they leave a movie theater, leaving one reality for another. That's why it's a good sign if a psychotic person yawns: It shows he is trying to maintain contact with the outside world, and probably is in an accessible mood.

For the same reason, Lehmann said, a yawning audience should hardly dismay a speaker. "Those who yawn are at least making some effort to follow him," Lehmann wrote recently in an article published in the *Bulletin of the Menninger Clinic*. "The others may be letting their thoughts wander unchecked or may be asleep with their eyes open."

But a good thing can go too far. A person who yawns too widely may dislocate his jaw. And there have been mysterious cases in which people have yawned for up to two months, a condition known in earlier times as "chasmodia." Lehmann says such paroxysms of yawning are hysterical reactions.

Still, yawning is extremely contagious even for the ordinarily calm; no one really knows why.

And Lehmann says that if someone imitates your yawning, you should take it as a compliment. "We only follow a yawning suggestion by someone who has aroused our interest," even subconsciously and even through such superficial means as eye-catching clothing or an unusual gesture.

"It's a very complex body language," he said. "If I made a motion in a committee, and I know certain people have yawned when I yawned, I know they will be with me."

Lehmann made his own investigation into yawning 35 years ago because he was annoyed when people yawned at him. He also was amused at the descriptions of yawning in physiology textbooks.

As a young doctor working in a psychiatric hospital, he noticed that the hospital patients didn't yawn. He observed people on buses, in restaurants, and at scientific meetings, and decided that something wasn't right.

The next thing he knew, he recalls, he was spending time in medical libraries and administering sedatives to groups of patients to see why some were stimulated to yawn and not others.

"My paper was rejected by two journal editors because it wasn't scientific enough," Lehmann says now. "It was too philosophical."

But a colleague who heard Lehmann speak of it 10 years ago thought it was an ideal way to prove to his technology-spoiled students that good research could be done with no expensive technology at all.

"I had lost all the references; it was difficult to get it together again," Lehmann said. Still, this time he got the paper published.

YAWNING

A Homeostatic Reflex and Its Psychological Significance

Heinz E. Lehmann, M.D. *

Here is the first page from the journal article that Dr. Lehmann wrote for a professional audience.

Yawning is a common phenomenon that is an expression of certain physiological and psychological states, yet it has received remarkably little attention in the medical literature. Dumpert (1921), Hauptmann (1920), and Lewy (1921) reached some conclusions regarding the nature of yawning in connection with observations of patients with encephalitis lethargica; however, after the 1920s the subject was again disregarded. On the basis of certain clinical and experimental observations which may have some psychiatric significance and which, to my knowledge, have not yet been described, a review of the matter of yawning appeared justified.

Physiological Aspects of Yawning

Physiology textbooks furnish scanty information regarding the nature of yawning. Under a common heading with laughing, crying, sighing, coughing, and sneezing, yawning is usually described as a modified respiratory movement, characterized by a prolonged inspiration with wide open mouth followed by shorter expiration and often associated with stretching movements of the muscles of the trunk and extremities.

Phylogenetically and ontogenetically, yawning is an old phenomenon. Dogs, cats, and even crocodiles yawn; turtles and birds show movements resembling yawning (Vischer 1959). Yawning and stretching seem to be intimately associated in their phylogenetic origins. Although lower mammals stretch without yawning, they almost never yawn without stretching. In man, stretching is also probably an essential part of the yawning act but is often voluntarily suppressed. The early ontogenetic occurrence of yawning is confirmed by the observation that infants yawn when only a few days old (Preyer 1923).

*Professor of Psychiatry, McGill University, Montreal, Quebec, Canada.
Copyright © 1979 Menninger Clinic. First page of article and references (p. 51) from *Bulletin of the Menninger Clinic*, 43(2), 1979, 123–138. Reprinted by permission.

EXERCISES

Good research begins with curiosity and a genuine desire to answer some questions prompted by your observation or reflection. In the article "It's (Yawn!) The Natural Thing To Do," Barbara Brotman reports on research conducted by Dr. Lehmann, who as a young man became curious about why we yawn. Following Brotman's article, which was published in a daily newspaper, is the first page of Dr. Lehmann's original paper, which was published in a medical journal. Read both before you respond to these questions:

A. Dr. Lehmann's research
   1. Why did Dr. Lehmann begin to investigate yawning?
   2. How did he gather information? Did he conduct primary research? secondary research?
   3. What surprising conclusion did he reach about the reason why we yawn?
   4. Why did he have trouble getting his research published?
   5. Why was he encouraged to resubmit the paper many years after it was rejected?
   6. Who might benefit from the research he conducted? Are there practical aspects to the research?
   7. Did Dr. Lehmann solve the question of why we yawn?
B. Barbara Brotman's article
   1. What research do you think Brotman did before writing this article?
   2. What aspects about her reading audience did she have to keep in mind while writing the article? For instance, how is the reader of a newspaper different from the reader of a textbook?
   3. How does she begin the article in a way that will catch the reader's interest?
   4. Does the article explain what is meant by the title? In what ways is yawning a "natural thing to do"? Can you think of some other catchy, yet informative, titles for this article?
   5. How have people turned yawning into a form of body language?
   6. Does Brotman use any names or terms that are unfamiliar to you? How would you find out more about them?
   7. Complete a brief summary of the article by filling in the blanks with wording of your own:

In "It's (Yawn!) The Natural Thing To Do," Barbara Brotman reports on the research of Dr. Heinz Lehmann, who began to study yawning when _____ . After gathering information by _____ _____ and _____ , Dr. Lehmann concluded that _____ . He believes that humans have "taken the reflex and made it into a means of expression." For example, the yawn can express _____ or _____ . Although he had difficulty in getting his paper published when he was a young doctor, _____ .

C. Dr. Lehmann's original paper
   1. How is the reading audience of a professional journal different from the audience of a newspaper?
   2. What different techniques do Lehmann and Brotman use to help their readers understand what they are saying and to convince these readers that they are right?
   3. What seems different about the style, tone, and format of the original paper?
   4. What difference is there between the way that Lehmann cites his sources of information and the format that Brotman uses?
D. Read one or more of the Anthology selections listed below and explain what you think might have happened in the writer's life to trigger the need to research and write. In other words, what do you think was the real life stimulus for the pieces of writing?
   1. "Animal Rights"
   2. "Am I Blue? . . ."
   3. "What's Wrong with Animal Rights?"
   4. "The Facts about Animal Research"
   5. "Better Health Care Doesn't Justify Animal Research"

Worksheet 1 _____ **EXPLORING**

Name _____   Date _____

1. Are there any reflex actions, such as sneezing or scratching, that would be fun to investigate?
2. Have you observed any human behaviors, social conditions, or natural events that make you curious?
3. What questions can you ask about the following observations?
Example:

Observation	*Question*
Many students come from one-parent families.	How well do students from one-parent families perform in school?

Observation — *Question*

a. Many factories are closing in my state.

a.

b. Quite a few athletes take performance-enhancing drugs.

b.

c. TV shows contain many violent episodes.

c.

d. Many unwed teenagers seem to be having babies.

d.

e. Smoking is being banned in many public places.

e.

f. Many businesses now offer stress management programs to their employees.

f.

CHAPTER 1

Getting Started

CHECK THE REQUIREMENTS

Before you begin to search for a topic you should make sure you have all the details of the assignment. The requirements in each class will vary; therefore, you must always check the instructor's specifications.

1. What type of paper is required: report? thesis? primary research?
2. Is the topic assigned or limited in any way?
3. Is there a suggested number of sources to be consulted?
4. Are certain sources required or prohibited?
5. Are there any special requirements: an interview? a survey? a case study? an observation? an experiment?
6. Is there a minimum or maximum length?
7. What documentation style is required?
8. When is the final draft due?
9. What are the due dates for the preliminary stages of the paper?

SET UP A SCHEDULE

Regardless of whether your instructor requires preliminary materials to check your progress, you should set deadlines for completing each stage of the research process. Generally, the most time-consuming steps are locating the information you need and taking notes on your reading. You must allow ample time to get materials through interlibrary loan if your college library does not have what you need.

Schedule

COMPLETION DATE	TASK
_____	1. Develop possible topics.
_____	2. Undertake preliminary search for sources.
_____	3. Write proposal.
_____	4. Read and take notes.
_____	5. Create provisional thesis and outline.
_____	6. Prepare draft(s) of paper.
_____	7. Do final revision and bibliography.

DEVELOP POSSIBLE TOPICS

The topics that you develop must relate to the course in which the paper is required and must fit the guidelines provided by your instructor, particularly the directions which indicate whether the paper should be a report or a thesis. The THESIS paper requires you to interpret and draw conclusions; therefore your topic must be one that leaves room for analysis. For example, if you were interested in mortgages and wished to prepare a REPORT on that topic, you might ask: What types of mortgages are available? However, if you had to do a THESIS, you would want to rephrase the question to give it an argumentative edge: Are middle-class families being squeezed out of the housing market? You are looking for a topic where there is some difference of opinion among the experts, but a difference that is grounded in facts.

Depending on the course you are taking, one or more of the following suggestions will be helpful to you.

1. *Survey the course syllabus and textbooks.* Chapter headings or subdivisions may suggest topics such as inflation (economics), sibling rivalry (psychology), immigration laws (history), or search and seizure (law enforcement). Suggestions for further reading are often listed at the end of a chapter.

2. *Browse through magazines in the bookstore or library.* Most college libraries and bookstores carry an assortment of periodicals, everything from mass audience magazines such as *Time* and *Newsweek*, to popular magazines aimed at special audiences such as *Forbes*, to professional journals such as *Journal of Consulting and Clinical Psychology*. Somewhere within that selection are articles that you would enjoy reading and which might spark a research question. For example, spotting an article titled "Growing Up Scared" could lead to a research question about the impact of violence on children; or "The Facts about Animal Research" might suggest the issue of using animals in medical research.

3. *Skim through the subject headings in an index that lists articles published in periodicals.* There are indexes for popular magazines, such as *Readers' Guide,* and specialized indexes for academic disciplines, such as the *Humanities Index.* The procedure for using these indexes and the comparable computerized data bases is explained in Chapter 2. Examining an index will not only give you ideas for topics but will let you know how many articles have been published on a particular topic in a given year. A related source is an abstract, a compilation of brief summaries of articles and papers that have been presented during the year by researchers in a specific field.

4. *Brainstorm with classmates, friends, and family.* Discuss topics that you know something about, ones that you wish you knew about, ones that have been written about frequently.

5. *Brainstorm for questions.* Learning to ask questions is essential to research. Questions are a way of activating our curiosity and getting us really interested in a topic. Later, when reading sources, questions help us to focus on the information that we need to record. How do you get research questions? Where do they come from? To begin with, you can draw on your own experience. When we are relaxing with friends, we spend most of our time talking about three things: *people, places, and events.* We can use this interest, apparently built into all of us, to make up questions. For example, take a topic such as animals. Begin by asking all the questions that you can think of about *people* you associate with the topic:

> How difficult is it to become a *veterinarian?*
> What techniques do *animal trainers* use?
> Why have *Frank Perdue's* marketing techniques been so successful?

Then make up questions about *places* associated with the topic:

> How are *nursing homes* using pets?
> Are *zoos* good or bad for wild animals?
> Can *laboratories* conduct research without using animals?

Next, try to create questions about *events* associated with the topic:

> Does the *circus* exploit animals?
> How do *pet shows* set fashion?
> How has the *decrease in wetlands* affected migratory birds?

Here is another useful list to generate questions:

> *Cause and effect* (What caused X or why did X happen? What will X lead to?) For example, why do we have a taboo against eating some animals, such as the dog, which are eaten by people in other cultures?
> *Comparison and contrast* (How is X similar to or different from Y?) For example, do vegetarians and animal rights activists share a similar set of values?

Analysis (What does X consist of?) For example, what are the strategies that animal rights activists have used?

Process (How does X occur or work?) For example, how did the animal rights movement develop?

6. *Consider topics that other students have found interesting.* In case the suggestions above do not lead you to possible topics, here is a list of questions based on topics that students have researched in the past. We have grouped the questions by subject area, but some questions might fit into more than one field of study. Many of the questions would need to be made more specific in order to fit the requirements of your instructor.

THE ARTS (FILM, DANCE, LITERATURE, MUSIC, AND THE VISUAL ARTS)
a. What were the major influences on a particular artist, writer, composer, director, or musician?
b. How did the public respond to the work of a particular artist, writer, or musician?
c. How was a particular style or element used by an artist, writer, or musician?
d. What controversies or debates are there about the meaning or significance of a particular work?
e. What is the role of the arts in a society?
f. Is censorship ever justifiable?
g. How is the artistic value or monetary worth of an art work determined?
h. How was a particular group of people (women, minorities) portrayed in the work of a particular artist or period?

BUSINESS
a. Have employment opportunities increased for certain groups (youth, minorities, women, handicapped)?
b. Does the small, independent business have a future in the United States?
c. Should the regulations governing unemployment compensation, affirmative action, or the minimum wage be changed?
d. Are Japanese management practices more effective than ours?
e. Will a unified European market benefit the American economy?
f. How do employers screen potential employees?
g. Has the power of labor unions declined in the United States?
h. What factors contributed to the success or failure of a particular advertising campaign?

EDUCATION
a. How are children with learning disabilities being helped?
b. What is the school's role in dealing with domestic violence?
c. Should private schools be tax-exempt?
d. Does gender affect academic success in certain subjects?
e. Does bilingual education enhance achievement?

f. How did the Montessori Method influence early childhood education?
g. Do college sports exploit student athletes?
h. What changes have taken place in the teaching of a particular subject (reading, writing, math, etc.)?

HEALTH FIELDS
a. Are Americans overmedicated?
b. What progress is being made in treating a particular disease (AIDS, Alzheimer's, etc.)?
c. Why should we be concerned about food additives?
d. Are the claims of health benefits from certain foods or exercise programs exaggerated?
e. How should expensive medical procedures be financed?
f. How has the medical profession been affected by the increase in law suits?
g. Is alcoholism a disease?
h. How can we reduce teen suicide?

NATURAL SCIENCES (BOTANY, BIOLOGY, CHEMISTRY, ECOLOGY, ETC.)
a. What are the moral implications of genetic research?
b. Has any progress been made in the control of acid rain?
c. What is the impact of diminishing forests?
d. Are humans overpopulating the earth?
e. How will we dispose of toxic waste?
f. How certain is the evidence of global warming?
g. How is a certain factor contributing to the pollution of the atmosphere, a body of water, or an area of land?
h. Will we ever be able to accurately predict earthquakes or volcanoes?

SOCIAL SCIENCES
a. Why are some people attracted to religious sects?
b. Is the jury system overburdened?
c. Are IQ tests racially slanted?
d. Are the legal rights of the mentally ill and retarded adequately protected?
e. Should juvenile offenders be punished more severely?
f. How should our legal system deal with the insanity plea?
g. Have Political Action Committees distorted the political process?
h. Why do women and ethnic minorities still face barriers in getting elected to public office?

TECHNOLOGY
a. Can air travel be made safer?
b. How is the computer affecting the workplace?
c. How is the computer affecting education?
d. Have we lost control over the use of medical technology?
e. Have satellites improved the accuracy of weather forecasts?

f. What dangers are posed by computer crimes?
g. Are building codes impeding the application of new technologies?
h. What are the latest developments in the creation of artificial intelligence?

ADDITIONAL IDEAS

Consult this book, which was prepared by a reference librarian: Kathryn Lamm, *10,000 Ideas for Term Papers, Projects, and Reports,* 2d ed. (New York: Prentice Hall, 1987).

TOPICS AND QUESTIONS TO AVOID

Some questions are unsuitable as research questions because they can be answered with a factual statement: How many manned flights to the moon have taken place? Who invented polio vaccine? Other questions are unsuitable because they fall at the opposite extreme; they are impossible to answer given the current state of knowledge: Is there life after death? Are UFO's evidence of extraterrestrial life? In between these extremes lies a spectrum of suitable questions, ones that give you the opportunity to analyze and synthesize information.

Some questions or topics may be too broad or too narrow to meet your instructor's requirements. For example, a topic such as censorship is probably too broad. You would need to narrow the topic to a particular time, place, and issue such as censorship of rock lyrics in contemporary America. On the other hand, it is possible to start with a topic that is actually too narrow in the sense that not enough sources are available. A good research paper must be based on more than just one or two main sources.

Avoid topics and questions that elicit strong personal opinions and about which you already have a bias. A research project should be approached with as much objectivity and open-mindedness as you can muster. Consequently, writing about the morality of certain issues, such as abortion, may be inappropriate. Often there are suitable research questions that can be asked about controversial topics. For example, it might be possible to research the psychological effects of abortion. Of course, there is no way that a person can be completely unbiased. We are not always aware of our own predisposition to look at issues from a certain slant. The very choice of a topic implies a set of values that says one topic is more important than another. Nevertheless, it is important to aim for the greatest amount of objectivity possible.

Avoid topics and questions that are worn out by overexposure in the media. At any given time, there are certain issues that catch public attention. Although the topics may be interesting to you, your instructor may be tired of reading papers on the same subject. If you use the techniques we have suggested, you will generate a sizeable list of possible topics. Through consultation with your instructor, you will be able to discard those topics which are unsuitable.

EXERCISES

A. Evaluate the questions below. Which would make good research questions? Would some be better for a report than a thesis? Can you detect any bias in the questions? If the question is not a suitable research question, try to improve on it.
   1. What is plea bargaining?
   2. What is the highest mountain peak in the continental United States?
   3. What causes obesity?
   4. How can "goonism" in professional hockey be controlled?
   5. Why is modern art such a fake?
   6. What can be done about teenage alcohol addiction?
   7. What is the hospice movement?
   8. Why has the United States lagged behind other industrialized nations in providing affordable day care?
   9. Why is euthanasia wrong?
   10. Should we regulate the type of advertising on children's TV programs?

B. For each of the following topics, make up a question you associate with a person (or people), a place, and an event.
   1. Physical fitness
      a. A person (who?) _____
      b. A place (where?) _____
      c. An event (what?) _____
   2. Television news
      a.
      b.
      c.
   3. Medicine
      a.
      b.
      c.
   4. The environment
      a.
      b.
      c.
   5. Children
      a.
      b.
      c.

C. For each of the topics above, try to make up questions about cause and effect, comparison and contrast, analysis, and process.

D. The following topics are too broad. For each topic, list three more specific aspects that would be more suitable for a research topic.
   1. Sports

2. Education
3. Science fiction movies
4. Crime
5. The depiction of women in American fiction

E. Consider these titles of readings in the Anthology:

"Why Worry about the Animals?"
"What's Wrong with Animal Rights?"
"Does Conservation Justify Keeping Animals in Zoos?"
"Better Health Care Doesn't Justify Animal Research"

Use the basic framework provided by each title to suggest other research paper topics by filling in the following blanks:

"Why Worry about (the) _____?"
"What's Wrong with _____?"
"Does _____ Justify _____?"
"_____ Doesn't Justify _____"

Worksheet 2 _____ **DEVELOPING TOPICS**

Name _____ Date _____

A. Find the display of current magazines and journals in the library. Browse through magazines of interest to you or journals in a specific discipline such as business or psychology. Find five articles that you would like to read sometime. For each article, list the information in the format shown in the example. Then list a topic or question suggested by the article.

Example:

Article	*Topic or Question*
Author: Cook, William J. Title: "Thefts of Computer Software" Periodical: <u>FBI Law Enforcement Bulletin</u> Volume Number: 12 Date of Issue: December 1989 Pages: pp. 1–4	How easy is it to steal computer software?

Article *Topic or Question*

1.

2.

3.

4.

5.

B. List topics or questions that you have developed by brainstorming.

C. List topics or questions that you have developed by surveying a textbook from one of your courses.

D. List five of the questions from pp. 16–18 that interested you.
  1.

  2.

  3.

  4.

  5.

CHAPTER 2

Locating Information in Print

WHERE TO BEGIN

There are two ways to answer the question of where to begin: geographically and strategically. Geographically, you start in the reference section of your library. Strategically, you start by considering possible constraints on your project: the instructor's requirements and the kinds of information that may, or may not, exist about your topic and that you are aiming to find.

THE LIBRARY REFERENCE SECTION: YOUR FIRST STEP

If you think of the library as an organism, the reference section is its brain and its nervous center. Here are the encyclopedias, guides, indexes, almanacs, and various other reference sources, including specially trained librarians, that identify where and how you can locate the information sources in the rest of the library. The reference section is geographically where you begin.

SPECIFIC CONSTRAINTS

First, check the instructor's requirements. Some instructors may not want you to use an encyclopedia because of its general level of information; others may prohibit the use of articles that appear in mass market magazines, such as *Psychology Today*, because they want you to become familiar with scholarly publications such as the *Journal of Consulting and Clinical Psychology*. Also, it helps at the beginning to know what documentation system your instructor requires so that when you start making bibliography cards (see below) you will be setting them up in the most useful format. Documentation systems are explained in detail in Chapter 9. At this point all you need to know is what system you will ultimately be using.

Second, consider how recent the information is that you are seeking. Information in a library is processed over time into different kinds of publications. Information usually enters the library as current newspapers or pamphlets. As scholars and other people read, think, and write about them, time passes, and this information reappears in magazines and journals. More time passes, and the information continues to get processed from magazines and journals into books, and ultimately into textbooks and encyclopedias. The library, accordingly, has layers of information processed over time. Consider, then, which layer you will probably need most. A student writing a critical review of Donald Trump's *The Art of the Deal* would need to rely on newspapers and magazines in order to read up on recent developments in this New York real estate developer's personal and professional life. A student investigating the disappearance of the Maya in Mexico and Central America would consult books and scholarly journal articles. Aiming in the right direction will make finding what you need more likely.

KEEPING TRACK OF SOURCES: BIBLIOGRAPHY CARDS

As you locate information you will need to record it. Every research paper must include a formal bibliography, which is a list of the sources that were consulted in preparing the paper. The list is usually arranged alphabetically using the author's last name. If you put this information on cards as you go along, then later you can simply shuffle the cards into the correct order and write out the bibliography.

One alternative is to put the information on a sheet of paper. If you use just one side of the paper, then you can cut it up and shuffle the slips of paper into alphabetical order.

Another alternative is to enter the information on a computer. Some computer programs, like Squarenote or Pro-Cite, exist solely for this purpose. Otherwise, even without one of these special programs, you can simply open a new file for your cards.

In this chapter we will give you examples of bibliography cards that use the MLA system. For more details about documentation, see Chapter 9.

Here is the first set of examples, for bibliography cards using encyclopedias.

Bibliography Cards for General and Specialized Encyclopedias

List in this order (in a column):

1. *Author's name reversed.* Brackets indicate that you are adding something to the original to get a complete name (not just initials). Some general encyclopedias identify the author only by initials. If so, then you will need to consult the list of contributors, usually at the beginning or end of the encyclopedia (not the article), and decipher the abbreviations. For example, the article below on "Solar Heating and Cooling" was signed only J. I. Y. The list of contributors at the beginning of this encyclopedia identified his full name.
2. *Subject within quotation marks.* Quotation marks indicate that you are referring to an excerpt of a larger publication.
3. *Name of encyclopedia underlined.* Underlining indicates that it is the title of a publication that stands on its own.
4. *The year of the edition you are using* (not the number of the edition). You can find the year in several places, but the handiest is often the back of the title page at the beginning of the particular volume you are using.

Here is a sample bibliography card for a general encyclopedia:

```
Bibliography

Y[ellott], J. I.

''Solar Heating and Cooling''

McGraw-Hill Concise Encyclopedia of Science and Technology

1989
```

Notice that the volume number is not necessary. Page reference is only needed occasionally—when you cite one page of a multipage article.

Specialized encyclopedias and reference works require more information, particularly books that are not frequently updated.

Here is a sample bibliography card for a specialized encyclopedia. If in doubt whether an encyclopedia is general or specialized, ask a reference librarian or your instructor.

```
Bibliography

Zaslow, Robert W.

''Bonding and Attachment''

Encyclopedia of Psychology

Ed. Raymond J. Corsini

New York

Wiley

1984

pp. 160-162
```

REFERENCE WORKS

We have shown you bibliography cards for encyclopedias because a reference work is the kind of text that most students consult first in a research paper project. Not all reference books are called "encyclopedias," but they all function the same way: to give you condensed information as efficiently as possible.

Encyclopedias and dictionaries are, of course, arranged alphabetically. So are many other reference books. But if you want to consult one with another arrangement, be prepared to check the index at the back of the volume or the table of contents at the front to find out which pages will be most useful to you.

These specialized reference books are collected in the reference section of the library, and they usually don't leave the library.

Hint: Often a good investment at this stage is photocopying the few pages on your topic in these encyclopedias so you can have your own copy.

Caution: Not all subjects can be found in such works. A student interested in the rapid growth of private health clubs and figure salons could not find health clubs in the encyclopedia. Nevertheless, it is often worthwhile to consider the historical perspective and check under a more general heading, in this case, physical education.

How Encyclopedias Can Help You

1. Even if you have been discussing your subject in class, or reading about it in your textbooks, an encyclopedia will refresh your memory and give you a broader overview of the subject by including such information as definitions, history, current statistics, and connections to other subjects. Encyclopedia articles are often divided up under headings or with subtopics in the margins. These subdivisions may suggest how you might limit your own topic. By identifying specific problems or issues associated with the subject, an encyclopedia may give you a handle on it, again suggesting research questions or approaches you might want to take yourself.

2. An encyclopedia will identify key terms related to your topic. Working on unfamiliar vocabulary at this point will pay off particularly well later. These are the terms you will encounter in all your other reading on the subject, and the quicker you learn them, the better. For example, a psychology major with an interest in altered states of consciousness might read an encyclopedia article on hypnosis and not feel too sure about some of these words in the article:

empirical
placebo
inference
pharmacological

The student's own desk dictionary, such as the *American Heritage Dictionary* or *Webster's New Collegiate Dictionary*, would probably give adequate definitions. But specialized dictionaries also exist to clarify technical terminology applicable to a particular field or audience, and you should be prepared, if necessary, to consult them. Examples include the *American Political Dictionary*, *Dictionary of American Slang*, *Dorland's Illustrated Medical Dictionary*, *Dictionary of Education*, *Mathematics Dictionary*, and *McGraw-Hill Dictionary of the Life Sciences*.

3. Encyclopedia articles often include a short bibliography of their own, that is, a list of recommended readings that are considered basic to an understanding of the subject. These readings are often helpful as a shortcut if you find yourself swamped with material and are not sure how to select readings to concentrate on or begin with.

At this point, don't worry about taking notes. Later you may want to return to the encyclopedia to take notes, but right now your job is to read, to get a quick overview of the subject and its scope, and possibly to gain some idea of what books and magazines others have written about it.

People, Places, Events

Remember how our curiosity often takes the form of asking questions about people, places, and events? We can follow up these interests in connection with a possible research paper topic by consulting appropriate reference texts. Here is a list of the most commonly used ones:

PEOPLE
Dictionary of American Biography
Who Was Who in America
The Dictionary of National Biography (for the United Kingdom)

PLACES
The Europa World Year Book. A World Survey
National Geographic Atlas of the World
Rand McNally Cosmopolitan World Atlas

EVENTS
Chronology of World History: A Calendar of Principal Events from 3000 BC to AD 1976 by G. S. P. Freeman-Grenville
Harper Encyclopedia of the Modern World: A Concise Reference History from 1760 to the Present

Specialized Encyclopedias and Other Reference Books

As a glance through the reference section in a library shows, there are specialized reference books about almost everything. We recommend strongly that you consult one or more of them. For example, if you were planning to write on some aspect of women's studies, perhaps the "glass ceiling" restricting opportunities for women in business and politics, you might want to consult one or more of these:

The Good Housekeeping Woman's Almanac
Encyclopedia of Feminism
The Nature of Woman: An Encyclopedia and Guide to the Literature
Womanlist

Or, if you were investigating matriarchalism among single-parent African-American families, in addition to consulting these sources about women, you might also refer to the following reference books about African-Americans:

Dictionary of Black Culture
Encyclopedia of Black America
The Negro Almanac: A Reference Work on the African-American
World Encyclopedia of Black Peoples

Here is a sampling of just some specialized academic reference books:

ART
The Britannica Encyclopaedia of American Art
Encyclopedia of the Arts
Encyclopedia of World Art
McGraw-Hill Dictionary of Art
Oxford Companion to Art
Praeger Encyclopedia of Art

ARCHITECTURE
The Architecture Book: A Companion to the Art and Science of Architecture
Dictionary of Architecture and Construction
Historic Architecture Sourcebook

BIOETHICS
Encyclopedia of Bioethics

BIOGRAPHY
Dictionary of American Biography
Dictionary of National Biography
McGraw-Hill Encyclopedia of World Biography
Who's Who

CURRENT ISSUES AND POPULAR CULTURE
Editorial Research Reports
Handbook of American Popular Culture

DRAMA
McGraw-Hill Encyclopedia of World Drama
The Oxford Companion to the Theatre
The Reader's Encyclopedia of World Drama

ECONOMICS
Encyclopedia of American Economic History

EDUCATION
Encyclopedia of Education
International Encyclopedia of Higher Education

ENVIRONMENT
McGraw-Hill Encyclopedia of Environmental Sciences

FILM
The Film Encyclopedia
The Oxford Companion to Film

FOREIGN RELATIONS
Encyclopedia of American Foreign Policy
Encyclopedia of the Third World

HISTORY
Dictionary of American History
Dictionary of the History of Ideas

LITERATURE
Encyclopedia of World Literature in the 20th Century
A Handbook to Literature
Oxford Companion to American Literature
Oxford Companion to English Literature
The Reader's Encyclopedia

MINORITIES AND ETHNIC GROUPS
Harvard Encyclopedia of American Ethnic Groups
Negro Almanac: The Afro-American

MUSIC
The New Grove Dictionary of Music and Musicians

PAINTING
Encyclopedia of Painting: Painters and Paintings of the World from Prehistoric Times to the Present Day

PHILOSOPHY
Dictionary of the History of Ideas
The Encyclopedia of Philosophy
Philosophical Dictionary

PHOTOGRAPHY
Encyclopedia of Photography

PSYCHOLOGY
Encyclopedia of Psychology
International Encyclopedia of Psychiatry, Psychology, Psychoanalysis, and Neurology

SCIENCE
Encyclopedia of Chemical Technology
McGraw-Hill Encyclopedia of Science and Technology
Van Nostrand's Scientific Encyclopedia

SOCIAL SCIENCES
International Encyclopedia of Population
International Encyclopedia of the Social Sciences

THEOLOGY AND RELIGION
Encyclopedia of Religion and Ethics

WOMEN
Nature of Women: An Encyclopedia and Guide to the Literature
Women's Action Almanac

ZOOLOGY
Grzimek's Animal Life Encyclopedia

How can you tell which reference work you need? Two shortcuts can help you find the most useful specialized reference books for your project:

1. A librarian, especially reference librarians—they have been trained to locate and explain reference sources, and part of their job is to help you find and use them easily. Just ask.

2. The *Guide to Reference Books* by Eugene P. Sheehy—this is the reference librarians' "bible," a trade secret that anyone can use.

As its title suggests, the *Guide to Reference Books* is an annotated list of specialized reference books (dictionaries, encyclopedias, almanacs, etc.). Materials are arranged by broad disciplines, and within each discipline and subdiscipline by type of reference work (atlas, dictionary, etc.). The index at the back includes authors, titles, and subjects. You can also consult the table of contents, checking under a broader heading. For example, if you were researching a paper on hypnosis, you could look up "Hypnosis" in the index:

Hypnosis, CD108

Then by checking the reference CD108 you would find this:

Gordon, Jesse, E., ed. Handbook of clinical and experimental hypnosis. N.Y., Macmillan; London, Collier-Macmillan, [1967]. 653p. **CD108**
Presents information on the background, research and clinical applications, theories, and new developments in hypnosis.
RC495.G6

Here is a longer example from Sheehy's *Guide to Reference Books*. If you looked up "Afro-American" in the Index you would find many references:

Afro-American artists, T. D. Cederholm, BE180
Afro-American fiction, E. Margolies and D. Bakish, BD485
Afro-American folk culture, J. F. Szwed and R. D. Abrahams, CF87
Afro-American history, D. L. Smith, CC397
Afro-American literature
  bibliography, BD476–BD479
  drama, BD480–BD482, BD486
  fiction, BD483–BD485
  poetry, BD486–BD488
Afro-American literature and culture, C. D. Peavy, BD478
Afro-American novel, H. R. Houston, BD484
Afro-American poetry and drama, BD486
Afro-American religious music, I. V. Jackson, BH25
Afro-Americans
  bibliography, CC97, CC359–CC403
  biography, CC426–CC428
  dictionaries and encyclopedias, CC410–CC413
  directories, CC414–CC417
  dissertations, CC404–CC407
  education, CB50, CB52
  handbooks, CC418–CC423
  library resources, BB315, CC376–CC377, CC385, CC417
  periodicals, CC408–CC409; indexes, AE251–AE253
  yearbooks, CC424–CC425
  By occupation or profession: artists, BE180; athletes, BJ1; motion pictures, BG214; music, BH16, BH18, BH204, BH209; theater, BG32, BG65
Afro-Americans and Africa, W. B. Helmreich, CC375

If you then consulted the section on handbooks (CC418–CC423) you would find this information. Note how Sheehy also provides interpretive information about whether or not and how the text might be useful:

Handbooks

Bergman, Peter M. The chronological history of the Negro in America. N.Y., Harper, [1969]. 698p.   **CC418**

A year-by-year presentation of facts and miscellaneous information relating to the Negro in America (mainly United States, but including occasional references to other parts of the Americas). Offers an impressive gathering of information, but dates, etc., are often too inexact or statements too sketchy to be truly satisfactory; some inaccuracies have been noted. Detailed index, but no subheads nor strict pattern of arrangement within yearly listings to make for easy scanning.   E185.B46

The black American reference book. Ed. by Mabel M. Smythe. Englewood Cliffs, N.J., Prentice-Hall, 1976. 1026p.   **CC419**

Sponsored by the Phelps-Stokes Fund.

A revised and updated edition of *The American Negro reference book* edited by J. P. Davis (1966).

Scholars and specialists have contributed 30 chapters intended to provide "a reliable summary of current information on the main aspects of Negro life in America, and to present this information in sufficient historical depth to provide the reader with a true perspective."—*Pref.* Some chapters carry bibliographies; others employ bibliographic footnotes; several include useful tables. Reference value and depth of coverage of the individual chapters vary considerably. Detailed index.   E185.D25

Diggs, Ellen Irene. Black chronology from 4000 B.C. to the abolition of the slave trade. Boston, G. K. Hall, [1983]. 312p.   **CC420**

Rev. ed. of *Chronology of notable events and dates in the history of the African . . .* (1970).

A chronology from the beginning of the first Egyptian empire to the emancipation of Brazilian slaves in 1888. Bibliographic references; index.   DT17.D5

The Ebony handbook, by the Editors of Ebony. [Editor: Doris E. Saunders] Chicago, Johnson, 1974. 553p.   **CC421**

1966 ed. had title: *The Negro handbook.*

While this work covers much of the same ground as the *Black American reference book* (above), the general presentation, together with a good deal of directory-type information and the inclusion of considerably more statistical tables, makes this handbook more useful as a ready reference tool. In addition to general updating in the new edition, there has been extensive rearrangement and much of the text is new or considerably revised.   E185.E22

Garrett, Romeo B. Famous first facts about Negroes. N.Y., Arno Pr., 1972. 212p.   **CC422**

A topical listing of American Negro "firsts." Index of names and subjects.   E185.G22

The Negro almanac; a reference work on the Afro-American. Comp. and ed. by Harry A. Ploski and James Williams. 4th ed. N.Y., Wiley, [1983]. 1550p. il. **CC423**

1st ed. 1967.

Covers a wide range of topics in the social sciences, with numerous statistical tables and charts illustrating various aspects of Negro life, history, and culture. Selected bibliography; index.

E185.N385

IDENTIFYING SUBJECT HEADINGS: YOUR SECOND STEP

When you are ready to move outside the reference room in order to find particular sources other than reference works, you depend on the library's classification system to actually track down and locate material in the rest of the library: books on shelves in the stacks, magazines and journals in the reading room, microfiches in their collection, pamphlets in the vertical files, etc. If you think of the reference section as the library's brain, then the catalog and its subject headings are the library's nerves which run out from its brain to other parts of the organism.

You can look up a subject in an encyclopedia under almost any heading. However, when you look up a subject in a card catalog in order to find out whether your library has a particular source, you must use an official Library of Congress (LC) heading.

For example, if you wanted to find out what has been written about breakfast foods you wouldn't find anything in the catalog under "breakfast foods." It is not an official subject heading. Information about breakfast foods is identified under the heading "Cereals, Prepared." A specialized reference book, *Library of Congress Subject Headings*, identifies these alternatives. It is a large, red multi-volume set placed conveniently near the catalog. Here, for example, is what you find if you look up "Breakfast foods" in the *Library of Congress Subject Headings*:

Breakfast foods
See Cereals, Prepared

"Cereals, Prepared" is the official subject heading that describes information about breakfast foods, and "Cereals, Prepared" is what you look under to find sources about your topic of breakfast foods.

If the term you have in mind is an official subject heading, it will be printed in boldface type, for example, **Animal experimentation.**

In the example below, notice that related subject headings are identified.

"sa" means "see also"
"x" and "xx" mean "other related subject headings"

> **Animal experimentation** *(Indirect)*
> sa Animal models in research
>   Diseases—Animal models
>   Laboratory animals
>   Vivisection
> x Experimentation on animals
> xx Laboratory animals
>   Research
> —Law and legislation *(Indirect)*

Only when you have determined the appropriate LC subject heading for your search can you use the catalog to find appropriate sources in your library.

LOCATING BOOKS

Books are catalogued in a card file (drawers of cards that you can flip through), in an electronic system (a computer does the looking for you), or on microfiche (pieces of film which must be magnified on a machine called a microfiche reader). All three systems use the same basic principle to catalog the books:

1. You can search for a book by looking under

the author's name
the title
the subject heading

2. The catalog will give you a call number for the book. The call number tells you where the book is located. Your library will have a map showing where books with different call numbers are located.

Deciphering Catalog Information

Here is an example of a card from a file drawer:

```
                REF
                LB
Author's name   2369  Turabian, Kate L.
Title            .T8    A manual for writers of term papers, theses, and dissertations
Edition         1987   Kate L. Turabian. — 5th ed. / revised and expanded by Bonnie
Publication            Birtwistle Honigsblum. -- Chicago : University of Chicago Press,
information            1987.
                         ix, 300 p. ; 23 cm. -- (Chicago guides to writing, editing, and
                       publishing)
                         Bibliography: p. 281-282.
                         Includes index.
                         ISBN 0-226-81624-9
                         1. Dissertations, Academic.
                         2. Report writing. I. Honigsblum, Bonnie Birtwistle.
                       II. Title III. Series

                       19 NOV 87  1394; 40  MHGAsl                           86-19128
```

Here is information on the same book, this time a printout of a display on a computer screen for an on-line system, but it contains the same basic information as a paper card or a microfiche. Note that the same information could be retrieved by asking for it under the author's name (Turabian Kate L.), the title (*A Manual for Writers of Term Papers, Theses, and Dissertations*), or one of the two official LC subject headings (Dissertations, Academic; Report Writing).

```
Current Search: fnt kate turabian              ORION/UCLA Libraries
COMMAND -->

   Type STATUS for circulation information or to request an item.
              Type HELP or press PF1 for options.

--Short Display Screen (for more information, type LONG) ---------------
    Record D4 of 14        Screen 1 of 4
                                                  ORION Number: 4159334MC
          Author: Turabian, Kate L.
           Title: A manual for writers of term papers, theses, and
                  dissertations / Kate L. Turabian.
         Edition: 5th ed. / revised and expanded by Bonnie Birtwistle
                  Honigsblum.
       Published: Chicago : University of Chicago Press, 1987.
     Description: ix, 300 p. : ill. ; 23 cm.
          Series: Chicago guides to writing, editing, and publishing
      Subject(s): Dissertations, Academic.
                  Report writing.
LIBRARY: AUPL            Call number: LB 2369 T84m 1987
                                          Press ENTER for the Next Screen
```

If no author is named, then catalog information is collected under the title, as in this example:

```
Current Search: f nt publication manual american psychol  ORION/UCLA Libraries
COMMAND -->

   Type STATUS for circulation information or to request an item.
              Type HELP or press PF1 for options.

--Short Display Screen (for more information, type LONG) ---------------
    Record D5 of 8         Screen 1 of 4
                                                  ORION Number: 2349807MC
           Title: Publication manual of the American Psychological Association.
         Edition: 3rd ed.
       Published: Washington, D.C. : The Association, c1983.
     Description: 208 p. : ill. ; 26 cm.
      Subject(s): Writing (MeSH)
                  Communication in psychology.
                  Psychology--Authorship.
LIBRARY: BIOMED          Call number: PE 1475 P978 1983
                            Location: All Year Reserve
  Status: Non-Circulating
  Status: Circulation Restricted
                                          Press ENTER for the Next Screen
```

A tip—stack stalking: The term "stack stalking," which we first heard used by distinguished historian J. H. Hexter, refers to a random, but often very fruitful, exploration of the library stacks. Once you know the call number of a possible source, you can find that place in the library stacks and investigate neighboring books. Often you will discover something useful on the library shelves that you didn't otherwise know even existed.

BIBLIOGRAPHY CARD FOR A BOOK

In a bibliography card for a book, seven items of information are contained in this order (in a column):

1. Name of author reversed. Omit if none; if more than one author, reverse only the first author's name.
2. Title of book underlined. Capitalize first letters of major words, except articles and prepositions.
3. Name of editor or other named person involved in the publication. Omit if none.
4. Place of publication.
5. Publisher.
6. Date of publication (and number of edition if not the first edition).
7. Add the call number for your own convenience.

Example:

```
                         Bibliography

   REF    Turabian, Kate L.
   LB     A Manual for Writers of Term Papers, Theses, and Dissertations
   2369   Revised and expanded by Bonnie Birtwistle Honigsblum
   .T8    Chicago
   1987   University of Chicago Press
          1987
          5th edition
```

ARTICLES IN MAGAZINES AND JOURNALS

Periodical Indexes

The periodical indexes keep track of which magazine articles have been published on what subjects, when, by whom, and where. Periodical indexes do *not* print the articles themselves. But they do give you all the information you need to find them.

Some indexes cover articles in general magazines, the kind you find on newsstands, for example, *The Readers' Guide to Periodical Literature.* Other indexes, like the *Social Sciences Index,* the *Humanities Index,* or the *Education Index,* are more specialized and cover articles in academic journals. We will demonstrate how to use these indexes with examples from *Readers' Guide* because it can be found in public, as well as college, libraries.

Each index consists of several volumes, with one volume added each year. Supplements keep the present year's listings up to date.

The indexes are arranged alphabetically with cross references, like card catalogs, under subject and author (but not titles).

Most often you will be looking under the subject heading. You can get help in figuring out the correct subject heading to use in your search by consulting either the *Library of Congress Subject Headings* (see pp. 33–34) or the guide to subject headings prepared by the index. Check the introductory section of the index to learn how subjects are listed. Be careful, too, to decipher the abbreviated information correctly.

Here are two entries from *Readers' Guide,* the first a subject entry and the second an author entry.

The entries are easy to understand once you are familiar with the way information is listed.

1. The first item in an entry is always the title. This is true for subject and author entries.
2. The second item is usually the author's name. There are two exceptions. The author's name will not be repeated if the article is listed under his name. If the author's name did not appear in the magazine, it will not be given in the entry.
3. Abbreviations, such as "il" (to indicate that the article is illustrated), sometimes appear. Every volume of an index will have a page at the beginning that translates these abbreviations for you.
4. The name of the periodical in which the article appeared is frequently abbreviated. The beginning of every volume has a page that lists all the periodicals that are indexed and shows the abbreviation. You must give the full title in your bibliography, so be sure to translate the abbreviation.
5. Immediately after the name of the magazine is a series of numbers. The number before the colon is the volume number, which is important because all the issues of a particular year are bound together and given a volume number. Following the colon are the pages on which the article will be found.
6. The final item is the date of the issue in which the article appeared. Again, you will find abbreviations that you must translate for your bibliography.

Other One-Step Indexes

Readers' Guide is called a one-step index because using it involves only one step: looking up a subject heading or author entry. Any relevant articles are identified immediately.

College students also depend on other, specialized one-step periodical indexes. Here are some of the most widely used ones:

Social Science Index
Humanities Index
Education Index
Applied Science and Technology Index
Business Periodicals Index
Public Affairs Information Service Bulletin

These specialized indexes work in exactly the same way as *Readers' Guide* (see a representative page from *Readers' Guide* on page 39).

ANATOMY
  See also
  Physiology
ANDERSON, DANIEL R., 1944-
  How TV influences your kids. il *TV Guide* 38:24-6+ Mr 3-9 '90
ANDERSON, DENISE, D. 1990
  about
  Obituary
    Jet il por 77:55 Mr 12 '90
ANDERSON, JAMES W.
  Sorting out fiber. il por *The Saturday Evening Post* 262:26+ Mr '90
ANDERSON, PHILIP WARREN, 1923-
  Some thoughtful words (not mine) on research strategy for theorists. por *Physics Today* 43:9 F '90
ANDIAMO! (NEW YORK, N.Y.: RESTAURANT) *See* New York (N.Y.)—Restaurants, nightclubs, bars, etc.
ANDREEN-HERNANDEZ, SCILLA
  about
  The wonder years. J. Calhoun. il *Theatre Crafts* 24:50-3+ F '90
ANDRE'S MOTHER [television program] *See* Television program reviews—Single works
ANDROGENS
  See also
  Testosterone
ANEMIA
  See also
  Sickle cell anemia
ANESTHESIA AND ANESTHETICS
  Equipment
  Implanting anesthetics [SynchroMed infusion system] il *USA Today (Periodical)* 118:12 F '90
ANESTHETICS *See* Anesthesia and anesthetics
ANEURYSMS
  Poison berries [brain aneurysm] E. Rosenthal. il *Discover* 11:80-1+ F '90
ANGELOU, MAYA
  about
  Touches of grace from three writers. B. Thompson. *The Christian Century* 107:237-8 Mr 7 '90
ANGELS
  Angels: a short visit with our heavenly hosts. T. Unsworth. il *U.S. Catholic* 55:30-3 Mr '90
ANGELS (MUSICAL GROUP)
  Angels finally fly. D. Fricke. il *Rolling Stone* p56 Mr 8 '90
ANGER
  Can getting mad get the job done? K. S. Black. il *Working Woman* 15:86-8+ Mr '90
ANGIOSPERMS, FOSSIL
  An Aptian plant with attached leaves and flowers: implications for angiosperm origin. D. W. Taylor and L. J. Hickey. bibl f il *Science* 247:702-4 F 9 '90
  Flowers for the dinsoaurs. *Science News* 137:85 F 10 '90
ANGLING *See* Fishing
ANIMAL BEHAVIOR *See* Animals—Habits and behavior
ANIMAL COMMUNICATION
  Animal body talk. il *National Geographic World* 175:3-5 Mr '90
ANIMAL DEFENSES *See* Defense mechanisms (Biology)
ANIMAL EXPERIMENTATION
  Laws and regulations
  Pet causes [controversy surrounding medical research] F. Barnes. *The New Republic* 202:23 Mr 12 '90
ANIMAL LANGUAGE *See* Animal communication
ANIMAL MODELS OF HUMAN DISEASES *See* Diseases—Animal models
ANIMAL RIGHTS MOVEMENT
  Are animals people too? [cover story] R. Wright. *The New Republic* 202:20-2+ Mr 12 '90
  Pet causes [controversy surrounding medical research] F. Barnes. *The New Republic* 202:23 Mr 12 '90
ANIMAL SOUNDS
  See also
  Animal communication
ANIMALS
  See also
  Ear—Animals
  Pets
  Pregnancy in animals
  Wildlife
  See also names of animals
  Civil rights
  See Animal rights movement
  Food and feeding
  See also
  Grazing

Habits and behavior
  See also
  Defense mechanisms (Biology)
  Extrasensory perception in animals
  Food sharing in vampire bats [altruistic behavior] G. S. Wilkinson. bibl il *Scientific American* 262:76-82 F '90
  Language
  See Animal communication
  Protection
  See Wildlife conservation; Wildlife sanctuaries
  Treatment
  See also
  Animal experimentation
  Animal rights movement
  Hunting—Ethical aspects
ANIMALS, PREDATORY
  See also
  Coyotes
ANIMALS AS CARRIERS OF INFECTION
  Can your pets transmit disease? [views of Gary White] il *USA Today (Periodical)* 118:8 F '90
ANIMALS IN CAPTIVITY *See* Zoos
ANIMATED CARTOONS *See* Television broadcasting—Cartoons
ANNENBERG, WALTER H., 1908-
  about
  Annenberg announces gift of $50 million to UNCF. il por *Jet* 77:14-15 Mr 19 '90
ANNUAL MEETINGS, STOCKHOLDERS' *See* Stockholders' meetings
ANNUALS (PLANTS)
  A white border [cover story] C. A. Rossell. il *Organic Gardening* 37:32-4 F '90
ANNUITIES
  Growing old without growing poor. S. E. Kuhm. il *Fortune* 121:28+ Mr 12 '90
  What's in 'em for you? J. Kosnett. il *Changing Times* 44:65-72+ F '90
ANT (FIRM)
  'Have I got a used tank for you' [scandal highlights resistance to private cooperatives in Soviet Union] R. Brady. il *Business Week* p54 Mr 12 '90
ANTARCTIC REGIONS
  Climate
  Can we fix the ozone hole? C. Claiborne. map *National Wildlife* 28:42 F/Mr '90
ANTENNAS (ELECTRONICS)
  See also
  Television antennas
ANTHROPOLOGY
  See also
  Evolution
  Man
ANTI-COMMUNIST MOVEMENTS
  See also
  United States—Foreign relations—Anti-Communist measures
ANTI-NUCLEAR MOVEMENT
  Idaho says no [protest against proposed Special Isotope Separation project at Idaho National Engineering Laboratory] K. Schneider. il *The New York Times Magazine* p50+ Mr 11 '90
  The thawing of the freeze movement. B. Turque. il *Newsweek* 115:30 Mr 12 '90
ANTI-SATELLITE WEAPONS
  Industry complaints prompt Pentagon to amend ASAT competition rules. P. A. Gilmartin. *Aviation Week & Space Technology* 132:25 Mr 5 '90
ANTI-SEMITISM
  History
  See also
  Holocaust, Jewish (1939-1945)
  Soviet Union
  Whispers of hatred. il *Time* 135:41 Mr 12 '90
ANTIGENS AND ANTIBODIES
  See also
  Major histocompatibility complex
  Monoclonal antibodies
ANTIQUARIAN BOOK DEALERS *See* Booksellers and bookselling—Rare books
ANTIQUE AUTOMOBILES *See* Automobiles, Antique
ANTIQUE DEALERS
  Great Britain
  See also
  Sotheby's (Firm)
ANTIQUE SAMPLERS *See* Samplers
ANTIQUES
  Collectors and collecting
  Expensive habits: antique antics. P. Mayle. il *Gentlemen's Quarterly* 60:43+ F '90

Computerized Indexes

Information about articles may be found through a computerized database. There are several different systems in use at libraries throughout the country. You can get a printout of articles on a particular subject or by a specific author. Usually, the computer program begins by asking for a general heading, such as

STRESS

It will then tell you how many articles have been found. If the number is too large to look through, you can limit the topic by typing in a second word, such as

MANAGEMENT

```
                                                    Academic Index
                         Subject Guide
STRESS ANALYSIS
STRESS AND HEALTH
STRESS INDUCED REACTIONS
STRESS MANAGEMENT
  --analysis
  --evaluation
  --innovations
  --methodology
  --problems
  --research
  --technique




             to select subjects, use ↑ ↓
             to view citations, press ENTER
```

Once you have an appropriate number of sources, you can call up the list on the screen. Scanning the list, you may jot down information to locate a few sources that look promising, or print out the list if it seems that many of the sources are relevant.

LOCATING INFORMATION IN PRINT   41

STRESS MANAGEMENT   Academic Index
  --technique

    How Japan's workers relax. ("brain massages" at Tokyo's Brain Mind Gym)
  by Mark Alpert il   v121
  Fortune   April 23 '90 p17(1)
                    LIBRARY SUBSCRIBES TO JOURNAL

    Simple holiday stress relievers. by Joe Mullich il
  v135 Reader's Digest   Dec '89 p49(4)
                    LIBRARY SUBSCRIBES TO JOURNAL

    Ambition without anxiety. (stress management and includes related
  articles on problem solving and faulty thinking) by Pam Miller Withers
  il   v14
  Working Woman   Sept '89 p123(4)
    51B4318   46U3941
                    LIBRARY SUBSCRIBES TO JOURNAL

STRESS MANAGEMENT   Academic Index
  --research

    Chronic occupational stressors, self-focused attention, and well-being:
  testing a cybernetic model of stress. by Michael R. Frone and Dean B.
  McFarlin il   v74   Journal of Applied Psychology Dec '89 p876(8)
    By using a cybernetic approach to occupational stress, it was
  hypothesized that the relationship between chronic work stressors
  and strain would be stronger among individuals high in private
  self-consciousness than among individuals low in private
  self-consciousness. Moderated regression analyses using a sample of
  135 blue-collar workers, revealed strong support for this hypothesis.
  This finding is antithetical to prior research showing that
  self-focused attention may buffer the effect of acute life events
  (Mullen & Suls, 1982; Suls & Fletcher, 1985). The results of the
  present study in conjunction with prior research suggest that the type
  of stressor (acute vs. chronic) examined may be a boundary condition
  influencing the direction of Stressor X Self-Focused Attention
  interactions. Implications for future research and stress management
  are discussed.

  (Reprinted by permission of the publisher.)
                    LIBRARY SUBSCRIBES TO JOURNAL

    Modest treatment yields heartfelt benefits. (heart attack
  survivors) by B. Bower   v136 Science News Oct 21 '89 p261(1)
    51M0142
                    LIBRARY SUBSCRIBES TO JOURNAL

BIBLIOGRAPHY CARD FOR AN ARTICLE

In a bibliography card for an article, seven items are listed in this order:

1. Name of author reversed. Omit if none; if more than one author, reverse only the first author's name.
2. Title of article within quotation marks, capitalizing first letter of each word except articles and prepositions.
3. Complete title of magazine itself, underlined.
4. Volume number.
5. Issue number if any.
6. Date of issue.
7. Inclusive pages of the article.

ANIMAL RIGHTS MOVEMENT
Are animals people too? [cover story] R. Wright. *The New Republic* 202:20-2+ Mr 12 '90
Pet causes [controversy surrounding medical research] F. Barnes. *The New Republic* 202:23 Mr 12 '90

Example:

```
Bibliography

Wright, R.

''Are Animals People Too?''

The New Republic

volume 202

12 March 1990

pp. 20-22
```

ABSTRACTS

Using indexes of abstracts involves two steps to get from the author or subject heading to information about specific articles. This procedure is more complicated, but there is an additional benefit. Along the way you also get not only a bibliographical citation identifying the article and source, but also a short description or brief summary of its contents. Consequently, you can often weed out unsuitable articles and save time. An example of a two-step index is *Psychological Abstracts,* but college students rely on many others, including, for example:

Women's Studies Abstracts
Sociological Abstracts
Food Science and Technology Abstracts
Computer and Control Abstracts

The Two-Step Procedure

STEP ONE. Look up your topic under an appropriate subject heading in an *index* volume. Find the number for the abstract of a suitable article. This number is *not* a page number. Each abstract has its own number. Here is an example from *Psychological Abstracts:*

Hypnosis [See Also Autohypnosis]

suggestive nature of trance experience & future of hypnosis as "shared delusion", 9693

STEP TWO. Look up the abstract number in a separate volume. The abstract will give you a summary of the article. It will also refer you to the original source of the article, which you can then consult if it looks promising.

9693. **Gibbons, Don E.** (Allentown Coll of St Francis De Sales) **Hypnosis as a trance state: The future of a shared delusion.** *Bulletin of the British Society of Experimental & Clinical Hypnosis,* 1982(Apr), No 5, 1-4. —Argues that unless the subjective nature of trance experience is fully appreciated, the relationship between suggestor and S may itself take on some of the aspects of a shared delusional system, with both believing in the objective reality of the hypnotic trance and of its supposed "properties." If the true potentials of the human imagination are to be fully realized, it is necessary that trance experience be recognized for what it is: an experience rather than an objectively identified "state" with a fixed set of physiological and mental correlates. If the experience of hypnosis implies to a sufficiently hypnotic S that he/she either will or will not be amnesic, these expectations tend to function as self-fulfilling prophecies unless such expectations are countered by explicit suggestions to the contrary. (9 ref)—*C. P. Landry.*

This citation from Psychological Abstracts *and that on page 48 are reprinted with permission of The American Psychological Association publisher of* Psychological Abstracts *and* The PsycINFO Database *(Copyright © 1967–1983 by The American Psychological Association) and may not be reproduced without its prior permission.*

NEWSPAPERS AND OTHER SOURCES

For current or very recent information, you may need to consult a newspaper. The *New York Times* is one of the most important and useful newspaper sources because it covers national and international news, as well as local city and state news. It also gives complete transcripts and texts of important speeches and documents.

To find a useful newspaper article on your topic, consult subject headings in the *New York Times Index*, which arranges references to specific articles chronologically as they appear during a particular year and provides a brief description of them.

Here is an example from the 1989 volume:

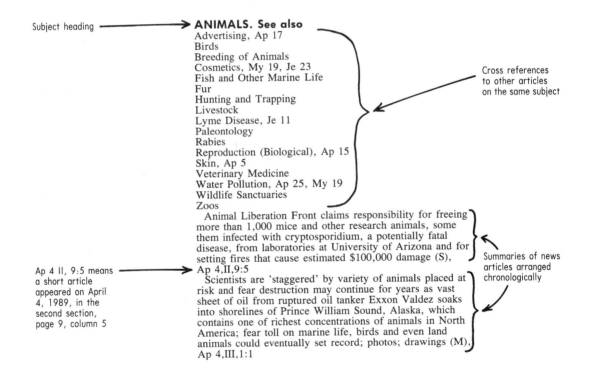

Other newspapers (*The Wall Street Journal* and *Christian Science Monitor*) also prepare indexes. Check to see if your library has indexes for these papers.

LOCATING INFORMATION IN PRINT 45

Facts on File

Facts on File is just what it says—a looseleaf arrangement of important up-to-date facts. This is a useful source if you need to know a very current bit of information, for example, who won the Academy Awards or when the national budget was submitted to the President.

Editorial Research Reports

Editorial Research Reports are collections of research reports, published weekly and compiled annually by Congressional Quarterly Inc., and are extremely useful for students engaged in a research paper project. This research service reports and analyzes emerging issues of national interest across a broad range of social, scientific, political, and economic fields. For example, recent collections include information on whether or not women should serve in combat, homelessness, smoking, zoos, and AIDS. The *Editorial Research Reports* synthesizes and duplicates information, and also provides suggestions for further reading and research.

Gallup Poll Reports

Results and interpretations of the well-known Gallup Poll survey are available in report form.

Audiovisual Materials

Many libraries stock educational videos and audio-cassettes. Ordinarily, these will be listed, along with books and pamphlets, in a catalog.

SUMMARY OF INFORMATION SOURCES IN THE LIBRARY

The following are the major information sources in a library:

1. Books—card catalog
2. Magazine articles—indexes and abstracts
3. Newspaper articles—indexes
4. Pamphlets—file cabinets
5. Librarians
6. Interlibrary loan—just that. If your library doesn't have a book, your librarian will arrange to get it for you from another library.
7. *Facts on File*
8. *Editorial Research Reports*
9. *Gallup Poll Reports*
10. Audiovisual materials

There are many other sources of information in the library. Everybody has favorites and they vary slightly from library to library, but the ones listed on page 45 are the old reliables for college students.

Here is a flow chart diagram which outlines steps in a research strategy for locating library information:

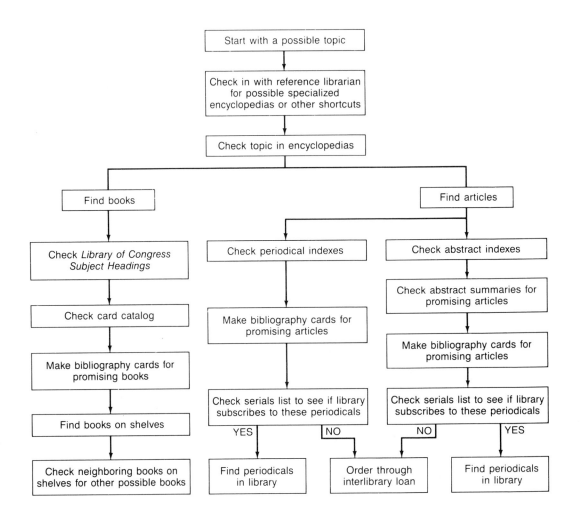

SEARCHING COMMERCIAL COMPUTER DATABASES

Just as bibliographical information is collected in various printed reference texts in the library's reference section, and represented in the library's catalog, so, too, is it increasingly available on-line with a microcomputer or computer terminal at home or the office. If you have access to a computer and a modem, you can use one or more commercial services, like

BRS After Dark or Knowledge Index, to track down possible sources at any time of the day or night. The computer can search through hundreds of thousands of references in a few minutes and present you with a list of books and articles that might be suitable for your particular research project. These services, which charge a fee, can often also provide abstracts of sources.

ASSESSING POTENTIAL SOURCES

If you were building a house, it would be only as strong as the construction materials—wood, nails, pipes, etc.—that you used. In the same way, too, the quality of your research paper is dependent on the quality of your sources. Sometimes at this stage you can benefit from weeding out one or more potential sources as inferior or inappropriate, and therefore not wasting your time on reading and taking notes on them. Here are three questions to ask about each source:

1. *Is it current?* Unless you have a special reason, restrict your attention to recent publications, for two reasons. First, the authors of very recent publications will have read and thought about previous sources, so their work will reflect and encompass earlier studies and will thereby provide you with a shortcut to more information. Second, sometimes older publications turn out to be wrong or biased. More recent studies correct the older ones. For example, when the nuclear power industry got going after World War II, it evoked tremendous enthusiasm for an energy source that seemed clean and cheap. Since the accidents at Three Mile Island, Chernobyl, and elsewhere, and the growing problem of radioactive wastes from nuclear power plants, opinion is now often quite different from that initial enthusiasm.

2. *Is it authoritative?* First, is the author entitled to address the topic because of appropriate credentials such as academic degrees or professional experience? You can check in a biographical reference source for authors of books. *The Directory of American Scholars* presents information about authors in the humanities. *American Men and Women of Science* does the same things for science, including the social sciences. Magazine articles usually include a biographical note about authors.

Second, consider the scope and quality of the source's evidence. If there is more emphasis on opinion rather than reasons for the opinion, be suspicious. Also, if reasons are given, for example, facts and figures, be even more suspicious about where these facts and figures come from.

Third, consider the source's affiliation. Is the publication sponsored by an organization? For example many scholarly organizations have a journal or press. *Religion* is an academic journal sponsored by the Department of Religious Studies, University of California, Santa Barbara, and commands a different kind of respect than would a newsletter from a group of "creation scientists." Some publications are clearly dedicated to advocating a party line. For example, *The PETA Newsletter* is published by the organization People for the Ethical Treatment of Animals. Obviously any articles in this publication will reflect the organization's beliefs and biases.

Bias is not necessarily bad. Any important issue will evoke a range of opinion. The important thing is to be aware of it, not to assume that everything in print is objective fact, and to realize that other angles on the topic might exist, too.

3. *What is its reputation?* Particularly for books, important new work is reviewed, and these reviews can provide a useful assessment of strengths and weaknesses. To find reviews of your book sources, look in the reference section of your library for specialized guides to book reviews. These guides list the reviews alphabetically by author of the book reviewed. Some have title and subject indexes and a few include a reviewer index. In order to locate a book review, you need to know the book's date of original publication. This indicates when the book could have been reviewed.

Here are the main guides for book reviews:

Book Review Digest
Book Review Index
Current Book Review Citations
New York Times Book Review Index, 1896–1970

In addition, professional journals often include reviews of new books and important articles. Usually the index you are using will identify these reviews. Here is an example from *Psychological Abstracts:*

> suggestive nature of trance experience & future of hypnosis as "shared delusion", comment on D. E. Gibbons's article, 9701
> suggestive nature of trance experience & future of hypnosis as "shared delusion", comment on D. E. Gibbons's article, 9702

REFINING YOUR BIBLIOGRAPHY

So far you have been tracking down sources of information for your paper and keeping a record on bibliography cards of what you have found. Soon you will be working in depth with these sources, reading them in detail and taking notes. Now is the time for weeding some out. You need to decide which sources you really want to get to know and which to screen out. There are two ways to do this, one by forming your own general impression, the other by consulting authorities you trust.

The same thing happens when you meet new people. You quickly form a general impression of what they are like on the basis of their appearance and behavior. And you may change your mind later. To get even more information about them, so you know whether or not to invite them to a party, for example, you might ask some mutual friends for their opinion, too. This way you find out about their reputation.

The next assignment requires you to form an initial impression of your sources in two ways: First, to describe them by summing them up briefly, and second, to evaluate them by offering your first-impression opinion.

An Annotated Bibliography

Professional researchers and librarians learn a special format for this activity. You don't need to worry about that now. What you are aiming at, however, is to provide several sentences for each of the sources identified on your preliminary bibliography.

Begin by identifying the source with complete bibliographical information. Then write one or two sentences to *summarize* the main point or points of the source objectively. Then add one or two more sentences to *evaluate* how good or useful you think it is likely to be.

Here are four examples of annotated bibliography items, prepared by a student working on a research paper about genetic engineering. Notice that this student has used quotations from the original source as a shortcut to make his points.

ARTICLES

Dembart, Lee. ''Fears on DNA Studies Fade, but Won't Die,'' Los Angeles Times, April 12, 1980, Part I, p. 1 ff. Dembart claims that fears of ''Andromeda Strain'' are unfounded. There is an interesting quote by James D. Watson, codiscoverer of DNA, who says over the genetic controversy, ''I think the whole thing is lunacy....I helped raise these issues, but within six months I was acutely embarrassed. There's no evidence that anyone has gotten sick from any of this.'' On the other side, Dembart quotes Robert Sinsheimer, who acknowledges fears are less justified than originally thought, but also suspects that genetic engineering could conceivably result in a new route for the transmission of cancer. This seems like a pretty balanced, up-to-date overview of the whole issue.

Rich, Vera. ''Soviet Claims,'' Nature, July 3, 1980, pp. 6-7. The Soviet newspaper Pravda claims that the U.S. is working on ''ethnic viruses.'' They are supposed to be bacteriological weapons which would selectively attack memebers of particular races or ethnic groups. This ridiculous claim could at least be used to demonstrate the paranoia generated by the government's hush-hush attitude toward this issue.

BOOKS

Howard, Ted, and Jeremy Rifkin. Who Should Play God? New York. Dell, 1977. According to its dustjacket, this book ''lifts the cloak of secrecy from genetic experiments'' and explores, among other things, ''who is performing the research and who profits from it.'' It's clearly anti-genetic engineering; its chapter titles give a good idea of the direction and flavor of the book, for example, ''Eugenics,'' ''Eliminating 'Bad' Genes,'' ''Bio-Futures,'' ''Scientists and Corporations.'' This looks like the place to go for the social arguments from the political left wing.

Wade, Nicholas. The Ultimate Experiment: Man-Made Evolution. New York. Walker and Company, 1977. This seems to be a more balanced book than Howard and Rifkin's, for example, the chapter: ''Assessing the Hazards.'' The book explains the significance of the Conference at Asilomar in 1975 which set guidelines for genetic research, I think. There is a description of *E. coli* bacteria which all the sources refer to. Wade admits that estimating dangers is still largely guesswork; he raises issues but remains noncommittal. He does make a point of distinguishing genetic engineering from other technologies. One interesting point I stumbled across here: ''Despite the yodeling about medical benefits, the most important contributions of the gene splicer's craft may well come from some unexpected quarter, such as in the adaptation of microorganisms to convert sunlight into machine-usable forms of energy.'' Thus genetic engineering <u>may</u> be connected with solar power and the whole dilemma of fuel.

The bibliographical material on genetic engineering was compiled by Professor Malcolm Kiniry from student work generated in his English 3 class at UCLA, 1983.

A PROFESSIONAL SHORTCUT (USE CAUTION)

As we have explained in this chapter, we recommend that you begin by consulting one or more encyclopedias or other specialized references. The purpose is to provide you with a context showing where your topic fits into our current understanding and how related issues are connected to it. That is, after all, why many research papers are assigned—to provide you with an opportunity to learn about a topic in some depth and detail.

Professional scholars, however, have already gone through this learning stage. They already know this background information. When they undertake a research paper, they need to go immediately to a network of other scholars working on the same specialized problem and to consult their work. To access this information most efficiently, they often begin by turning to one or more very recently published articles on the subject and consulting the references cited in these sources. These references provide a ready-made set of benchmarks defining scholarly opinion in a narrow field, and it is these sources that the would-be researcher consults and concentrates on, tracking backward, as necessary, through the references cited in these cited sources, until an adequate picture of the problem or issue is formed and the researcher shapes a personal thesis.

You, too, may want to use this approach. It is certainly fast, but it does have drawbacks for the beginner. The major drawback is that once you find a current, central article (not easy in itself), you might not be able to understand the problematic aspects under discussion, especially if the topic is quite technical. Much knowledge will be implied. The authors concerned will be thoroughly familiar with it, and will assume the same familiarity in their readers. They will be addressing their professional colleagues, not you. Because this knowledge will be missing in your academic background, you may misunderstand the issues, or, worse, not understand them at all.

Here, for example, is the list of references for Dr. Lehmann's article, "Yawning: A Homeostatic Reflex and Its Psychological Significance" in the *Bulletin of the Menninger Clinic*.

References

DARWIN, C. R.: *The Expression of the Emotions in Man and Animals.* New York: Appleton & Co., 1873.
DUMPERT, V.: Zur Kenntniss des Wesens und der Physiologischen Bedeutung des Gähnens. *J. Psychol. Neurol. (Lpz)* 27:82–95, 1921.
GEIGEL, R.: Das Gähnen. *Münch. Med. Wschr.* 55:223–24, 1908.
HAUPTMANN, A.: Wie, Wann und Wozu Gähnen Wir? *Neurol. Zbl.* 39:781–82, 1920.
HEUSNER, A. P.: Yawning and Associated Phenomena. *Physiol. Rev.* 26:156–68, 1946.
LEWY, E.: Über das Gähnen. *Z. Ges Neurol. Psychiat.* 72:161–74, 1921.
MAYER, C.: Physiologisches und Pathologisches Über das Gähnen *Z. fur Biol.* 73:101–14, 1921.
OPPENHEIM, H.: *Lehrbuch der Nervenkrankheiten.* Berlin: Karger, 1931.
PEIPER, A.: Das Gähnen. *Dtsch. Med. Wschr.* 58:693–94, 1932.
PENFIELD, WILDER & ERICKSON, T. C.: *Epilepsy and Cerebral Localization.* Springfield, IL: Thomas, 1941.
PREYER, W.: *Die Secle des Kindes.* Leipzig: Th. Grieber, 1923.
RUSSELL, H.: *Yawning* (Delsarte Series, No. 1). New York: U.S. Book Co., 1891.
VISCHER, A. L.: Über das Gähnen und Seine Spontanen Mitbewegungen. *Schweiz. Med. Wschr.* 89:1356–59, 1959.
WEINBERGER, J. L. & MULLER, J. J.: The American Icarus Revisited: Phallic Narcissism and Boredom. *Int. J. Psychoanal.* 55(4):581–86, 1974.

Although another psychiatrist would probably recognize and be able to understand this evidence for Lehmann's position, an undergraduate would find the references baffling. Better for the undergraduate to start, as we recommend, with a reference text and work up to this level if, later, it is necessary.

EXERCISES

I. Catalog information
   A. Examine the following printout of a computer screen cataloging a library book and answer these questions:
   1. Who is (are) the author(s)?
   2. What is the exact title?
   3. How long is the book?
   4. Has there been a previous edition?
   5. Who is the publisher?
   6. Where was it published?
   7. What is the call number?

```
Current Search: fnt manual of style            ORION/UCLA Libraries
COMMAND -->
   Type STATUS for circulation information or to request an item.
            Type HELP or press PF1 for options.
-- Short Display Screen (for more information, type LONG) --------------
   Record D1 of 133      Screen 1 of 2
                                                ORION Number: 2977217MC
          Author: Achtert, Walter S.
           Title: The MLA style manual / by Walter S. Achtert and Joseph
                  Gibaldi.
       Published: New York : Modern Language Association of America, 1985.
     Description: viii, 271 p. ; 24 cm.
      Subject(s): Authorship--Style manuals.
                  Humanities--Authorship--Handbooks, manuals, etc.
                  Scholarly publishing--Handbooks, manuals, etc.
LIBRARY: COLLEGE           Call number: PN 147 A28 1985
           Notes: reference and stacks
                                           Press ENTER for the Next Screen
Current Search: fnt manual of style            ORION/UCLA Libraries
COMMAND -->
   Type STATUS for circulation information or to request an item.
            Type HELP or press PF1 for options.
-- Short Display Screen (for more information, type LONG) --------------
```

B. Now make a bibliography card for this book.

II. Bibliography cards

A. Make proper bibliography cards for each of these four books:

1. A book entitled *The Case for Animal Experimentation: An Evolutionary and Ethical Perspective* by Michael Allen Fox. It was published in Berkeley, California, in 1986 by the University of California Press.

2. A book entitled *Animal Rights: Opposing Viewpoints.* It was edited by Janelle Rohr, published in 1989 by Greenhaven Press in San Diego.

3. A book by Sue Brebner and Debbi Baer entitled *Becoming an Activist: PETA's Guide to Animal Rights Organizing.* It was published by PETA in Washington, D.C., in 1989.

4. A second edition in 1990 of Peter Singer's *Animal Liberation,* published by the New York Review in New York.

B. Make proper bibliography cards for each of the following items from *Readers' Guide to Periodical Literature:*

1. Alternatives to animals in toxicity testing. A. M. Goldberg and J. M. Frazier. *Scientific American* 261: 24–30 Ag '89

2. Necessary evil? K. Barrett and R. Greene. *Redbook* 173:160–1 S '89

3. Will relief for lab animals spell pain for consumers? J. Carey *Business Week* p. 43–4 O 30 '89

4. Universities fight animal activists. C. Holden. *Science* 244:1253 Je 16 '89
5. Agriculture and animal rights. R. McGuire. *Vital Speeches of the Day* 55:766–8 O 1 '89
6. Fight animal welfare emotion with emotionalism. *Successful Farming* 87:41 D '89
7. What's wrong with animal rights? B. G. Harrison. *Mademoiselle* 95:76 Jl '89

III. Deciphering one-step indexes

A typical page from the *Readers' Guide to Periodical Literature* appears on page 39. Study it and then answer the questions that follow:
1. Does this page list any magazine articles about anti-semitism in Russia?
2. Under what other subject heading could you look for magazine articles about anti-semitism?
3. Under what subject heading would you look for magazine articles about animals in captivity?
4. Under the heading "Animals, Predatory," the *Readers' Guide* refers us to "Coyotes." Why are there no other predatory animals, like wolves, lions, or sharks, listed here?
5. ANDERSON, JAMES W. is an author entry. What subject heading would give you exactly the same information about Anderson's article in *The Saturday Evening Post?*
6. What is the title of the article about Walter Annenberg? Is there a picture of him?
7. What is the title of the article written by Philip Warren Anderson?
8. Who is the author of the article on anger titled "Can Getting Mad Get the Job Done?" On what pages did it appear? What volume? What date?

IV. Finding information in newspapers

Find a copy (probably on microfiche or microform) of a newspaper from the day you were born.
1. What is the date of the newspaper?
2. What is the name of the newspaper?
3. What was the main headline in the paper that day?
4. Name one movie that was playing at the time.
5. Find one advertisement that lists a price. What is the item and how much did it cost the year you were born?

V. Analyzing annotations

A. For each of the following annotated items, identify the two main parts: (1) the summary of what it is about; and (2) an evaluation of its worth or usefulness.
1. Bresler, Robert J. "The Bargaining Chip and SALT." *Political Science Quarterly,* volume 92, 1977, pp. 65–88. Bresler explores the dangers and advantages of using bargaining chips

during strategic negotiations. He points out that the U.S. uses this ploy often. The article is good because it examines a not often mentioned aspect of SALT.

2. Burt, Richard. "The Scope and Limits of SALT." *Foreign Affairs*, volume 56, 1978, pp. 751–776. From a pro arms control point of view, Burt points out the substantive limitations of SALT II: the failure to address the issues of MIRV, cruise missiles, and new technology. This article is a good liberal critique of SALT II.

3. Gray, Colin S. "SALT: Time to Quit." *Strategic Review*, volume 4, 1976, pp. 14–22. Gray takes the view that SALT was of dubious worth and that SALT II is definitely bad for the national security of the United States. He calls for the discontinuation of SALT before further damage is done. Gray presents an excellent conservative critique of SALT.

4. Kinter, W. R., and R. L. Pfaltzgraff. "Assessing the Moscow SALT Agreements." *Orbis*, volume 16, 1972, pp. 341–360. The authors hold the conservative view that SALT cannot halt the slipping nuclear advantage of the United States. They conclude that the United States needs a national reassessment of defense policy. They further conclude that the only utility of SALT is in developing a dialogue with the Soviets. This is a good conservative critique of SALT I.

5. Kruzel, J. "SALT II: The Search for a Follow on Agreement." *Orbis*, volume 17, 1973, pp. 9–18. Kruzel favors SALT. He points out that SALT II is concerned with converting the interim agreement of SALT I into a permanent treaty and also with both quantitative and qualitative reductions. This is a useful overview of the early SALT II negotiations.

6. Lodal, Jan. "SALT II and American Security." *Foreign Affairs*, volume 57, 1979, pp. 387–410. Lodal takes a favorable view of SALT II. He argues that SALT II enhances American national security by preserving our technological advantage and at the same time limiting Soviet arms development. He presents a good liberal defense of SALT II.

7. Scoville, H. "Beyond SALT I." *Foreign Affairs*, volume 50, 1972, pp. 488–500. Scoville presents a pro-SALT view which argues that SALT I was only the first step and that SALT II is necessary to complete the process. He offers a fine liberal argument for SALT II.

The annotated items on SALT were prepared by Professor Patricia Chittenden for her Library and Information Science 110 course at UCLA, 1984.

B. Look back at Sheehy's annotations on the Handbooks listed on p. 32. Examine each sentence. Which sentences are objective summary? Which sentences are interpretive evaluation?

Worksheet 3 _____ **USING AN ENCYCLOPEDIA**

Name _____ Date _____

Find an article on one of your possible topics in an encyclopedia in the library and read it. Then answer the following questions.

1. What is your research question or provisional topic?

2. What is the exact title of this article? Fill in below:

3. Is there an author of this article? (circle) Yes   No

4. If there is an author, who?

5. What is the exact and complete title of the encyclopedia you are using?

6. When was this edition published?

7. Are there any cross-references in the article that look interesting and are possibly worth following up? What are they?

8. Are there any vocabulary words or technical terms mentioned in the article that you are not familiar with? If so, list them below.

9. Is there a bibliography listed at the end of the article? (circle)
   Yes   No

10. If there is a bibliography, give the author and title of the first book listed there:

11. Make a bibliography card for the encyclopedia article, using the format shown on p. 25 (or p. 26) as a model.

12. Try to develop a research question suggested by this article. In other words, can you formulate a specific question or problem or issue which is raised by the article, that *focuses* on the subject in a particular way?
    Your question:

Worksheet 4 _____ **TRANSLATING CARD CATALOG INFORMATION**

Name _____ Date _____

1. In the space below, copy exactly *everything* on one catalog card for a library book on your subject.

2. In the space below, translate the appropriate part of this information from the catalog card to the proper bibliography card.

Worksheet 5 _____ **USING PERIODICAL INDEXES**

Name _____ Date _____

Topic _____

Find any one-step index (*Readers' Guide* or those listed on p. 38), and look up your topic.

1. What is the subject heading you have looked up?

2. Copy *exactly* the reference to the first article listed under this heading. Keep the abbreviations exactly as they are.

3. In this citation that you have just copied, what is the title of the article?

4. What is the full name of the periodical in which this article appeared?

5. What is the date of the periodical issue in which this article appeared?

6. On what page(s) did the article appear?

7. On the back of this page, make a correct bibliography card for this particular article. Take the abbreviated information you copied above and translate it into the correct format.

Worksheet 6 _____ COMPILING A PRELIMINARY BIBLIOGRAPHY

Name _____ Date _____

Check the information available for the different topics you listed on Worksheet 2. Start with the topics that are most interesting to you. Explore all the resources discussed in this chapter. A topic cannot be considered feasible unless you can spot ten sources. You will have to balance interest and feasibility to decide on the topic for your paper.

Topic: _____
_____

List ten sources on this topic. Put the information in bibliography card format.

Worksheet 7 _____ **ANNOTATING YOUR BIBLIOGRAPHY**

Name _____ Date _____

Directions: Look at your preliminary bibliography, Worksheet 6. Pick two articles and two books from it. Annotate the two articles in the space below. Follow the format illustrated in the examples on pp. 49–50 and 53–54.

Article 1:

Article 2:

For each of your books, find and read a review.

Book 1: Which guide did you use to find out about the review?

Where was this review published? (That means, in what other book or magazine?)

Annotate your book in the space below. Follow the format illustrated in the examples on pp. 49–50.

Book 2: Which guide did you use to find out about the review?

Where was this review published?

Annotate your book in the space below. Follow the format illustrated in the examples on pp. 49–50.

CHAPTER 3

Collecting Firsthand Information

We recommend that every student engaged in a research paper project at least consider this step of collecting firsthand information. There are several straightforward ways. In addition to reading about your topic in the library, you can telephone, write a letter, observe a public meeting or event, conduct an interview, or use a questionnaire to survey opinion.

BENEFITS OF FIRSTHAND INFORMATION

Although it is not appropriate for every topic, taking your project outside the library has three potential benefits.

1. *Firsthand information is often the most up-to-date.* Remember the time lag involved in publication. Being on the spot can sometimes provide information that only later will get processed into books and magazine articles. For example, one student had worked as a volunteer during a political campaign. For her research paper she wanted to check out the possibility that a "glass ceiling" thwarted the political ambitions of women on the campaign trail. Her own volunteer experience had led her to believe so. She still had a number of contacts in the headquarters of the political party concerned, and by talking to these people she was able to collect a considerable amount of detailed information about job descriptions for men

and women in that particular campaign. She was then able to use this detailed information to illustrate the general concept of the "glass ceiling" that she had learned about in class.

2. *Firsthand information can also help you shape your thesis and even sometimes change it.* For example, another student was writing about the issue of flag desecration and First Amendment protection. She was able to interview a group of veterans, many from the Vietnam War, at a July 4th parade. Their responses showed her a wider range of opinion than she had expected, and more aspects to the problem than she had anticipated from reading mainly newspaper editorials up to that point. As a result she refined the working definition of "patriotism" that she had started out with. This was a major change in her argument.

Another student thought he might look into the medical uses of hypnosis, but changed his mind about this topic after talking to his dentist for a few minutes during a routine visit. The dentist said that he would never consider replacing anesthetics with hypnosis and dismissed the possibility out of hand. The student probably shouldn't have let this one person alone change his mind, but the example does show the power of firsthand information.

At the very least, talking over your ideas with someone else, or listening to them talk, can help you test these ideas out and shape your argument.

3. *Collecting firsthand information can be exciting.* Students often complain that research papers are dull and dry. Taking the project outside the library can be a personally moving—if not disturbing—experience. For example, one student wanted to look into the effectiveness of antismoking campaigns. She was particularly concerned about her younger brother in middle school and worried that he would become addicted to nicotine because his friends were starting to smoke. She narrowed down her topic to antismoking campaigns in middle schools, and talked to several school teachers, counselors, and administrators about their effectiveness. This was an extremely satisfying experience for her because she learned how she could help reinforce the message that her brother was getting at school.

Another student in a sociology class had no choice about his paper. He was assigned a research paper on the extent to which research on AIDS has been limited by public perception of it as a disease of homosexuals who are stigmatized members of society. The assumption he was investigating claimed that if AIDS had affected the general population, much greater effort would have been made to find a cure. Not gay himself, he approached this required assignment with a mixture of indifference and resentment. Soon, however, he became caught up in his research, especially after talking to some gay activists, and totally outraged at the inadequate medical response to this terrible disease. Far from being bored by his research paper project, he became consumed by it.

TELEPHONING

This resource is not suitable for all topics, but it is very valuable for some, and is often overlooked by students. For example, one student interested in single-parent adoption called a local adoption agency that was very helpful in sending copies of state regulations and the agency's application forms.

You can also use your telephone call as an opportunity to ask for an interview. For example, another student called Planned Parenthood to ask if they counseled pregnant women about fathers' rights in abortion, and was invited to come in and discuss the matter with a counselor. He did so, and he got quite a lot of information as well as a reference to a journal article about this topic.

The various sections of your local telephone book include appropriate numbers. There is also a *National Directory of Addresses and Telephone Numbers,* a reference book that gives "50,000 most wanted addresses and telephone numbers in the U.S."

What to Say

Begin by briefly identifying yourself and explaining why you are calling (because you are working on a college research paper project). Then ask if you have called at a convenient time, and offer to call back later if that would be more convenient. Then ask if you have called the appropriate number to request information. If not, call the correct source. Go ahead and ask for information related to your topic, emphasizing that it would probably be most helpful to you if the authority would send you printed data, pamphlets, and so on in the mail. Otherwise, be prepared with one or two specific questions. One tactic you might use is to ask the person if he or she agrees with something you have read so far about the topic. Then ask why.

WRITING A LETTER

A local telephone call will do the same thing, but for out-of-town sources, write a letter. Besides making sure that you follow standard business letter format (typed on one side of white paper), there are three other points to consider: *who* to write, *where* to send your letter, and *what* to include in it. A good tactic is to begin by referring not only to your research paper project, but also to the class and the instructor. Here is an example of part of such a letter:

Chris DeRose
Director
Last Chance for Animals
18653 Ventura Blvd.
Suite 356
Tarzana CA 91356

Dear Mr. DeRose:

My English instructor, Dr. Mimi Hotchkiss, at Cal State Long Beach, has suggested that I write to you in connection with my term paper for her class. I'm investigating the subject of animal experimentation, and I'm particularly interested in the ALF, which as you know is the Animal Liberation Front. I read your name in the L A Times as someone who supports the ALF, and I thought you might be able to give me some information about them. It is very difficult to find any ALF members to talk to.
 I would appreciate it if you could send me any of your organization's information that might help me with my research paper. It would be really helpful to get a lead on someone in the ALF to interview. If that's not possible, could I interview you? I could call you at a convenient time. You can let me know or leave a message on my machine by calling......

Sincerely,

(Type and sign your name)

You will probably be writing to one of the following sources. In addition to the *National Directory of Addresses and Telephone Numbers,* there are specialized library reference books that will give you addresses. Here is a sampling:

1. *A business: Million Dollar Directory,* produced by Dun and Bradstreet. A student who was researching fast-food restaurants found the correct address for McDonald's Corporation in this directory.
2. *An organization: Encyclopedia of Associations.* One student was researching legal rights of the mentally ill. By checking "Mental Health" in the index of this book, he found out about the existence of a Center for the Study of Legal Authority and Mental Patient Status and its address.
3. *A person: Who's Who* and other specialized directories. One nursing student was intrigued by the historical figure of Dr. Samuel Mudd, the physician who treated the broken leg of Lincoln's assassin and was subsequently convicted of treason. She found from her preliminary reading in an encyclopedia that Samuel Mudd's grandson has been trying to clear his grandfather's reputation. The encyclopedia also indicated that Mudd's grandson is a physician, so the

student looked him up in the *American Medical Association Directory,* found his address, and wrote a letter. The present Dr. Mudd was very interested and helpful, and sent copies of such things as his letter to the President presenting reasons for exonerating Samuel Mudd.

OBSERVING A PUBLIC MEETING OR EVENT

Again, not all topics lend themselves to this source of information, but some do—for example, any issues about local government. The student researching zoning and land use policy attended a zoning commission meeting. Most local government committee meetings are open to the public, and are held at regularly posted times. Call your town hall or government center for dates and places.

Sometimes out-of-town experts give local talks or presentations to which the public is invited. Another student, who was researching the influence of different kinds of toys on preschool children, attended a public meeting that was part of a regional social services seminar. A nationally known authority on child development spoke, and the student was able not only to take notes on what she said, but was also able to ask a question. Calendars in newspapers, both campus and town or city, are good places to find out about this possibility.

A more unusual but sometimes quite possible source of information is firsthand observation. This requires tact, careful planning (a telephone call or letter beforehand), and sometimes a letter of introduction from your instructor. Nonetheless, it is often worth pursuing. One student researching judicial reform observed a court in session; another student obtained an invitation to ride in a police patrol car.

CONDUCTING A PERSONAL INTERVIEW

The advantages of a personal interview are, first, that you can follow up an answer with more questions, testing ideas of your own against someone else's experience. Second, the authority you are interviewing can often give you practical suggestions about further reading, or comments on your thesis and approach to the topic. In other words, you will be gathering more facts about the subject as well as expert opinion.

Arranging the Interview

Begin with a telephone call to request an interview. Explain who you are and your reasons for calling (your research project). Set a specific date that is mutually convenient. Before you arrive, prepare a short list of questions, based on your reading so far, and the ideas that you want to check out. Write your questions on a notepad, leaving enough room for answers. Be on time, even a few minutes early. Take a tape recorder if you wish, but ask permission before you use it.

What to Say

If the other person does not take the initiative, begin by asking your first question. Jot down answers in abbreviated form. If you miss something important, ask the person to repeat it. Don't hesitate to say that you don't understand. It is quite normal to ask for clarification of a point or further explanation. On the other hand, don't annoy the person by trying to take down each word. Don't waste time recording the obvious.

How to Get the Person to Talk

You can ask both direct and indirect questions. A direct question is one that begins with *why, when, where, who, what, how*—for example, "What medicine is routinely given to the patients to counteract depression?" An indirect question is an open-ended opportunity to respond: "I wonder if there are any other realistic alternatives to medication for depressed patients?"

Two thoughtful techniques can help you avoid the unpleasant impression of grilling the person at your interview. The first is to use the person's name: "Dr. Brown, why does your agency disapprove of interracial adoption?" The second technique is to introduce your question courteously: "May I ask you what you think of this statement I just read . . . " or "If you wouldn't mind, I would appreciate hearing your perspective on interracial adoption."

After the Interview

Don't stay too long. An hour would be a maximum, but many interviews will not take that long. When you get home, write a short letter thanking the person again. This courtesy is appropriate because the person has willingly given time to help you and, insofar as you automatically represent other students, by showing your genuine appreciation you will make it easier for other students to obtain an interview in the future. Examples of students who have gathered information through interviews include those working on depression among the elderly (interviewing a nurse in a nursing home); religious cults (a priest); wild animals as pets (an animal trainer at an aquarium); hedges against inflation (a stockbroker).

SURVEYING OPINION WITH A QUESTIONNAIRE

Some elaborate, complicated research projects—for instance, the ones undertaken by graduate students—often depend on gathering firsthand statistical data through questionnaires and experiments. Designing them requires special training and techniques. In most introductory courses you are not expected to gather data this way now. However, without feeling overwhelmed by technical difficulties, you can still experiment with a questionnaire to use on an appropriate sample of people. If the results are not rigorously scientific, they can still be very suggestive and therefore useful.

For example, one student was writing a paper on anorexia nervosa. The slant that she wanted to take on this subject had to do with the mothers of anorexic girls, and she suspected that perhaps the most important factor in this relationship had to do with mothers' ambitions for their daughters. She accordingly constructed a questionnaire about this relationship and asked the other members of her dorm to help her test this hunch by providing information about their own mothers.

Another student was concerned about the authorities in her small town who were trying to strictly regulate, if not close down, the only video arcade. She enjoyed playing the games there and thought that the public had somehow got a wrong impression, based on wrong information. She wanted to get some firsthand information besides her own opinion, so she made up a short questionnaire with these questions:

```
1. How many hours a week do you spend here? _____
2. How many hours a week do you spend on homework? _____
3. How many hours a week do you spend on sports? _____
4. How many hours a week do you spend watching TV? _____
5. Do you come here alone? (yes or no) _____
6. Do you come here with friends? (yes or no) _____
7. How much money a week do you spend here, on average? _____
8. If you were not spending it here, what would you be spending it on?
   _____
9. A lot of people criticize video arcades. What benefits do you get from
   coming here? _____
```

The important thing on a questionnaire is to create questions so that most of them give comparable answers. That means that they can be counted up and averaged: so many "yes's," so many "no's," so many hours, so much money. The first seven questions here are like that; the last two questions are more open-ended.

Once the student had made up a number of copies of this questionnaire, she went to the video arcade and asked players to answer her questions, one questionnaire for each player. She explained her purpose, read the questions out loud, and jotted down the player's answers. She then went home, tallied up the answers, and averaged them into a profile of the typical player. This all provided excellent information for her research paper on video arcades.

EXERCISES

1. Consider the power of these questions about animal experimentation in a recent issue of *Glamour* magazine. Experiment with their usefulness in various contexts by practicing with them in one or more of the following ways:
   a. Telephoning: Call someone (for example, a relative, a former teacher, a present science or philosophy instructor, a priest, minister, or rabbi) and ask for responses. (You take notes and follow up.)
   b. Conducting an interview: Arrange to meet someone face-to-face to ask these questions. (You take notes and follow up.)
   c. Surveying opinion with a questionnaire: Copy these questions on a sheet of paper with enough space for written answers. Copy the sheet and distribute it to a sample of people (for example, in one of your classes or to your family members) and ask them to fill it in.

Tell Us How You Feel about This Issue

No sane person is in favor of hurting animals; no sane person wants to stop medical progress. What can be difficult is staking out a position somewhere between those two poles. These questions may help with the sorting-out process. In addition, we'd like you to let us know what you think; we'll share your ideas in a future issue.
1. Do you approve of using animals in medical research if they are treated as humanely as possible?
2. What if the animal is spared pain, but ultimately dies?
3. Who should decide whether a study or experiment involving animals is necessary or valuable?
4. Guerrilla raids on laboratories often disrupt research. Are such raids right or wrong?
5. Is the life of a dog or cat more important than the life of a rat or guinea pig? Is the life of an animal as valuable as the life of a human being?
6. What question would you like to ask an animal-rights activist? What question would you like to ask a medical researcher using animals?

Optional: Tell us your name and age, and how we can get in touch with you. Please mail your responses to Animal Rights, *Glamour*, 350 Madison Ave., New York NY 10017. Or fax it to (212) 880-6922.

Courtesy Glamour. Copyright © 1990 by Conde Nast Publications, Inc. Reprinted by permission.

2. Look back at the research questions on pp. 16–18. For each question suggest the best way, or ways, of getting firsthand information. In each case, what kinds of information would be most helpful, and what kinds of questions would be most likely to get this information?
3. Consider Molly O'Neill's newspaper article on "Animal Rights" (pp. 310–313). Where and how do you imagine she got her information? Scrutinize each quotation and suggest a possible source. To what extent did she use firsthand information?

Worksheet 8 _____ **GETTING FIRSTHAND INFORMATION**

Name _____ Date _____

At this stage in your research paper project, collect some firsthand information in one or more of the ways detailed below:

Making a telephone call
Sending a letter
Observing an event
Attending a public meeting
Conducting an interview
Surveying opinion with a questionnaire

1. Give complete information on the source.

2. Specify what you expect to learn from this source. What questions do you want answered?

CHAPTER 4

Critical Reading

Reading efficiently and perceptively is such an important part of the research process that we want to spend a chapter giving you some suggestions and practice with the essential skills of academic reading. Many students think that once they have located some of their sources, the next step is to start taking notes, but you may end up wasting a good deal of time unless you have a strategy and know how to read with insight. Often the material you must read is complicated. Unless you have some skill at reading difficult material, you will end up copying down passages that you do not understand. That lack of understanding will then be reflected in your paper. We will present suggestions about what to do before you begin reading, **Pre-Reading;** what to do while reading, **Active Reading;** and what to do after you have read the material, **Post-Reading.**

PRE-READING

Pre-reading activities will help to make reading more efficient.

Develop a Reading Strategy

Preview the sources to determine the order in which you will read them. Usually, it is advisable to begin with background information in a textbook or encyclopedia. (See pp. 27–33 about encyclopedias.) Furthermore, these sources are likely to be easier reading than some of the articles in professional journals. Once you have read the background material, the next step would be to read the most recent publications. Obviously, recent publications are likely to incorporate earlier research findings on your topic. Looking at the bibliographies listed at the end of recent publications may alert you to earlier materials that you did not come across during your library search.

Beyond these two basic principles, other considerations to keep in mind as you develop a reading strategy are the comprehensiveness of the source and its relevance to your particular topic. For example, while investigating the nature of hypnosis, a researcher might locate many books and articles, among them *Hypnosis: Developments in Research and New Perspectives* and *The Origin of Consciousness in the Breakdown of the Bicameral Mind.* Although the second book has some relevant sections on the essence of hypnosis, the first book is clearly more comprehensive and relevant to the subject of hypnosis. Checking the table of contents in a book or skimming the sections of an article will give you a good idea about how useful any one source is likely to be. The materials that look especially difficult should be set aside and read after you have begun to develop some familiarity with the terms and concepts that are a part of your topic.

Set Goals for Your Reading

1. Develop a context for your research through background reading. As indicated earlier, you need to have a sense of the big picture, of basic knowledge in the field, and how your particular research queston fits into this body of knowledge. At this stage, your primary goal is to get an overview of the topic you will research. In many cases, this preliminary reading will take place while you develop a topic and search for materials. However, if you are working with a technical or highly specialized subject, you may need to do further background reading in a textbook or encyclopedia before you begin the more focused reading.

2. Determine in advance whether you need to read the whole of a particular source or can skim it for relevant information.

3. Establish a reading schedule. What periods of time do you have available for close, uninterrupted reading? What significant chunks of material can you read during those periods?

4. Ask questions that will help you to focus your reading. As you begin your research, your questions will be general ones: When were breakfast cereals introduced? What are the ingredients in cereals? How is the nutritional value of cereals determined? As you progress in your research, your questions will become more specific: What led to the promotion of oat bran? What regulations are there on advertising claims for foods? Are the regulations different for other products, such as drugs?

ACTIVE READING

Active reading is a way to improve your reading comprehension. You have already taken the first step by engaging in pre-reading activities that require decisions. You have already moved beyond being a passive consumer of someone else's ideas. What we want to concentrate on in this second step are techniques to increase your understanding through close reading of a particular source. In this section, we will assume that you have already selected a significant piece of material to read (a book, a chapter from a book, or an article) and that you have gone through the pre-reading steps already described.

Steps in Active Reading

1. Develop an overview of the source.
    a. Examine the title to see whether it gives just the topic ("Immigration Laws Up for Review") or also gives the author's main point ("The Need to Liberalize Immigration Laws").
    b. Look for subdivisions, often in bold face, which will give you a sense of the organization of the piece.
    c. Skim the first and last few paragraphs of an article or chapters in a book. These are the places where an author will state the thesis, purpose, scope, conclusions, or implications of the work. You should be able to distinguish between the related terms—topic, purpose, and thesis—and use them correctly:

TERM	MEANING	EXAMPLE
Topic	The subject	Police use of hypnosis
Purpose	Author's intention	To show how police use hypnosis
Thesis	A position, claim, or opinion	Police use of hypnosis may lead to injustices.

    Although main ideas are often found at the beginning or the end of a work, this is not always the case. Articles and books intended for a professional audience almost always have a clear statement of purpose, but sometimes the writer who is addressing a more general audience will imply or suggest a position without ever stating it directly. A writer makes the decision about stating the thesis directly based on a sense of the reading audience.
2. Interact with the print on the page.
    a. Look for main ideas in paragraphs and think about how each paragraph furthers the author's purpose.
    b. Look for signal words that help you anticipate what is coming next. (See pp. 216–218 for a list of signals and transitions.)

c. Look for supporting details and evidence.
   d. Pay attention to the places where opinions are expressed.
   e. Consider whether sufficient facts have been presented to support the opinions and the thesis.
   f. Think about whether the author has failed to address relevant questions or aspects of the topic.
   g. If you are reading library materials, stop periodically to make notes.
   h. If you are reading a photocopy or book of your own, you can underline, check, or highlight important sections. Use this technique sparingly or else you'll find yourself marking practically everything on the page. You can also write key words, comments, or questions in the margin.

To illustrate the application of these techniques, we have marked and annotated an essay. In Chapter 7, Organizing Your Research, we show you how to take notes from a reading selection. In this section, we are concentrating on reading comprehension.

TO TRUST, PERCHANCE TO BUY

Donald J. Moine

The title suggests a connection between trust and buying. Questions I will ask as I read: How does trust lead to buying? Who can I trust?
The epigraph seems to sum up an important idea: persuaders use hypnotic techniques. I'll have to check on the identity of Willy Loman and Dr. Mesmer.
The author begins by describing a scene in which a salesperson is talking to a customer.
Starting with a bit of narrative is a way for the author to get my interest.
An explanation of the scene is given. The author is moving from a specific example to a generalization about salespeople.
Author states his conclusion. This is the thesis that he develops in the article. "Psycholinguistic" is an unfamiliar term, but I can break it down: psycho = mind linguistic = about language.

Maybe what Willy Loman needed was lessons from Dr. Mesmer. The best persuaders build trust by mirroring the thoughts, tone of voice, speech tempo, and mood of the customer—literally the techniques of the clinical hypnotist.

The real-estate agent, who normally speaks quickly and loudly, is responding in a slow, soft, rhythmic voice to her slow-speaking, quiet customer. The agent opened the sales interview with a series of bland and flatly accurate remarks about the cool weather and the lack of rain. Now she is explaining her hesitation in showing her customer a particular house: "I know you want to see that house, but I don't know whether I should show it to you. It is expensive, and"—an imperceptible pause—"*just looking at it will make you want to buy it.*" A bit later she repeats something that, she says, a previous customer told her about a house he'd bought: "The house has been worth every penny. My wife and I just enjoy it so much"—another pause—"*we can't understand why we took so long to buy it.*"

The agent, an extremely successful saleswoman, is instinctively using weapons from the arsenal of the skilled clinical hypnotist, whose initial aim is to create in a subject a state of intensified attention and receptiveness, leading to increased suggestibility. All successful persuaders produce such an effect, probably without understanding the exact nature of the techniques that accomplish it. Our real-estate woman is lulling her customer into a mood of trust and rapport by taking on his verbal and emotional coloring, and her techniques are almost identical to those that therapists like Herbert Spiegel use with patients who come to them to be hypnotized out of, say, their fear of cats.

The conclusion that a successful sales presentation is an intuitive form of indirect hypnosis is the most provocative finding of a psycholinguistic analysis that I performed in 1981. My initial study focused on eight life-insurance salesmen, four of whom were identified as "top producers" by the presidents of their companies, and four as only average. The two groups were closely matched on such characteristics as age and experience.

Donald J. Moine received his Ph.D. in psychology from the University of Oregon for his study of successful sales people. He lives in Redondo Beach, California.
Reprinted from *Psychology Today Magazine,* Copyright © 1982 American Psychological Association.

Author gives info about how research was conducted.

Taking the role of the customer, I spoke with the eight men, recorded their comments, and analyzed those comments for the 30 techniques of persuasion that Richard Bandler and John Grinder had identified in the work of the master hypnotist Milton Erickson. I next examined the work of 14 top sellers of real estate, luxury automobiles, stocks, commodities, and trust deeds. Since 1981, I have tested my findings with more than 50 other people, who sell, among other products, jets, computers, and oil and gas leases. My basic finding was confirmed: Superior sellers use the techniques of the clinical hypnotist; mediocre ones do not.

Getting in Sync

Heading identifies one of the techniques: "hypnotic pacing."

The best sales people first establish a mood of trust and rapport by means of "hypnotic pacing"—statements and gestures that play back a customer's observations, experience, or behavior. Pacing is a kind of mirror-like matching, a way of suggesting: "I am like you. We are in sync. You can trust me."

Identifies a type of pacing: "descriptive pacing"

Gives examples

The simplest form of pacing is "descriptive pacing," in which the seller formulates accurate, if banal, descriptions of the customer's experience. "It's been awfully hot these last few days, hasn't it?" "You said you were going to graduate in June." These statements serve the purpose of establishing agreement and developing an unconscious affinity between seller and customer. In clinical hypnosis, the hypnotist might make comparable pacing statements: "You are here today to see me for hypnosis." "You told me over the phone about a problem that concerns you." Sales agents with only average success tend to jump immediately into their memorized sales pitches or to hit the customer with a barrage of questions. Neglecting to pace the customer, the mediocre sales agent creates no common ground on which to build trust.

Signal words = "A second type"

Examples of "objection pacing"

A second type of hypnotic pacing statement is the "objection pacing" comment. A customer objects or resists, and the sales agent agrees, matching his or her remarks to the remarks of the customer. A superior insurance agent might agree that "insurance is not the best investment out there," just as a clinical hypnotist might tell a difficult subject, "You are resisting going into trance. That's good, I encourage that." The customer, pushing against a wall, finds that the wall has disappeared. The agent, having confirmed the customer's objection, then leads the customer to a position that negates or undermines the objection. The insurance salesman who agreed that "insurance is not the best investment out there" went on to tell his customer, "but it does have a few uses." He then described all the benefits of life insurance. Mediocre sales people generally respond to resistance head-on, with arguments that presumably answer the customer's objection. This response often leads the customer to dig in his heels all the harder.

Signal words = "most powerful forms of pacing"

The most powerful forms of pacing have more to do with how something is said than with what is said. The good salesman or -woman

CRITICAL READING 81

Explanation and examples

has a chameleon-like ability to pace the language and thought of any customer. With hypnotic effect, the agent matches the voice tone, rhythm, volume, and speech rate of the customer. He matches the customer's posture, body language, and mood. He adopts the characteristic verbal language of the customer ("sounds good," "rings a bell," "get a grip on it"). If the customer is slightly depressed, the agent shares that feeling and acknowledges that he has been feeling "a little down" lately. In essence, the top sales producer becomes a sophisticated biofeedback mechanism, sharing and reflecting the customer's reality—even to the point of breathing in and out with the customer.

"Do not...pace" tells me that he is explaining an exception.

I have found only one area in which the top sales people do not regularly pace their customers' behavior and attitudes—the area of beliefs and values. For example, if a customer shows up on a car lot and explains that she is a Republican, a moderately successful salesman is likely to say that he is too, even if he isn't. The best sales people, even if they are Republicans, are unlikely to say so, perhaps because they understand that "talk is cheap" and recognize intuitively that there are deeper, more binding ways of "getting in sync" with the customer.

Heading suggests a second major technique will be discussed.

The Soft Sell

Only after they have created a bond of trust and rapport do the top sales people begin to add the suggestions and indirect commands that they hope will lead the customer to buy. One such soft-sell technique is using their patently true pacing statements as bridges to introduce influencing statements that lead to a desired response or action. For example: "You are looking at this car and you can remember the joy of owning a new reliable car," or "You are 27 years old, and we figure that your need for life insurance is $50,000." These pacing-and-leading statements resemble the way a hypnotist leads a client into hypnosis. "You are sitting in this chair, and you are listening to my voice"—the unarguable pacing statements—"and your eyelids are getting heavy, and they are beginning to close. . . ."

Pacing leads to "indirect commands."

Examples of the technique: "pacing statements" are a "bridge" to buying suggestions.

Further explanation of how "bridge" creates a "sales logic"

There does not have to be any logical connection between the pacing statement and the leading statement. They can be totally unrelated, yet when they are connected linguistically, they form a "sales logic" that can be powerfully effective, even with such presumably analytic and thoughtful customers as doctors and college professors.

The power of these leading statements comes from the fact that they capitalize on the affirmative mental state built by the undeniably true pacing statements, with which the customer is now familiar. Customers who have agreed with sales people expect, unconsciously, further agreement, just as customers who have disagreed expect further disagreement. The "traditional" truth of these pacing statements rubs off on the leading statements, and, without knowing it, the customer begins to take more and more of what the sales agent says as both factual and personally significant. Using hypnotic language, the agent activates the customer's desire for the product.

A second method: to give "indirect commands"	Average sellers combine pacing and leading statements less frequently and with less skill than do their superior colleagues. They also speak in shorter, choppier sentences, and thus fail to create the emotional web of statements in which the truthful and the possible seem to merge. One of the most subtle soft-sell techniques is to embed a command into a seemingly innocuous statement. "A smart investor knows how to *make a quick decision, Robert.*" "I'm going to show you a product that will help you, *Jim, save money.*"
Explanation of the technique is given and illustrated with examples.	Sales people insure that their embedded commands come across by changing the tone, rhythm, and volume of their speech. Typically, as they pronounce the commands, they intuitively slow their speech, look the customer directly in the eyes, and say each word forcefully. A clinical hypnotist does the same thing deliberately. "If you will *listen to the sound of my voice,* you will be able to relax." The placement of an individual's name in a sentence seems like a trivial matter, yet the position of a name can make a significant difference in how strongly the sentence influences the listener. Placed before or after the command portion of a sentence, it gives the command an extra power. By changing their speech rate, volume, and tone, the best sales agents are able to give certain phrases the effect of commands. "If you can *imagine yourself owning this beautiful car,* and *imagine how happy it will make you,* you will want to, *Mr. Benson, buy this car.*" The two phrases beginning with 'imagine' become commands for the customer to do just that. Owning the car is linked to the leading statement of how happy it will make the customer. Finally, the statement carries the embedded command: "*Mr. Benson, buy this car.*"
	The Power of Parables
Signal words = "a final soft-sell technique": using stories and metaphors	A final soft-sell technique of the best sales people is the ability to tell anecdotes, parables, and stories, and to frame their comments in metaphors. For thousands of years, human beings have been influencing, guiding, and inspiring one another with stories and metaphors, so it should be no surprise that sales people routinely use them to influence customers. What is surprising is the frequency and skill with which they do so.
Purpose of telling stories is explained and illustrated.	Some sales agents I have studied do almost nothing but tell stories. They tell them to get the customer's attention, to build trust and rapport, and even to deliver product information. A piece of information that in itself might be boring takes on a human dimension and stays in the customers' memory when placed in the context of a story. "I sold a receiver like this a week ago to a surfer from Torrance and what he liked best about it was its FM sensitivity of 1.7 microvolts." Metaphors and stories are used to handle customer's resistance and to "close" on them without endangering rapport. A top insurance agent was attempting to close a deal for a policy with a young man who was considering signing with a smaller company. As part of his clinching

argument, the salesman wove the following metaphor into his pitch: "It's like taking your family on a long voyage across the Atlantic Ocean, and you want to get from here to England, and you have the choice of either going on this tugboat or on the Queen Mary. Which one would you *feel safe* on?" Had the saleman tried to make his point with a litany of facts and figures, he might never have focused his customer's attention; the discussion could have descended into a dispute about numbers. Instead, his story spoke directly to the customer's concern about his family's safety and implied that it was now in the customer's power to decide between two choices that were clearly unequal.

Note, too, that the salesman used conjunctions to link the metaphor in one unbroken chain and give it a hypnotic cadence. Mediocre sales people who know such a story would probably tell it as several separate sentences. In addition, they probably would give no special emphasis to the phrase "feel safe" even if they had heard better sales people do so. The skill in telling it is more important than the material itself.

> *Conclusion links these techniques to other groups of persuaders.*

The same can be said about all the skills that constitute the intuitively hypnotic arsenal of the best sales agents. But obviously, these skills are not exclusive to sellers. They are common to others—politicians, lawyers, even preachers. No less than sales people, these persuaders try to influence their audiences. No less than sales people, they attempt to implant in their audiences a resolve to do something. And, like sales people, all of them use, to some extent, variations of the techniques of Mesmer, Cagliostro, and Rasputin.

> *Here are some other names I'll have to check on.*

TECHNIQUES FOR READING DIFFICULT MATERIAL

In addition to the suggestions we have already given, you may have to use some special techniques when you run into materials that are especially difficult. As indicated earlier, you should postpone reading difficult materials until you have become somewhat familiar with your chosen topic. Each bit of reading that you do builds your vocabulary of special terms and your familiarity with the key concepts related to the topic.

The source of difficulty usually comes from two or three areas:

1. Vocabulary
    a. Sometimes we can figure out the general meaning of an unfamiliar word through its context in the sentence.

        For example: "Early investigators assumed that women enter hypnosis more readily than men, but this has not been borne out in most studies; similarly, *hypnotizability* is not especially related to intelligence nor to education" (Orne & Hammer, 1974, p. 138).

        The first part of the sentence contains the phrase "enter hypnosis more readily," which would clue a reader unfamiliar with *hypnotizability* that it means the ease with which an individual can by hypnotized.

    b. If the context does not provide a clue, you may be able to break the word into components that are more recognizable.

        For example: *hypnotizability* is made from two words—hypnotize + ability. In this case, we would have to think about whether the word referred to someone's ability to hypnotize others or the person's ability to be hypnotized. Apart from the context of the sentence, we can call up our prior knowledge of similar words. For instance, excitability means the capacity to be excited, not the ability to excite others. Extrapolating from what we know to the unknown, we can determine that hypnotizability means the capacity to be hypnotized.

        It is important to make use of these two techniques the first time you read through a difficult section. If you have to stop to look up too many words, you will not be able to follow the train of thought in the passage.

    c. Use a dictionary or reference work. You should check your guesses about the meaning of words after you have read a section of the material. Obviously, you will have to check sooner if you are unable to guess at the meaning. The amount that you read before checking depends on just how difficult the material is. Perhaps you can understand enough of the ideas, so that you will need to consult a dictionary only after you have finished reading several pages. At other times, the material may seem so dense that you will need to check after each paragraph.

        In addition to a general dictionary, there are specialized dictionaries and glossaries for different academic fields. See pp. 28–30 for a list. For names of people, places, and events that you cannot find in one of these sources, you may need to consult an almanac or fact book. Some of the most useful ones are listed on p. 27. You can also ask a reference librarian for help in finding an appropriate book.

2. Sentence structure

    a. If a sentence is longer than what we are used to, we may have trouble understanding it. However, a long sentence is just a short sentence that has been expanded. You can learn to look for the kernel (the simple subject and predicate) and see how other parts of the sentence are related to the kernel. One way to identify the kernel is to ask:

        Who is doing what (to whom)?

        Example: Although initially interested in his theories, the scientific community, after witnessing his treatments, dismissed Mesmer's theories, concluding that his cures were due to the imagination of his patients and not to a physical cause.

Complex sentences, such as the one above, consist of a series of simple sentences that have been embedded in a kernel sentence.

Kernel: The scientific community dismissed Mesmer's theories.
Embedded sentences: The scientific community was initially interested in Mesmer's theories.
The scientific community witnessed his treatments.
The scientific community reached a conclusion.
The conclusion was that the cures were due to the imagination of his patients.
The conclusion was that the cure was not due to a physical cause.

Long sentences are not necessarily good or bad, but they are often written to express the close relationship between ideas. Learning to take apart long sentences goes hand-in-hand with learning to construct sentences that will adequately express the complex ideas of your own that you will develop about your research topic and express in your paper.

b. If a sentence is arranged in an unfamiliar pattern, we may have difficulty understanding it. A common pattern in academic writing, particularly scientific reports, is the use of the passive voice. In the passive voice, the doer of the action (who?) is not identified or is mentioned at the end of the sentence.

Example: Suggestability, which has been considered an essential part of the hypnotic state, can be achieved through directions given to subjects who are fully awake.

Kernel: Subjects can achieve suggestability.
Embedded sentence: The subjects are fully awake.
Directions are given to subjects.
Suggestability is considered an essential part of the hypnotic state.

POST-READING

After careful reading, you should check your understanding through one or more of the following types of response:

- Identify the author's purpose or thesis.
- Understand how individual sections (paragraphs or chapters) relate to the purpose or thesis.
- Paraphrase important sections.
- Summarize key points.

— Relate what you have read to other knowledge that you have of the topic.
— Compare what the author has stated with what others have said on the same topic.
— Evaluate the author's reasoning and use of evidence.

You can test your understanding informally by writing in your journal or talking to other students in your research group. More formal ways of expressing your understanding are note-taking, which is explained in Chapter 7, or writing short papers, such as a summary, which are explained in Chapter 6. Ultimately, your understanding will be expressed in the formal research paper that you write. However, as part of the research process, your instructor may want to check your skills. At this point, we want to concentrate on the critical thinking skills required to paraphrase, summarize, compare or contrast, and evaluate.

PARAPHRASING

Paraphrasing means putting information into your own words without distorting the meaning of the original. A paraphrase is a sentence by sentence translation of important passages. Unlike a summary, a paraphrase does not leave out any information. A paraphrase does not contain your opinions on the topic or your evaluation of the author. Instructors prefer to have students paraphrase, rather than quote directly, because putting information into your own words is a good indication that you have digested the ideas. Many writing assignments in college rely on the ability to paraphrase from your reading. Direct quotation should be used sparingly in any college paper. Whenever you use an author's wording, even if it is just a part of a sentence, you should use quotation marks.

Steps in Paraphrasing

1. Use the pre-reading and active reading strategies that we have suggested. You need to have a sense of the whole before you can adequately paraphrase a specific section.

2. Select key passages that you want to paraphrase. Limit yourself to a paragraph at a time.

3. Read the paragraph one more time and then set it aside. Without looking at the paragraph, jot down all that you can remember. Unless you have a photographic mind, you will have put most of the information into your own words. An alternate strategy is to make up a question based on the information in the paragraph and then write the answer without looking at the paragraph.

4. Use a dictionary to find synonyms for words that you cannot translate on your own. Be very careful to use a synonym that fits the

context of the sentence. Many words have more than one meaning; consequently, words listed as synonyms may not match the way the word was used by the author. Sometimes there is no accurate substitute for a word used by the author, in which case you must repeat the word in your paraphrase.

5. Check your first effort at a paraphrase against the original. Is the paraphrase accurate and complete? Have you left out important pieces of information? Have you inadvertently repeated the author's original phrasing without using quotation marks? If your paraphrase seems too much like the original, try rearranging the sentences. You can switch the sequence of words within sentences, break up long sentences, or combine short sentences. You can also reorder the sentences in the paragraph.

Example: Here is a paragraph from "To Trust, Perchance To Buy," found on pp. 79–83. It is an important passage because it states the author's thesis and explains how his research was conducted.

Original passage: The conclusion that a successful sales presentation is an intuitive form of indirect hypnosis is the most provocative finding of a psycholinguistic analysis that I performed in 1981. My initial study focused on eight life-insurance salesmen, four of whom were identified as "top producers" by the presidents of their companies, and four as only average. The two groups were closely matched on such characteristics as age and experience. Taking the role of the customer, I spoke with the eight men, recorded their comments, and analyzed those comments for the 30 techniques of persuasion that Richard Bandler and John Grinder had identified in the work of the master hypnotist Milton Erickson. I next examined the work of 14 top sellers of real estate, luxury automobiles, stocks, commodities, and trust deeds. Since 1981, I have tested my findings with more than 50 other people, who sell, among other products, jets, computers, and oil and gas leases. My basic finding was confirmed: Superior sellers use the techniques of the clinical hypnotist; mediocre ones do not.

First effort at paraphrase: The author conducted a study of the techniques used by top salesmen. He interviewed life insurance salesmen and discovered that they used the same techniques as hypnotists do. He continued to study other salesmen and found that his initial results were confirmed.

Comparing this paraphrase with the original, we can see that some of it is not quite accurate and information has been left out. However, the most important step has been taken; the author's words have been translated into the reader's own words. The next step is to correct any inaccuracies. In this case, it is incorrect to say that the author "interviewed" the salesmen. His method was to act like a customer and then note what they said. A second inaccuracy comes from failing to notice that the author expanded his study from *salesmen* to *sales people*. This first effort is also incorrect in that is does not clearly indicate that the salesmen used the hypnotic techniques without being aware that they were hypnotic techniques.

Revised paraphrase: The author studied top salesmen to find out what techniques they used. He began by comparing a group of four top life-insurance salesmen with a comparable group of four average salesmen. He pretended to be the customer and made notes on what they said. Then he compared the way they handled a customer with the techniques used by a famous hypnotist, Milton Erickson. His tentative conclusion, reached in 1981, was that the top salesmen instinctively used the techniques of the hypnotist, but the average sellers did not. He further tested his conclusion by studying over 64 sellers of several other products, such as computers and investments, and found the same results.

SUMMARIZING

When you summarize material, you are reducing it and making judgments about what information can be cut out without distorting the original meaning. What gets eliminated always depends on the purpose of your summary, but generally when you summarize material, you are "boiling it down" to the main ideas and cutting out the details. Like the paraphrase, a summary translates material into your own words, sticking to the text and not including your opinions or evaluations.

Examples of summaries are plentiful in academic writing. Most professional journals require that writers include a summary or abstract of the article that is being submitted. Indexes of abstracts in specific disciplines are described in Chapter 2. If you check your textbooks, you will find that many of them contain summaries at the beginning or end of a chapter. A sample summary paper is included in Chapter 6.

To summarize effectively, you must be able to identify the main point in a paragraph and understand how the point is developed. There are several basic methods of development. An author may use one or a combination of these. In the following examples of paragraph development, the main point has been underlined:

1. Illustration with specific detail or examples

Example: Some people can be hypnotized more easily than others. Contrary to what was first thought, women and unintelligent individuals are not necessarily more suggestible. However, children and adults who must follow directions from others are good subjects for hypnosis. Surprisingly, well-adjusted individuals are more hypnotizable than neurotics. The most important factors seem to be an individual's willingness to trust others, a belief that one can be hypnotized, and confidence that the procedure is safe.

2. Analysis of component parts

Example: According to a study by Donald Moine, top salespeople use techniques that resemble those of the clinical hypnotist. One technique is known as ''pacing'' and consists of mirroring the customer's mood, doubts, and mannerisms. After the salesperson has created a bond with the customer, a second technique is introduced: subtle suggestions to buy the product are linked with the pacing statements to form a ''sales logic.'' The sales pitch is augmented by a third technique, the use of stories and metaphors that carry an important message to the customer.

3. Comparing and contrasting

Example: The hypnotic state has often been compared to sleep. In fact, the term hypnosis comes from a Greek word for sleep. The similarity between hypnosis and sleep was promoted by the famous Russian researcher, Ivan Pavlov, who argued that both states were characterized by inhibition of neural processes. Contemporary researchers have also stressed that the inner experience of hypnosis parallels the experience of deep relaxation. However, the differences between the two states may be greater than the similarities. The most obvious difference is that sleep is a physiological necessity for everyone, whereas hypnosis is not. Certain nonvoluntary responses, such as the knee jerk, are suppressed during sleep but not during hypnosis. Furthermore, studies of brain waves have shown far less activity in the cortex during sleep than during hypnosis.

4. Narration/description

Example: Although Freud was interested in hypnosis and used it for a while in his treatment of patients, he eventually dropped it. As a medical student, Freud had become convinced that the controversial technique had merit. In 1885 he visited Paris where he studied with the master hypnotist Jean Martin Charcot. He listened to Charcot skillfully engage the audience by detailing his train of thought and confessing his doubts. Then he watched the consummate performer demonstrate how he could induce and cure paralysis while a patient was in a hypnotic state. Freud brought the tool of hypnosis back to Vienna with him where he used it to treat a variety of physical symptoms caused by hysteria. However, Freud found hypnosis a less reliable technique than the method of free association that became his trademark.

Steps in Summarizing

1. Use the pre-reading and active reading strategies that we have suggested so that you have a sense of the whole piece.

2. Select a section to summarize. This may be a single paragraph, a cluster of paragraphs, an article, or chapter in a book. Remember that the amount that you reduce the original will depend on the purpose of your summary. You can summarize a paragraph or a book in a single sentence; the difference is the amount that is being left out.

3. Identify the main idea and the method of development.

4. Paraphrase the main idea, using the techniques explained on pp. 86–87.

5. Decide on how much additional material will be included in the summary.

6. Check your summary against the original for accuracy of information and to be sure that your word choice and sentence structure do not closely resemble the original. Also, make sure that you have put quotation marks around any phrases or sentences that are worded just like the original.

To illustrate the process of summarizing, we will use a cluster of paragraphs from Moine's article on pp. 79–83.

Notice that the first paragraph in this section identifies a main idea: that good sales people develop trust with the customer by communicating in ways that mirror the customer. The following paragraphs develop this idea by analyzing the different forms of pacing and giving examples of each.

Getting in Sync

The best sales people first establish a mood of trust and rapport by means of "hypnotic pacing"—statements and gestures that play back a customer's observations, experience, or behavior. Pacing is a kind of mirror-like matching, a way of suggesting: "I am like you. We are in sync. You can trust me."

The simplest form of pacing is "descriptive pacing," in which the seller formulates accurate, if banal, descriptions of the customer's experience. "It's been awfully hot these last few days, hasn't it?" "You said you were going to graduate in June." These statements serve the purpose of establishing agreement and developing an unconscious affinity between seller and customer. In clinical hypnosis, the hypnotist might make comparable pacing statements: "You are here today to see me for hypnosis." "You told me over the phone about a problem that concerns you." Sales agents with only average success tend to jump immediately into their memorized sales pitches or to hit the customer with a barrage of questions. Neglecting to pace the customer, the mediocre sales agent creates no common ground on which to build trust.

A second type of hypnotic pacing statement is the "objection pacing" comment. A customer objects or resists, and the sales agent agrees, matching his or her remarks to the remarks of the customer. A superior insurance agent might agree that "insurance is not the best investment out there," just as a clinical hypnotist might tell a difficult subject, "You are resisting going into trance. That's good, I encourage that." The customer, pushing against a wall, finds that the wall has disappeared. The agent, having confirmed the customer's objection, then leads the customer to a position that negates or undermines the objection. The insurance salesman who agreed that "insurance is not the best investment out there" went on to tell his customer, "but it does have a few uses." He then described all the benefits of life insurance. Mediocre sales people generally respond to resistance head-on, with arguments that presumably answer the customer's objection. This response often leads the customer to dig in his heels all the harder.

The most powerful forms of pacing have more to do with how something is said than with what is said. The good salesman or -woman has a chameleon-like ability to pace the language and thought of any customer. With hypnotic effect, the agent matches the voice tone, rhythm, volume, and speech rate of the customer. He matches the customer's posture, body language, and mood. He adopts the characteristic verbal language of the customer ("sounds good," "rings a bell," "get a grip on it"). If the customer is slightly depressed, the agent shares that feeling and acknowledges that he has been feeling "a little down" lately. In essence, the top sales producer becomes a sophisticated biofeedback mechanism, sharing and reflecting the customer's reality—even to the point of breathing in and out with the customer.

I have found only one area in which the top sales people do not regularly pace their customers' behavior and attitudes—the area of beliefs and values. For example, if a customer shows up on a car lot and explains that she is a Republican, a moderately successful salesman is likely to say that he is too, even if he isn't. The best sales people, even if they are Republicans, are unlikely to say so, perhaps because they understand that "talk is cheap" and recognize intuitively that there are deeper, more binding ways of "getting in sync" with the customer.

A one-sentence summary: Good sales people develop trust in the customer by mirroring the customer through forms of ''hypnotic pacing,'' such as ''descriptive pacing,'' ''objection pacing,'' and nonverbal pacing; however, they do not try to pretend that they hold the same beliefs or values as the customer.

Clearly, such a summary leaves out a good deal of important information. If you wanted to test your understanding of the material, you would then add information to explain the different types of pacing.

A one-paragraph summary: Good sales people develop trust by mirroring the customer's experience, objections, and body language, a technique called pacing. ''Descriptive pacing'' mirrors the customer's experience in simple statements about the weather or something the customer has just said. ''Objection pacing'' is used to mirror the customer's concerns when the customer resists a sales pitch. Good sales people mirror how the customer communicates, not just the content of what the customer says. However, trying to mirror the customer's deeply held beliefs and values is not a technique of the successful sales person.

For an example of a summary of an entire article, see the Sample Summary paper on pp. 140–141.

COMPARING AND CONTRASTING

As you engage in the pre-reading and active reading techniques we have described, you will inevitably find yourself categorizing information: restatement of something that you already knew, a variation or extension of something that you already knew, or something that is quite new. Your mind is busy weaving the material you are reading into the network of knowledge that is already stored in your brain. The process of comparing and contrasting what you have just read with what you already know or with another selection on the same topic is a way of testing your understanding and strengthening your grasp of the material.

Although the terms are sometimes used interchangably, comparing means seeing the similarities and contrasting means seeing the differences. For example, when Moine was studying the comments of salespeople, he saw similarities in many of the comments and grouped them together as examples of what he called "hypnotic pacing." The similarity between them was that they "mirrored" the customer in some way. Within this category, however, were subgroups that differed from one another on the basis of what was being mirrored: commonplace observations, objections, or the nonverbal aspects of communication.

Steps in Comparing and Contrasting

1. Identify the material that will be analyzed. There must be some similarity or else the process is not worthwhile. You have probably heard the expression, "You can't compare apples and oranges," meaning that two different items cannot be discussed usefully. However, you are the judge of how much similarity is needed to make the process useful to you. For example, you could compare apples and oranges in terms of their nutrition, shelf life, or cultivation.

2. Search the two items for similar terms or concepts. Underline or take notes on these sections. Paraphrase and summarize the similarities.

3. Look for material that is not common to both items. Again summarize these passages. Do the differences illuminate various facets of the topic or do they indicate a difference of opinion about the topic?

4. Sum up the similarities and differences, indicating whether the writers are more in agreement or disagreement.

Let's examine two paragraphs on the same subject, looking for similarities and differences.

1. From "To Trust, Perchance to Buy": A final soft-sell technique of the best sales people is the ability to tell anecdotes, parables, and stories, and to frame their comments in metaphors. For thousands of years, human beings have been influencing, guiding, and inspiring one another with stories and metaphors, so it should be no surprise that sales people routinely use them to influence customers. What is surprising is the frequency and skill with which they do so.

2. From a paper on hypnotic suggestion: Indirect suggestions can be made during hypnosis through the use of stories and analogies. According to Erickson, stories and analogies function on two levels: 1. They focus the interest of the conscious mind, thereby minimizing distractions; 2. They evoke associations and patterns embedded in the unconscious. The result is that stories and analogies can produce responsive behavior in people who might resist overt directions or commands.

   COMPARING
   1. Both paragraphs refer to the use of stories.
   2. The use of metaphors is mentioned in the first paragraph and the use of analogies in the second. A metaphor is a type of analogy, so both paragraphs are discussing the same techniques.
   3. Both paragraphs claim that these techniques are successful ways to influence people.

   CONTRASTING
   1. The first paragraph is primarily concerned with the techniques of successful salespeople, whereas the second is about techniques used during hypnosis.
   2. The first paragraph is just making a claim that the use of certain techniques is effective. The second paragraph is explaining why the techniques work.

Sample comparison/contrast statement: Both writers agree that people can be influenced through stories and analogies. Moine is interested in the way that top sales people use these techniques, whereas the second writer explains that they are effective because they operate on the conscious and the unconscious portions of the mind.

For an example of a comparison/contrast paper, see the sample on pp. 144–146.

EVALUATING

Evaluating what you have read is a much more complex task than the process of paraphrasing, summarizing, comparing, or contrasting. In fact, you must include all of these steps as part of evaluating the material you have read. Although we have given you some practical tips on evaluating sources in Chapter 2, this section will contain a more detailed examination of the critical thinking skills needed to draw conclusions and form judgments about a piece of writing.

We draw conclusions and form judgments on a daily basis about many aspects of our lives—from the reliability of certain products to the performance of public officials. Our personal experience and the testimony of people we respect are filtered through a reasoning process that we have absorbed from our culture. The process used in the academic world is similar but more strictly defined. Its basis is the scientific method which has exacting standards for gathering the evidence (facts) and for logic (reasoning) used to draw conclusions about the facts. The scientific method has been enormously successful in advancing knowledge because the process has established and agreed-upon rules.

We suggest that you read with an attitude of *skeptical appreciation.* The appreciation will alert you to the effort that the writer is making to present information and its significance. At the same time, a bit of skepticism will prompt you to ask questions: Is this a reliable publication? What are the writer's credentials? Why should I trust this writer? Where are the facts? Where did they come from? What does all of this add up to? Could the facts be interpreted in some other way?

Steps in Evaluating

1. Carefully distinguish between factual and interpretive statements. A fact is an observation by a reliable reporter. A factual statement is one that can be verified or checked out. For example, Moine stated that two comparable groups of salesmen had been compared in his initial study. As a trained professional, Moine had a responsibility to keep records which could be used to verify the statements made in his research report. Anyone who doubted his statements could have asked for the records or for more specific information from the records. Often a writer is relying on facts that have been recorded by others, as Moine does when he uses the work of earlier researchers who had studied the techniques of a highly regarded hypnotist.

A factual statement can always be tested. It may turn out to be wrong, but there is always a way to verify it.

Example: The number of legal immigrants to the United States in 1989 was 612,110.

The actual number may be more or less, but we would be able to find out by checking government publications. In general, a statement of fact does not leave much room for disagreement. Here are a few more examples:

1. Twenty percent of the children in the United States live in low-income households.
2. The source of the Amazon River is in the Peruvian Andes.
3. An Egyptian novelist, Naguib Mahfouz, won the 1988 Nobel Prize in Literature.

An interpretive statement is one that comments on the implications or significance of the facts. An interpretive statement gives an opinion or judgment based on the facts.

Example: The United States needs to admit more immigrants in order to avoid labor shortages in the future.

Obviously, we could not verify this statement by checking records. We would have to look at the reasoning, as well as the facts, that had been used in drawing this conclusion.

Sometimes an interpretive statement will look like a factual statement because it has numbers in it:

Example: Within twenty years the United States faces a shortage of 1.2 million workers.

Although the statement looks factual at first glance, it is interpretive because it involves a projection into the future, an estimate about where current trends are leading. No reference will tell us whether the estimate is correct. Instead, we would have to examine the writer's arguments and information before we could decide on its accuracy.

Distinguishing between facts and interpretations is not always easy. Many of the statements that we read are a blend of both.

Example: A recent study showed that 30 percent of the children from two-parent families were high achievers, whereas only 17 percent of the children from one-parent families performed in that category.

We can verify whether there was a study that reported these figures, but it is another matter to assess the validity of the study. What was the purpose of the study? Who conducted it? Have the results been verified? What happens to the percentages if family income is considered? We would want more information before we accepted the results of this study.

2. Assess whether the author has sufficient facts to support the opinions or judgments which are expressed. Has the writer used up-to-date information? Does the information come from reliable sources? When writers interpret the facts to form conclusions, opinions, and judgments, they are reasoning about evidence. The errors that can creep into reasoning are discussed on pp. 155–158.

3. Determine whether the author has supported the thesis or argument of the piece. Almost every book and article has a thesis, either stated or implied, that determines what information will be included and how it will be presented. Even textbooks have a slant on their subject. Therefore, even if a book or an article does not seem to present an argument, try to figure out what the author is trying to prove. Again, look carefully at prefaces, introductions, and conclusions because these are the places where you are most likely to find a statement of purpose.

4. Compare and contrast what the author has said with what you know and with what other authors have said about the same subject. Does the author neglect to discuss certain aspects of the topic? Does failure to do so weaken the author's argument? Are the author's interpretations supported by other material that you have read?

Sample evaluation: ''To Trust, Perchance To Buy'' presents the findings of research that Donald J. Moine conducted to earn a Ph.D. from the University of Oregon. The magazine in which the article was printed, Psychology Today, is published by a reputable professional association. Consequently, the source of the information and the author's credentials are reliable. The article presents a description of Moine's conclusions, but not the raw data on which he based the conclusions; therefore, it is difficult to assess his use of facts. However, some questions can be asked about his interpretations. First, he claims that top salespeople intuitively use the techniques of the clinical hypnotist, but he does not discuss alternate interpretations: Are clinical hypnotists using the techniques of successful salespeople? Are hypnotists, in effect, skilled salespeople? Are these techniques truly intuitive? Second, would the results be different if sellers of other products were considered? Third, what factors other than hypnotic techniques might account for the success of top sellers: years of experience? knowledge of the product? amount of time and energy expended? Finally, there is the question of significance: does Moine's research have any relevance for sales people or consumers?

For an example of a more extensive evaluation, see the Sample Reaction Paper on pp. 168–171.

EXERCISES

I. Developing a reading strategy

Assume you are doing a research paper investigating medical uses of hypnosis. By looking up the subject "Hypnosis, Therapeutic uses" in various indexes and the catalog, you have found the following books and articles. With which ones would you start? This order would be provisional, because as you read each you would be informing yourself and developing insights and interests that you might then want to follow up in a different order. You might not even want to read them all. Nonetheless, it is good to have a preliminary strategy for tackling your sources.

Ambrose, Gordon, *A Handbook of Medical Hypnosis: An Introduction for Practitioners and Students* 1968.
Bower, B., "Post-Traumatic Stress Disorder: Hypnosis and the Divided Self," *Science News* 1988.
"Can Hypnotism Help Patients with Gastric Ulcers?" *RN* 1990.
Fross, Garland H., *Handbook of Hypnotic Techniques, with Special Reference to Dentistry* 1965.
Gibson, H. B., *Hypnosis: Its Nature and Therapeutic Uses* 1978.
"Hypnosis Hype," *New Scientist* 1988.
"Hypnosis," *Encyclopedia Britannica.*
"Hypnotherapy for Duodenal Ulcers," *American Family Physician* 1988.
"Hypnotism: Guilty of Fraud?" *Science News* 1982.
"Hypnotized by Hypnotism," *New Scientist* 1984.

Morris, D. M., and others, "Hypnoanesthesia in the Morbidly Obese," *Journal of the American Medical Association*.

Naish, Peter L. N. (ed.), *What Is Hypnosis? Current Theories and Research* 1986.

Nash, H. L., and others, "Baseball Breaks from Tradition in Player Care," *American Family Physician* 1987.

Nelson, S. " 'No Smoking Please': From Two-Packs-a-Day to Zero Overnight? It Was Easy for This 'Hypnotizable' Woman." *Health* 1988.

Rossi, E. L., *The Psychobiology of Mind-Body Healing: New Concepts of Therapeutic Hypnosis* 1986.

Spiegel, D., "The Healing Trance: After Years of Neglect, Hypnosis Is Winning Respect," *Science* 1984.

Wolberg, Lewis. *Hypnosis, Is It For You?* 1982.

II. Active reading
   A. Examine each title in the Anthology. Indicate for each, first, whether or not it identifies the topic, and, second, whether or not it identifies the author's thesis.
   B. Skim the first and last few paragraphs of "The Facts about Animal Research" by Robert J. White in the Anthology. Then determine Dr. White's topic, purpose, and thesis.
   C. Skim the other articles to determine thesis or purpose. Did you find any in which a thesis was not clearly stated?
   D. Choose one article to read closely. What signals or transitions did the author use?
   E. Paragraph development
      Read "Why Worry about the Animals?" Find good examples of paragraphs developed according to each of the following methods:
         illustration with specific detail or example
         analysis of component parts
         comparison/contrast
         narration/description

III. Post-reading
   List the five headings in Dr. White's article in the Anthology ("The Facts about Animal Research"). Then for each heading write one sentence that summarizes the key point in that particular section of his article.

IV. Vocabulary
   Read this passage about Nazi experiments in hypothermia from "Better Health Care Doesn't Justify Animal Research":

   > Human subjects—prisoners in concentration camps—were immersed in cold water to study their various reactions as they suffered and died. Such cruelty is horrifying. But it turns out that these experiments could provide useful data to help save people with hypothermia.

A. From the context, guess what "hypothermia" means.
B. If you break "hypothermia" into its components (hypo = thermia), what similar words can you suggest for each component?
C. Check "hypothermia" in a dictionary.

V. Finding synonyms
A. Read the following paragraph and use the dictionary to find synonyms for the words that are underlined.

> In studying the nature of the hypnotic trance, the question arises as to which <u>phenomena</u> are <u>primary</u> and <u>consistent components</u> of the trance state and which are <u>secondary derivatives</u>. Let us postulate that increased <u>motivation</u> is a <u>constant</u> accompaniment of the hypnotic state. The present phase of the research was designed to show that certain phenomena long viewed as part and parcel of the hypnotic state may more <u>parsimoniously</u> be viewed as derivative of increased motivation, and can be reproduced pari passu by other motivational <u>techniques</u> that have no direct <u>relationship</u> to hypnosis (Orne 290).

B. Can you guess the meaning of the Latin expression "pari passu" from the context of the passage and from your knowledge of comparable words like "par" (used in the expression "below par" or "on a par") or words like pass or passage? After trying to construct the meaning of "pari passu," check it in the dictionary.

VI. Paraphrasing
A. **Directions:** Write a paraphrase for each of the paragraphs. Be sure to change both the wording and the sentence structure of the original. Use quotation marks around any phrases that you cannot put into your own words.

1.
> The animal rights movement, which has mushroomed during the past decade, most conspicuously in the growth of PETA [People for Ethical Treatment of Animals] (membership around 300,000), is distinguished from the animal welfare movement, as represented by, for example, the Humane Society of the United States. Animal welfare activists don't necessarily claim that animals are the moral equivalent of humans, just that animals' feelings deserve some consideration; we shouldn't needlessly hurt them—with pointless experimentation, say, or by making fur coats. And just about every thinking person, if pressed, will agree that animal welfare is a legitimate idea. Hardly anyone believes in kicking dogs (Wright 21).

2.
> But by far the most fearsome form of skin cancer is malignant melanoma, which sometimes emerges from an existing mole or simply appears in an area of previously

unblemished skin. Melanomas are asymmetrically shaped, usually begin as mottled light brown or black blotches that eventually can turn red, white or blue in spots, become crusty and bleed. They grow rapidly, and once they have expanded to about the thickness of a dime, they have probably metastasized and become lethal (Jaroff 69).

3.
Roger Kobak, a psychologist at the University of Delaware, believes that distorted attachment patterns grow out of the way the child learns to deal with negative feelings. A secure child is able to communicate negative feelings like anger, hurt, jealousy, and resentment in a meaningful way. He can cry or shout, fall silent, or say "I hate you," confident of a sensitive response. The insecure child does not have this confidence. His mother, unable to handle her own negative feelings, either becomes dismissive or overreacts. As a result, his negative feelings are either walled off from his consciousness or revved up to the point where they overwhelm him. His ability to communicate his pain is gradually shrunken and distorted until it virtually demands misinterpretation (Daren 63).

B. **Directions:** Compare the paraphrase with the original and decide whether it is accurate. If it is inaccurate, write a better version. If the paraphrase contains a phrase that should be enclosed in quotation marks, indicate where the marks should be placed.

1. **Original:** "Because recent research suggests that some memories retrieved under hypnosis may be inaccurate, many states are re-evaluating the use of eye witness testimony obtained by hypnosis."

    Paraphrase: The state of hypnosis can cause eye witnesses to remember testimony incorrectly.

2. **Original:** "During hypnosis, imagined events can seem as authentic as reality, images can be extremely vivid and there is a heightened level of fantasy."

    Paraphrase: Hypnotic images, although a fantasy, are extremely vivid and authentic.

3. **Original:** "Most psychologists agree that hypnotised subjects are extremely susceptible to suggestions. The very language many hypnotists use with their subjects encourages guesses.

Paraphrase: The way a hypnotist talks to a subject can reinforce the subject's willingness to guess.

4. **Original:** "Hypnotised subjects correctly recalled twice as many items as did unhypnotised members of a control group but also made three times as many mistakes."

   Paraphrase: Twice as many hypnotised people remembered correctly and three times as many made mistakes.

5. **Original:** "The New Jersey Supreme Court, in 1981, approved guidelines for hypnotists to follow to avoid leading or influencing witnesses."

   Paraphrase: In 1981, the New Jersey Supreme Court helped hypnotists stay away from witnesses who were trying to lead or influence them.

Original statements in this section are taken from "Hypnosis on Trial" by Elizabeth Stark. Psychology Today, 18 *(February 1984), 2, 34–36.*

VII. Summarizing

Write a one-sentence summary for each of the paragraphs.

1. While busy Americans are eating almost as many meals out as ever, they are hunting harder for bargains. Surveying restaurant dining patterns across the country between December and February, the NPD Group, a Port Washington, N.Y. market research firm, reported that ethnic and quick-service outlets fared best. Some top eateries have shaved prices 10% to 20% to keep their kitchens busy. Many popular night spots that would have shunned families two or three years ago have added children's plates and have hung out the welcome sign. At home, catered dinners have largely been replaced by casual cookouts (Castro 57).

2. Although marked differences exist between the type of criminals who commit murders and those who commit computer crimes, their impact on society is great. A survey of 1,000 organizations revealed that the verifiable losses attributed to computer crime in 1985 were estimated between $145 million to $750 million. Estimates show that computer criminals in the

workplace alone may be costing businesses up to $3 billion a year. In fact, the possiblity of "corporate murder" is even more likely. Computer criminals can bring financial disaster to small business, as well as individuals, and can drastically affect many lives (Coutourie 19).

3.
Many Americans are devoted to serious, even ascetic, cultivation of the self in the form of a number of disciplines, practices, and "trainings," often of great rigor. There is a question as to whether these practices lead to the self-realization or self-fulfillment at which they aim or only to an obsessive self-manipulation that defeats the proclaimed purpose. But it is not uncommon for those who are attempting to find themselves to find in that very process something that transcends them. For example, a Zen student reported: "I started Zen to get something for myself, to stop suffering, to get enlightened. Whatever it was, I was doing it for myself. I had hold of myself and I was reaching for something. Then to do it, I found out I had to give up that hold on myself. Now it has hold of me, whatever 'it' is." What this student found is that the meaning of life is not to be discovered in manipulative control in the service of the self. Rather, through the disciplined practices of a religious way of life, the student found his self more grasped than grasping. It is not surprising that "self-realization" in this case has occurred in the context of a second language, the allusive language of Zen Buddhism, and a community that attempts to put that language into practice (Bellah 290–291).

VIII. Comparing and contrasting
    A. Compare and contrast the information and opinions expressed in each set of excerpts. Summarize the similarities and differences in a few sentences.
        1. Set 1
           a.
Finding markets for all the recyclable stuff being collected, however, is enormously difficult. So many old newspapers are now being set out at the curb that prices have collapsed. Last April, for example, Rhode Island could sell newspapers for $25 a ton; now, the price is $2. And other places, like New York, must actually pay brokers $10 a ton to take the papers. "Recycling doesn't pay for itself," Wright says. "If it was profitable, you wouldn't need the government to get involved." States like California and Connecticut are helping to create markets by requiring publishers to use recycled newsprint (Cook 61).

b.

Recycled paper has been even less popular than plastic. "In the East, cities are paying wastepaper companies to carry off the stuff," says William Franklin, who heads Franklin Associates, an environmental consulting firm. That's where Waste Management's* other joint venture comes in. Jefferson Smurfit will spin off its reclamation division, which includes 32 processing centers, to a new entity called Smurfit/WMI Recycling. Waste Management will chip in the 750,000 tons of old newsprint, boxes and other paper waste it collects each year. But finding a home for the recycled stuff will be tough. A paper glut has driven virgin newsprint prices down 13%, or $75 a ton, below year ago levels (Bremmer 49).

2. Set 2

a.

The plastics industry has been scrambling to support recycling, mostly out of fear that its ubiquitous products will otherwise be banned. But recycling has proved economical as well. Wellman, Inc., of Shrewsbury, N.J., for instance, buys plastic bottles and turns them into fiber for carpeting (35% of all polyester carpet is made from recycled soda bottles), filling for parkas and heavy felt used to stabilize railroad roadbeds. Wellman Vice President Dennis Sabourin estimates that about 110 million pounds of soda bottles are now recycled annually; he foresees markets for at least 430 million pounds (Cook 61).

b.

Then there's the problem of finding someone to use waste products. Only a paltry 1% of plastics are recycled, but Waste Management and DuPont may change that. They will invest a total of $25 million to build five plants to recover resins from plastic trash. The joint venture has a built-in customer for most of the plastic: DuPont itself, which will turn the resins into marketable carpet fibers and materials for auto parts and highway barriers. By 1994, DuPont and Waste Management hope to recycle 200 million pounds of plastic a year (Bremmer 49).

3. Set 3

a.

America, unhappily, is bullish on garbage. Our production of refuse, now about 160 million tons a year, will rise to 193 million tons by the end of the century if

*Waste Management is the name of a company that collects and recycles trash.

nothing is done. This growing effluence of affluence, 3½ pounds a day for every American and rising, is a byproduct of our consumer society, whose watchwords are "convenience," "ready to use" and "throw-away." And it has become a major national environmental issue, forcing citizens, elected officials and private companies to give serious thought to rubbish (Cook 61).

b. Calculating the total annual volume or weight of garbage in the United States is difficult because there is, of course, no way one can actually measure or weigh more than a fraction of what is thrown out. All studies have had to take shortcuts. Not surprisingly, estimates of the size of the U.S. solid-waste stream are quite diverse. Figures are most commonly expressed in pounds discarded per person per day, and the studies that I have seen from the past decade and a half give the following rates: 2.9 pounds per person per day, 3.02 pounds, 4.24, 4.28, 5.0, and 8.0. My own view is that the higher estimates significantly overstate the problem. Garbage Project studies of actual refuse reveal that even three pounds of garbage per person per day may be too high an estimate for many parts of the country, a conclusion that has been corroborated by weight-sorts in many communities. Americans are wasteful, but to some degree we have been conditioned to think of ourselves as more wasteful than we truly are—and certainly as more wasteful than we used to be (Rathje 100–101).

B. Read "At Issue: Does Conservation Justify Keeping Animals in Zoos?" Then in a few sentences summarize the differences and similarities (if any) in the information and opinions expressed by William G. Conrad and Michael W. Fox.

IX. Evaluating
   A. Decide which of the following sentences are factual and which are interpretive. If the statement is factual, what sources might you check to see if it is accurate? If the statement is interpretive, what facts or reasoning might be used to support it?
      1. Reducing cholesterol levels will cut deaths from heart disease by 20% to 30%.
      2. Women can handle stress better than men.
      3. Kellogg set aside 40 million dollars for a campaign to educate consumers about the principles of good health.
      4. Americans are overly concerned with physical fitness.
      5. A vegetarian diet cannot satisfy the nutritional needs of a growing child.
      6. Adidas produces more than 200 styles of sport shoes.

7. Bowling is not a fashionable sport.
8. The performance of women athletes has improved dramatically in the last twenty years.
9. If you want to be a good athlete, you have to begin training when you are young.
10. Professional football allows too much physical violence.
11. Vegetarian diets can feed more people from the same amount of land than a meat diet.
12. People are starving because of problems with food distribution, not because of inadequate food supplies.
13. For every five pounds a dieter loses, four will be regained within six months.
14. American women spend more on diet programs than men.
15. More money should be spent on cancer research.

B. One of the readings claims to present facts: "The Facts about Animal Research." Find sentences in it that are
   1. clearly factual
   2. a blend of interpretation and fact
   3. clearly interpretation
C. What else besides facts gives a piece of writing credibility? Read "Better Health Care Doesn't Justify Animal Research." Compare it to what you read in "Facts about Animal Research." Which reading do you find more convincing? Why?
D. Notice that the blank in the following sentence can be filled in with many possibilities:

"The use of animals in research is _____."

Possibilities:

   a. torture
   b. sometimes unnecessary
   c. essential for scientific progress
   d. the subject of heated debate
   e. being regulated by federal legislation
   f. immoral
   g. alarming some people

For each of these possibilities, indicate whether the resulting sentence is a fact or an opinion. What might a reader expect to follow each of these completed sentences? Can you suggest some ideas?

Now match each of these completed sentences to the best versions below. In each case be ready to defend your choice of following sentences:

Example: g. alarming some people. "The use of animals in research is alarming some people."

This version is a fact. The reader would expect some examples of alarmed people or some reasons for the alarm. The best sentence that fits (from the list that follows) is 3: "PETA (People for the Ethical Treatment of Animals) and ALF (Animal Liberation Front) are only two organizations that protest against such study."

"The use of animals in research is *alarming some people. PETA (People for the Ethical Treatment of Animals) and ALF (Animal Liberation Front) are only two organizations that protest against such study.*

Following sentences:
1. Animal rights activists claim that animals have rights, too, and that violating them constitutes oppression; while scientists insist that only by experimenting on animals can they improve our understanding of human diseases and ways to cure them.
2. Animals are often deliberately poisoned or dismembered without anesthetics or other treatments to relieve their pain.
3. PETA (People for the Ethical Treatment of Animals) and ALF (Animal Liberation Front) are only two organizations that protest against such study.
4. Animal rights activists point to the parallel with slavery in the American south.
5. The discovery of insulin, for example, resulted from experiments on dogs.
6. Major cosmetic companies have stopped using the Draize test on rabbits.
7. The Animal and Plant Health Inspection Service, an agency of the Agriculture Department, has issued regulations on medical experimentation on animals.

E. Read the following section from "Where Have All the Parents Gone?" and evaluate the author's use of facts. What claim is being made about America's children? What facts are given to support the claim? What questions might you ask about the facts and how they are used? Do the statements in this section contradict or support other material you have read on the same topic?

> . . . What's more, today's children will determine how successfully we compete in the global economy. They will be going head-to-head against Japanese, Korean and West German children.
>
> Unfortunately, American children aren't prepared to run the race, let alone win it. Many are illiterate, undernourished, impaired, unskilled, poor. Consider the children who started

first grade in 1986: 14 percent were illegitimate; 15 percent were physically or emotionally handicapped; 15 percent spoke another language other than English; 28 percent were poor and fully 40 percent could be expected to live in a single-parent home before they reached 18 (Whitehead 30).

F. Paragraph development
   1. Read "Why Worry about the Animals?" Find good examples of paragraphs developed according to each of the following methods:
      a. illustration with specific detail or example
      b. analysis of component parts
      c. comparison/contrast
      d. narration/description
   2. Write a one-sentence summary of "What's Wrong with Animal Rights?"
   3. Write a one-paragraph summary of "The Facts about Animal Research"

Sources for Exercises V, VI, VII, VIII, and IX

Bellah, Robert N., et al., *Habits of the Heart: Individualism and Commitment in American Life.* New York: Harper and Row Publishers, Inc., 1985.

Bremmer, Brian. "Recycling: The Newest Wrinkle in Waste Management's Bag." *Business Week* 5 March 1990.

Castro, Janice. "Hunkering Down." *Time* 23 July 1990.

Cook, William J. "A Lot of Rubbish." *U.S. News and World Report* 25 December 1989.

Coutourie, Larry, Lt. "The Computer Criminal: An Investigative Assessment." *FBI Law Enforcement Bulletin* September 1989.

Daren, Robert. "Becoming Attached." *Atlantic Monthly* February 1990.

Jaroff, Leon. "The Dark Side of Worshiping the Sun." *Time* 23 July 1990.

Orne, Martin T. "The Nature of Hypnosis: Artifact and Essence." *Journal of Abnormal and Social Psychology* 58 (January–May 1959).

Rathje, William L. "Rubbish!" *Atlantic Monthly* December 1989: 100–101.

Whitehead, Barbara Dafoe. "Where Have All the Parents Gone?" *New Perspectives Quarterly* 7(1) (Winter 1990).

Wright, Robert. "Are Animals People Too?" *New Republic* 12 March 1990.

CHAPTER 5

Planning and Proposing a Research Strategy

Once you have settled on a topic for your research and started to locate materials, you need to spend some time planning a research strategy. In general, this strategy involves conceptualizing and anticipating how your position on the topic is going to shape up; that is, it involves ways of thinking about your topic. Specifically, this strategy involves developing a tentative thesis (we stress "tentative") and taking inventory of your related interests, knowledge, and experiences. No one comes to a research project absolutely cold; everyone has some information and assumptions which predetermine their beliefs and provide a foundation on which they can build or remodel. Although often taken for granted, this background is a valuable resource which you can deliberately use to your advantage in this initial planning stage. Recognizing that you aren't starting from scratch can help to propel you forward with more confidence.

At this point instructors often assign a paper about your topic to get you to develop and describe such a strategy. The assignment can be short and informal, emphasizing your personal interest, in which case it is called a *statement of intent.* A longer, more formal version of the assignment is known as a *proposal.*

We want to stress that the type of research paper that we are showing you how to write is more than just a summary of your sources. You should read the sample research papers and pay attention to the way that the writers interpreted and commented on the information they gathered.

Although you cannot decide on the final shape of your thesis statement now, you need to know what you are aiming for so that you will avoid limiting your topic to something so cut and dried that it does not lend itself to interpretation.

AIMING AT A THESIS OF YOUR OWN

In the strict sense of the word, a thesis is an original insight. For example, a graduate student in speech pathology wanted to investigate the effect that eye contact had on a listener's reaction to a stutterer. After setting up a test situation and recording the results, the student concluded that poor eye contact, not stuttering by itself, caused a negative reaction in the listener. This was an original insight with important implications for therapists who work with stutterers.

It is not necessary to conduct primary research of the type just described to form an original thesis. Library research offers many possibilities for pointing out relationships that you think are important and significant. You might read about different methods that have been used to treat stutterers and make a connection between advances in knowledge about stutterers and changes in therapeutic approaches.

At this stage in your education, you are not expected to come up with a totally original slant on your subject. However, your thesis should reflect your thinking about the subject. A thesis is more than a rehash of what you have read and taken notes on. It points to some meaning in these facts and ideas, some perspective that your reading has caused to form in your mind. Your thesis should reflect what you believe is interesting and important.

As your research progresses and you focus on a particular aspect of the subject, you should begin to draw some conclusions and to make connections. "What is the point of all this?" you should ask yourself. The point is your tentative thesis statement, or what scientists call a hypothesis. A hypothesis is an educated guess or hunch about what the research will prove. It is a good idea to develop a tentative thesis/hypothesis so that you can focus the remainder of your research on deciding whether the available information does or does not support your initial hunch. For example, one student was interested in the proliferation of health food cereals, particularly oat bran products. After some initial reading, he developed a hunch that many of the health claims made for oat bran were exaggerated. As he continued his research, he focused on answering the question: Do the facts show that the claims made for oat bran cereals are exaggerated?

Be prepared to change your mind and your thesis if you cannot find sufficient information to support your original hunch. It is perfectly acceptable to reach the conclusion that a hypothesis was incorrect or that there simply isn't enough information to reach a decisive conclusion. For example, one student developed a hunch that most hyperactive kids could be treated without medication, but continued reading showed that drugs were a necessary part of the therapy for quite a few cases. After completing her research, she revised her thesis to state: Although medication is not always needed, it can be an important component of a treatment program for hyperactivity.

A thesis of your own is not likely to emerge automatically from your information. If it does, be cautious. You might simply be swallowing someone else's idea.

Strategies for Developing a Tentative Thesis

1. One way is to start with a research question like the ones on p. 15. For example, if you were researching the topic of teenage pregnancy, you might develop questions such as these:

```
Does fear of pregnancy discourage teenagers from sexual
experimentation?
  Is ignorance about sex a deterrent against sexual activity?
  Does access to contraceptive devices encourage sexual activity?
  Does sex education lead to sexual activity among teenagers?
```

After doing some preliminary reading, you formulate a tentative answer to one of the questions. For example, if you had found some solid research on the first question (Does fear of pregnancy discourage teenagers from sexual experimentation?), here are some tentative thesis statements which you might formulate:

```
Fear of pregnancy as a deterrent against sexual activity among teen-
agers varies with their attitudes toward abortion and access to it.
  Fear of pregnancy as a deterrent against sexual activity among
teenagers operates only among those who know enough anatomy to
understand and anticipate the cause and effect relationship.
  Any possible deterrent effect of pregnancy is overruled by
teenagers' curiosity about sex and by peer pressure to experiment.
```

2. Another way to aim at a thesis is to look at some data and speculate about it. Say to yourself, I wonder if _____ . For example, you might read some statistics about teenage pregnancy and discover that every year about 10 percent of American teenage girls, mostly unmarried, get pregnant. Start off, I wonder if teenagers get pregnant because _____ _____ , and then fill in the blank. Try out several versions, brainstorming as many possible thesis sentences as you can create. Then you can select the statements that seem most plausible to you, perhaps combining a few of them to consolidate your best ideas.

Guidelines for a Thesis Statement

1. A thesis must be a complete sentence. By definition, a thesis makes a claim about a subject. You have to stick your neck out and make a point. Therefore, a description of the subject is not sufficient.

Subject: The rights of adopted children.

Claim: (I think that) people who were adopted should have a legal right to information about their biological parents. Putting "I think that" in front of your statement is one way to be sure that you have made a claim and that it is worded as a complete sentence. When you state your thesis in your proposal or your paper, you should not use the phrase "I think that" because it is unnecessary and distracting to some readers.

2. A thesis must be an assertion, not a question. A question may be used effectively in your title or introduction as a way of creating interest, but a thesis is a statement that answers the question.

Question: Why are people hooked on credit cards?

Thesis: Credit cards are popular not only because they are a convenient substitute for money but because consumers have been brainwashed into thinking the credit card is a status symbol.

3. The thesis must not be a factual statement, but an interpretation of the facts or an opinion about them. A fact is something that can be verified as true or false; an opinion or interpretation must be supported and proven with the facts you have collected.

Fact: The burning of gas, oil, and coal contributes to the greenhouse effect.

Opinion: Governments must provide incentives to reduce burning fuels which contribute to the greenhouse effect.

4. A thesis on a controversial subject should not be wishy-washy. You may think that there are good arguments on both sides, but you should make some assessment of the issue.

Weak: Predictions about global warming have created a controversy among scientists.

or

Some scientists claim that global warming is a serious threat, but others disagree.

Better: The controversy over global warming stems from the difficulty of including all the relevant variables in the computer models used to make projections.

or

Although the extent of global warming is still uncertain, action must be taken now to prevent the possibility of serious harm.

5. A thesis should make a point, not just promise to do so.

Promise: There are many reasons why government should support solar energy.

Point: Government support for solar energy will provide jobs, lessen our dependence on foreign oil, and decrease the production of greenhouse gases.

6. Ideally, a thesis should be unified as a single sentence, not a series of sentences. Often your thesis statement will stem from a cluster of related ideas. Pulling them together gives the reader a clearer idea of your thinking.

Series: Japanese management techniques are superior to traditional American practices. The Japanese have a higher productivity rate among their workers. Japanese products have a reputation for high quality at competitive prices.

Unified: Japanese management techniques are superior to traditional American practices because the Japanese have a higher productivity rate and produce high quality goods at competitive prices.

7. The thesis should be a statement that can stand on its own. It should not be dependent on sentences that might come before or after it in an introductory paragraph.

Dependent: These changes have resulted in many young Americans being without a pension plan.

Independent: Many young Americans are without a pension plan because of shifts in the job market and the decline in unionized jobs.

WRITING A STATEMENT OF INTENT

From the instructor's point of view, this assignment has two purposes. It reassures the instructor that you are getting off to a good start, and it shows the instructor where help can be offered, if necessary, with any possible problems that may emerge at this stage.

Even more important, this assignment helps you move ahead on your research project. The very process of writing—putting pencil to paper or finger to computer keyboard—generates more ideas and helps clarify them. The first words written in a research paper project are the hardest. After completing this short paper, half the battle is truly won.

Basically, a statement of intent requires you to commit yourself, at least provisionally, to a topic. It requires you to identify a possible topic and explain why it interests you. It answers the instructor's questions "What do you want to write about and why do you want to do it?" As such it is a personal paper: the emphasis is on your topic and your reasons for choosing it. The most common problem with writing a statement of intent is losing sight of this basic personal aspect and starting to write the paper itself.

Here are some trigger questions to consider before you begin writing anything. Not all of them will apply, but try to provide answers to as many as you can:

What is it about your topic that interests you?
What other kinds of people have been interested or implicated in this topic? Why?
What places do you especially associate with this topic?
What event(s) seem to illustrate or occasion this topic?
Have you done any reading on this subject before? What was it? When?
What problem, puzzle, complication, or issue is connected with this topic?
What is your belief or opinion at this stage about this topic (your provisional thesis)?
Do you have any misgivings about your topic or your thesis? Fear it is too narrow? Too unoriginal? Too dry to sustain a reader's interest or your own?
What do you hope to learn from this research project?

SAMPLE STATEMENT OF INTENT

```
Statement of Intent
Donovan Grice
April 6, 1990
```

I come from a family background of business entrepreneurs. My grandfather was one of the original pioneers of today's Black haircare industry. Growing up in an atmosphere full of business professionals I was eventually introduced to workings of the financial products industry. During my freshman year of college I dabbled in stocks, bonds, and high yielding securities also known as Junk Bonds. Junk Bonds soon became the focal point of my financial perspective. In 1986 I followed this exciting trend of corporate takeovers fueled by Junk Bonds through the October crash of 1987 on to 1990, which presently seems to indicate an apparent demise of the high-yield security industry.

The subject of Junk Bonds and hostile corporate takeovers has proven to be extremely controversial in the community of Wall Street. I have never really researched this volatile and controversial time period of the 80s to find out if hostile corporate takeovers are really a device of greed conjured up on the part of a few corporate raiders to benefit at the expense of the American economy. Many conservative old-money institutions on Wall Street would have a person believe just that. Personally from my own observation on the actual mechanics of why a hostile takeover takes place I tend to disagree with the conservative viewpoint. My hypothesis is that hostile takeovers may actually be a sound means of restructuring for America's future.

I have followed this trend of the 80s by reading periodicals and newspapers, such as The Wall Street Journal and watching television sources for at least five years now, but I never recorded any of this information down for a personal use to answer a basic question about the good or evil of hostile takeovers for America. I suspect that the vast majority of my information will be coming from periodicals due to the extreme recentness of the issues involved.

On the surface, without looking at all the aspects of hostile takeovers, they seem to have a negative impact on the economy. The critics of takeovers claim that a raider is making a short-term profit at the expense of the target company, its shareholders, employees and the community in which the company is located. The critics also claim that takeovers and the expense they incur cause American industry, as a whole, to be less competitive in world markets. My research will show that the critics have placed the blame for plant closings and job loss on the wrong party. Also, raiders actually make their targeted companies _more_ competitive by streamlining and reducing waste, by redistributing resources to more productive areas and at the same time enhancing shareholder investment. In order to make my case in favor of corporate raiders and prove the eventual beneficial results of takeovers and attempted takeovers, I will be using specific case studies. The companies that will be discussed include Phillips Petroleum, Goodyear Tire and Rubber, American Can, Revlon, and TWA.

Presently I have no misgivings about the topic because this subject is a high interest of mine and I am very familiar with the issues involved. Yes, the subject can be very broad but I know what to look for. I have previously allocated much unofficial time to the subject of corporate takeovers and have even invested in a few projects. My topic will be original in that it takes the side of the mavericks of Wall Street and even though presently it seems the hostile takeovers days have finally stopped it will be interesting to see what has been left behind.

WRITING A PROPOSAL

This assignment goes beyond the Statement of Intent to frame your project in a more formal, objective, academic way. The emphasis is no longer on you, but on your thesis (still provisional, of course) and your research project.

Most real-world proposals are competitive (someone wins; others lose) and they usually request money. A proposal assignment for an undergraduate research paper is not competitive (everyone usually wins eventually), so you don't need to prove that your project is more deserving than someone else's. But you are requesting something valuable—the instructor's "go ahead" and ultimately course credit. Your goal in this assignment is to convince the instructor that your project is going to work.

Before you begin writing anything, consider these trigger questions. Notice that some of them overlap with questions for a Statement of Intent, but they will lead you toward the appropriate academic emphasis.

What is your topic?
What is your thesis?

What is the problem or complication or puzzle or issue about the topic that interests you?
Do you already have assumptions or opinions about this topic that you will be testing?
What other people are interested or involved in this topic?
Is there another slant on the topic besides your own? What is it?
Why does this topic matter?
How much do you already know about this topic?
Is this topic related to another class?
What kinds of sources will you need to consult?
What information do you need first?
What kind of source is likely to supply it?
Who could use the information you will be gathering?

Once you start drafting your proposal, you can assume that your reader is conscientious but rather rushed, possibly a little skeptical, and someone who gets very annoyed and impatient with proofreading or mechanical grammar mistakes. You have to get right to the point and really sell the instructor on this project. This means, specifically, that you must persuade your instructor that you have a clear idea in mind of what you want to do in your research paper, that the proposed paper is worth spending time and attention on, that it addresses an important problem or issue, that you are in a position to undertake it successfully, that you have thought through an appropriate method or approach, that you have at least a preliminary plan of how to undertake the paper (you know the kind of information you will need and you know how to get it), and that you will be able to complete the work in the allotted time.

Instructors know that this is asking a lot. Even if you don't feel very secure about this—remember it's negotiable at this stage—try to sound confident. You will undoubtedly modify your strategy as you proceed, but it is best to begin with some sort of plan. For the purpose of this proposal assignment remember that you're a salesperson, aiming to convince the instructor that the project is worthwhile and will work out well.

SAMPLE PROPOSAL

```
Proposal
Kevin Uriu
28 June 1988
```

During World War II, the U.S. government felt the necessity to intern nearly 110,000 Japanese-Americans from the west coast. Whole families were uprooted from their homes and taken, on short notice and with very few of their belongings, to live for three years in ''internment centers'' that were really like concentration camps. After the war, most of them had lost everything. Given the clarity of hindsight, it is obvious that this tragedy should never have occurred in the most democratic and free country in the world. The legality of this momentous decision is no longer in question, but exactly what the government can and should do to reconcile its mistake is a topic of heated debate.

More than forty years after the internment camps closed, this issue of redress is finally being discussed in Congress. What I find interesting is not the details of whether redress will be given, or how much should be given, etc., but how the Japanese-Americans feel about redress; not only those who are doing the fighting in Washington, but also those who are being fought for—those who have remained silent for so many years.

Although many support redress of some kind, some people feel that painful part of history should not be brought back up, or that one cannot put a price tag on the suffering and injustice inflicted, and doing so would only degrade the monstrosity of the act. There are some who feel that the U.S. government should officially recognize its error, formally apologize to those wronged, and learn from the experience. But there are others who feel that this is not enough, that a monetary award, though nominal in comparison, would help to offset the losses suffered during the war.

As a third generation Japanese-American, I feel it is important that we look at these human aspects of redress. Redress has been fought on moral and ethical grounds, trying to reconcile the injustice. But what about the personal aspect? How do the people most affected by redress feel about this method of compensation? Why have they kept quiet for so long?

After some preliminary research, I found that not much work has yet been done in this area. I am amazed that an issue that is so current, yet historical, and so threatening to the ''American'' sense of justice, has not been thoroughly researched on the human level. I would, therefore, like to start an exploratory study of this untrodden territory. Due to the limited amount of time and lack of previous research, this will be a very qualitative and reflective study. I hope to bring out some insights into how people feel about such an important issue, and especially shed some light on why the majority of victims have kept silent for so long.

For information on those lobbying for redress, I will consult the Pacific Citizen, a newspaper produced by the Japanese American Citizen's League. But for the feelings of those who have not been so vocal, I would like to conduct personal interviews. I have several valuable sources, such as Rev. Miyeko Uriu and Dr. Harry Kitano, who were all interned during the war, and Dr. Masashi Uriu, whose family moved out of California during the war.

EXERCISES

A. **Directions:** Make an assertion about each of the following subjects:
1. The future of the family farm in the United States.
2. Job opportunities for women in the business world.

3. The amount of violence on TV.
4. The consumption of alcoholic beverages.

B. **Directions:** Combine each set of related ideas into a single thesis statement. Try writing more than one version for each set of statements because your own thesis will probably go through several versions.

1. Soap operas attract viewers from all walks of life.
   Soap operas deal with contemporary problems.
   The plots of soap operas are full of old-fashioned suspense.
   Version 1:

   Version 2:

2. Nuclear power plants are opposed by some people.
   They claim that the plants are dangerous.
   There is always the chance of human error.
   The backup systems have not been adequately tested.
   Version 1:

   Version 2:

3. A growing number of people are opposed to using animals in medical experiments.
   They believe that animal rights are equal to human rights.
   They believe that there are alternatives to the use of animals.
   Version 1:

   Version 2:

C. **Directions:** Evaluate the following thesis statements as good, fair, or poor.
1. The two major reasons for legalizing drugs.
2. The worst junk food that teenagers ingest is their steady diet of mindless music.
3. The battle for affirmative action is not yet over.
4. Although the benefits of bilingual education are debatable, continuation of the programs has become a political necessity.

5. In England, where private ownership of handguns is illegal, crimes involving the use of guns have skyrocketed.
6. The poor academic performance of American students compared to that of students in other industrial countries.
7. People who smoke should be charged higher health insurance premiums because research has proven that they are more prone to illness.
8. The loss of interest in reading can be traced directly to the prevalence of TV.
9. Why have modern universities lost their vision of educating students to participate in a free society?
10. Although world temperatures dropped during the period between 1940 to 1970, a global warming trend has been taking place since the early 1800s.

D. **Directions:** Here is the beginning of an article, "Why Teenagers Get Pregnant," by William A. Fisher, in *Psychology Today, 17* (March 1983), pp. 70–71:

> Each year, 10 percent of American teenage girls (mostly unmarried) get pregnant—alarming proof that use of contraceptives by teenagers has not kept pace with their increased sexual activity. Even well-informed young people who have easy access to contraceptive devices often fail to use them.
>
> Some time ago, social psychologist Donn Byrne hypothesized that one major psychological barrier to teenage contraception was erotophobia, or fear of sex. Over the past six years, several studies that my colleagues and I have done have confirmed that hypothesis.

Reprinted from Psychology Today Magazine, *Copyright 1983 Sussex Publishers, Inc.*

1. What was the author's original research question?

2. What was the author's original hunch to fill in this blank: "I suspect that _____."
3. Underline the words in the passage that identify the author's hypothesis.

E. Determine the thesis (explicit or implied) in these readings in the Anthology:
   "Why Worry about the Animals?"
   "Am I Blue? . . . "
   "What's Wrong with Animal Rights?"
   "Facts about Animal Research"
   "Better Health Care Doesn't Justify Animal Research"

Then assess their effectiveness by matching them up with the guidelines for a thesis statement on pp. 112–113.

F. *Mini-research exercises*

These exercises allow you to practice synthesizing information from different sources.

1. **Directions:** Read the following three paragraphs, which are taken from different sources. Then complete the sentences in the synthesis paragraph, using your own words as much as possible.

   a. "Endangered Earth" announced the cover of *Time* magazine at the end of 1988. The Midwest had been parched by a drought, water was so low in the Mississippi River that navigation was impossible in places, and Yellowstone Park had been blackened by fires. Evidence was mounting that the temperatures around the world had been increasing since the mid-1970s. Scientists were piecing together a theory that the buildup of gases in the atmosphere could increase temperatures by as much as 9 degrees Fahrenheit in just 50 years. More recently, the computer models on which the projections were made, as well as the methods of measuring temperatures have been questioned (Manfred 1).

   b. Debate in the media reflects uncertainty among climatologists and geophysicists. Some of the world's eminent authorities on the atmosphere recently hurled verbal brickbats at one another in the pages of . . . *Science.* Their charges of "junk science" and "science by consensus" reflect the acrimonious nature of the debate within the scientific community. Some members of the National Academy of Sciences . . . charge that policymakers are being induced to take unwise actions on the basis of uncertain scientific evidence. Set against this view is the recent statement of the Union of Concerned Scientists urging action by the government. It was signed by 52 Nobel laureates and more than 700 members of the NAS (White 36).

   c. Environmentalists staged Earth Day to dramatize a simple message: The planet is threatened by a host of man-made ills, from toxic landfills to ozone depletion. But at least one part of the message—the theory that the buildup of carbon dioxide and other greenhouse gases in the atmosphere will cause global warming—has come under considerable attack. A small but vocal group of scientists contends that the case for warming is sketchy and based on inadequate computer models (Alexander 84).

   Synthesis paragraph: Environmentalists have been concerned about the possibility that _____. Scientists theorized that the _____ could cause _____. Many of them were so concerned about _____ that they signed a statement recommending _____. However, not all scientists agree _____. The dissenting scientists charge that _____.

2. **Directions:** Read each set of three sources. Decide on the common topic, jot down the important bits of information, and then write a sentence that summarizes the main idea of each set. Write a paragraph synthesizing the information in each set.

   a. Set 1

      (1) Scientists generally agree that an unchecked accumulation of greenhouse gases will eventually lead to warming, but no one knows when it will start, how much will take place or how rapidly it will occur. The most widely accepted estimate is a rise in the earth's average temperature of 1.5°C to 4.5°C (3°F to 8°F) as early as 2050. An increase in the upper part of that range could produce disastrous climatic effects, including rising sea levels and severe droughts in some areas (Alexander 84).

      (2) Modeling of global climate is being carried out intensively by at least 14 different groups. They have largely concentrated on examining effects of doubling the atmospheric content of greenhouse gases. As might be expected, the answers they get are functions of the models they employ. The spread is from 1.5° to 5°C; that is, there is great uncertainty. In addition, if one examines some of the scientific articles on the subject, one finds virtually unanimous agreement that the models are deficient. For example, they do not adequately incorporate effects of clouds, which are expected to increase with warming. Clouds have both negative and positive effects on warming. Clouds exert a negative effect on temperature in part by reflecting sunlight off into space. They have a positive effect by trapping heat from below. The sensitivity of computer models to the properties of clouds was illustrated in a recent paper. When the water content of clouds was recognized in the model, the predicted global average warming dropped from 5.2° to 1.9°C (Abelson 1529).

      (3) Just how much this doubling of carbon dioxide would increase temperatures, however, varied greatly from model to model. Some predicted as little as a two-degree F (one-degree C) increase, whereas others predicted increases of as much as nine degrees F (five degrees C). The difference in predictions became central elements in the debate about whether the models were sufficiently reliable to warrant policy actions. Further, it made a great difference whether the actual increase was at one or the other end of this range. At the low end, the normal resilience of society would probably be sufficient to accommodate the changed climate. Changes at the high end portended severe disruptions (White 39).

b. Set 2

(1) Roger Sedjo of Resources for the Future, a research center in Washington, D.C., estimates that planting 1.1 billion acres of new forest, roughly equivalent to the area of the contiguous states west of the Mississippi, would soak up all the 2.9 billion tons of carbon that gets added to the atmosphere each year. Says Sedjo: "We are talking big numbers, increasing the world's forests by some 16% at a cost of maybe $500 billion. But if this is an emergency and it's paid for out of a global checkbook, it can be done" (Nulty 105).

(2) In like manner, those interested in arresting population growth, especially in the Third World, point out that the climate-warming problem is probably not solvable as long as the number of human beings continues to rise. After all, it is people who consume natural resources and energy and who farm the land. Without population control, prospects for stabilizing the climate and arresting the deterioration of the habitability of the planet are abysmal (White 41).

(3) To his credit, Bush has already taken several steps that will help combat global warming. Among other things, the White House has 1) earmarked $1 billion for global climate research next year; 2) committed the U.S. to phasing out production of chlorofluorocarbons, potent greenhouse gases, by the year 2000; and 3) vowed to plant a billion trees, which would absorb CO_2 from the air. But Administration officials admit that Bush advanced most of the measures for reasons other than reducing global warming. And environmentalists argue that the Government should do much more to discourage the burning of fossil fuels. Among the possibilities: raise the gasoline tax or use financial incentives to encourage people to buy smaller, more efficient cars (Alexander 84).

c. Set 3

(1) The White House, however, worries about the economic consequences of forcing sudden, drastic curbs in fossil-fuel use. From the Administration's point of view, draconian action seems highly debatable so long as the scientific evidence for the greenhouse effect is sketchy. "We are not at the point where we can bet the economy," says a Sununu aide (Alexander 84).

(2) A recent report of the Council of Economic Advisors lends weight to this approach. It states that the cost of controlling carbon dioxide emissions and of taking other actions to address climate change would run into hundreds of billions of dollars. Because such reallocations of resources raise the spector of grave economic consequences, we need to be resonably sure such actions are worth the cost . . . (White 42–43).

(3) With so much at stake, the Bush Administration is wisely seeking international participation in any plan to roll back CO_2 emissions. The expense of unilateral reductions would put the U.S. at a disadvantage in world markets while its industrialized competitors and the Third World increase emissions in pursuit of economic development. Besides one country acting alone wouldn't have much effect. The U.S. is participating in an intergovernmental panel on climate control that will issue a scientific report in the fall on the dangers of global warming. Members, including Western European powers, Japan, and the Soviet Union, will try to get together on solutions. The model is the Montreal Protocol of 1988, in which 30 nations agreed to phase out CFCs (Nulty 104–105).

d. Set 4

(1) The idea that the actions of humanity might change the composition of the atmosphere and hence the world's climate has deep historical roots. As early as the 1860's, it was suggested that slight changes in atmospheric composition might bring about major variations in climate. Increases in carbon dioxide (CO_2) and other atmospheric gases can contribute to what has been called greenhouse warming because these compounds allow the sun's energy to reach the surface of the earth, thereby warming it, while preventing much of that energy from being reradiated to outer space (White 37).

(2) The facts about global warming are sparse but compelling. Certain gases in the atmosphere, principally water vapor and CO_2, trap heat radiating from the earth's surface. If they did not, the earth's average temperature would be roughly 0° instead of just over 59°, and everything would be frozen solid. Human activity creates greenhouse gases that include CO_2 (mainly from combustion), methane (from crops and livestock), and chlorofluorocarbons, or CFCs (from aerosol spray cans, air conditioners, and refrigerators) (Nulty 102).

(3) Though it comprises less than one-tenth of one percent of the total atmosphere, carbon dioxide plays a critical role in regulating global temperatures. CO_2 and other trace gases are responsible for what scientists have long called the "greenhouse effect." Greenhouse gases form a protective blanket that allows short-wavelength solar radiation to pass through but traps longer-wavelength thermal radiation near the earth's surface, where it warms the atmosphere. The process works in much the same way as a gardener's greenhouse: sunlight passes freely through the glass exterior but heat is kept inside, creating a hospitable climate for plants (Savage 12–13).

3. **Directions:** Using information from any combination of the sources in the preceding exercises, write paragraphs to support the following assertions:
   a. A wide range of programs will be needed to offset the greenhouse effect.
   b. The greenhouse effect may not turn out to be as serious a problem as initially predicted.
   c. There are numerous difficulties in making accurate predictions about the extent of the greenhouse effect.

Sources for Mini-Research Exercises (F)

Abelson, Philip H. "Uncertainties About Global Warming." *Science* 30 March 1990: 1529.

Alexander, Charles P. "A Sizzling Scientific Debate." *Time* 30 April 1990: 39–43.

Nulty, Peter. "Global Warming: What We Know." *Fortune* 9 April 1990: 101–105.

Savage, Harlin. "A Tree Grows in Guatemala." *The National Voter* June/July 1989: 12–15.

White, Robert M. "The Great Climate Debate." *Scientific American* July 1990: 84.

G. Write a statement of intent for your research project.
H. Write a proposal for your research project.

Worksheet 9 _____ **PROPOSING A STRATEGY**

Name _____   Date _____

1. State your research topic.

2. Explain why you are interested in the topic.

3. State the important question that your research will attempt to answer.

4. What are some of the different opinions on how this question can be answered?

5. List the sources that you have actually consulted so far.

6. State the hypothesis that you have developed on the basis of your preliminary research.

7. Explain the reasons why you have reached this tentative thesis.

CHAPTER 6

Writing Papers Based on Reading

Most of the papers you will have to write in college will be based on assigned readings. You will be asked to respond to your reading in various ways: summarize it, connect it to other readings, evaluate its reasoning, borrow evidence from it to argue a thesis of your own. Accordingly, there are some basic kinds of papers that you should be familiar with: the summary, the comparison/contrast, the argumentative essay, and the reaction paper. If you understand the principles behind these generic assignments, you will be able to see that most of your assignments will be variations on these basic types. Furthermore, the skills that are involved in writing these papers are esssential to writing a good research paper. If you build up your skills by writing these papers, you will probably be able to write the research paper with greater ease.

In Chapter 4, we explained and illustrated how to read closely. If you have not already studied that chapter, we suggest that you do so now.

WRITING A SUMMARY

A summary, sometimes referred to as an abstract or précis, is an objective condensation of the material in a longer piece of writing. The format for writing a research paper in many of the sciences requires that you begin with an abstract of the paper. When you are summarizing someone else's paper or book, the first step is to read carefully. In Chapter 4, we explained and illustrated how to read academic material closely. If you have not already studied the sections on pre-reading and active reading on pp. 75–78, we suggest that you at least read the section on the post-reading skills: paraphrasing, summarizing, comparing and contrasting, and evaluating.

Steps in Writing a Summary

1. Identify and paraphrase the author's thesis or purpose. Sometimes an author will not have a thesis. The book or article may be a report on the current information about a topic. For example, an author may be presenting factual information about the history of immigration to the United States. The author's purpose may be to give an accurate picture of the different periods of immigration and how the existing population reacted. Another possibility is that the author has shaped the presentation of the information in a way that leads the reader to the conclusion that although immigration waves have usually frightened the existing population, immigration ultimately benefited the U.S. economy. This thesis may be stated directly or may be implied by the way the author has presented the information.

2. Sketch the main sections of the article or book to trace its development and organization. Your sketch can be informal notes or an outline. An outline is like an X ray. It shows the order of the major parts and how specific points relate to one another. The table of contents for a book outlines the major parts but may not show how ideas are related. A formal outline begins with a statement of the thesis or purpose of the book or article. That main idea is then broken down into the major support points or sections, which are indicated with Roman numerals (I, II, etc.). The support for each of the ideas expressed after a Roman numeral is then listed using capital letters. Further subdivision of each of these ideas may be indicated with Arabic numerals and then lowercase letters, as illustrated in the following example. The movement from Roman numerals to capital letters to Arabic numerals to lowercase letters is a movement from general statements to increasingly more specific statements. The amount of specific detail that you put into an outline should be determined by the length of the summary that you are writing. At this point we do not want you to become preoccupied with the technicalities of outlining but to experiment with using it as a way of clearly expressing the relationship between ideas in a writer's work. As you construct an outline, try to follow the sequence of information as it appeared in the original. Some writers are not well organized and you may have to move bits of information to fit them into a logical outline.

SAMPLE OUTLINE. The following outline is based on "To Trust, Perchance to Buy," reprinted on pp. 79–83. You can refer to the article to see how the topic sentences from individual paragraphs are translated into outline form.

Thesis: The best salespeople use hypnotic techniques.
  I. Moine studied successful salespeople.
     A. 1981 study focused on eight life insurance salesmen.
     B. Initial findings were confirmed with additional subjects.
  II. Successful salespeople intuitively use hypnotic techniques.
     A. They create trust by using hypnotic pacing.
        1. Descriptive pacing creates a link with the customer.
        2. Objection pacing acknowledges the customer's concerns.
        3. Nonverbal pacing is the most effective approach.
        4. Values and attitudes are not paced.
     B. Their language is subtly suggestive.
        1. Leading statements are linked to pacing statements.
        2. Commands are woven into the sentence structure.
     C. They rely on parables and metaphors.
        1. Stories add a human element.
        2. Skill in storytelling is necessary.
  III. Hypnotic techniques are used by others whose business is to persuade.

3. Write a draft of the summary, using your sketch as a framework and paraphrasing the original material. Place information to identify the source in a heading: title, author, name of periodical, date of issue, and page numbers. The sequence of paragraphs in your summary should follow the original as much as possible. Don't leave gaps in your summary. It should be understandable to someone who has not read the original material. Use transitions and signal words (see pp. 215–218) to make connections between sentences and paragraphs.

4. Begin the summary by stating the title, author, and thesis or purpose. Although there are many ways to open a summary, here are two patterns that you can use to get started:

a. The THESIS of (give the title) by (give the author) IS THAT (state the main idea).

If you are referring to the thesis, do not introduce it with "how" or "why." The thesis is a claim and cannot be stated as a question.

Correct: The thesis of ''To Trust, Perchance to Buy'' by Donald Moine is that the best salespeople intuitively use hypnotic techniques.

Incorrect: The thesis of ''To Trust, Perchance to Buy'' by Donald Moine is what are the techniques used by the best salespeople.

b. The PURPOSE of (give title) by (give author) IS TO (use a verb phrase such as to show, to explain, to report) to state the author's intention).

Correct: The purpose of ''To Trust, Perchance to Buy'' by Donald Moine is to describe the results of his research on techniques used by top salespeople.

Incorrect: The purpose of ''To Trust, Perchance to Buy'' by Donald Moine is that he researched the techniques of top salespeople.

5. Condense the information by at least one-fourth. Anything less runs the risk of becoming a word-for-word substitution. Your summary should be as concise as possible, so trim any unnecessary words and combine sentences whenever possible in your summary.

6. Paraphrase as much as possible. A paraphrase must be accurate and adequate (essentially your own wording).

Example:

Original passage: The most powerful forms of pacing have more to do with how something is said than with what is said. The good salesman or woman has a chameleon-like ability to pace the language and thought of any customer. With hypnotic effect, the agent matches the voice tone, rhythm, volume, and speech rate of the customer. He matches the customer's posture, body language, and mood. He adopts the characteristic verbal language of the customer (''sounds good,'' ''rings a bell,'' ''get a grip on it''). If the customer is slightly depressed, the agent shares that feeling and acknowledges that he has been feeling ''a little down'' lately. In essence, the top sales producer becomes a sophisticated biofeedback mechanism, sharing and reflecting the customer's reality—even to the point of breathing in and out with the customer.

Inaccurate paraphrase: The good salesperson uses the effects of hypnosis and imitates the way the customer talks and feels.

Inadequate paraphrase: Top salespeople know that how something is said is more important than what is said, so they match the language, posture, and mood of the customer.

Accurate and adequate paraphrase: Successful salespeople know how to mirror the emotions, speech, and gestures of the customer.

For more information on paraphrasing, consult pp. 86–88.

7. Use direct quotation sparingly. There are three occasions when it is advisable to quote: when there is no way to accurately reword or condense the information (technical terminology, numbers, key phrases), when the author has stated an idea in a memorable fashion, or when the information is so surprising that a reader might question the accuracy of your paraphrase. Don't use a quotation to make a point. State the idea in your own words and follow with a quote to back up or illustrate what you have said. Use quotation marks when necessary and integrate the quoted material into your own sentence structure.

Incorrect: The states that have passed laws about weather control, ''almost all are regarded as inadequate.''

Correct: Most of the laws that states have passed on weather control ''are regarded as inadequate.''

Incorrect: Not everyone is happy about the prospect of weather modification. ''He asked that environmental consequences be studied before weather modification is accepted as a cure for the West's water problems.''

Correct: Not everyone is happy about the prospect of weather modification. Speaking at a recent conference, one scientist ''asked that environmental consequences be studied before weather modification is accepted as a cure for the West's problems.''

8. Signal the end of the summary by using phrases such as:
In conclusion, the author...
The author's last point is that...
The final section of the article covers...
9. Revise the draft, using the following checklist:

SUMMARY CHECKLIST

_____	Heading contains necessary information on source of the article.
_____	Introduction gives author (if available), title, and thesis.
_____	Paragraphs are organized around topic sentences and are clearly related to the outline.
_____	Sequence of ideas makes sense. Transitions have been used to show the connection between ideas.
_____	References to terms, names, etc., are explained.
_____	Summary is primarily paraphrase. Information is clear and accurate.
_____	Quotation marks are used around phrases and sentences which come from the article.
_____	Quotations are integrated into the text.
_____	No personal opinions are expressed.
_____	Paper has been carefully proofread for errors.

_____ **Application**

Writing a summary is not always a simple matter. Some materials will have a straightforward statement of thesis and clear organization, but others will require you to piece together the author's purpose and strategy. The article by Donald Moine, "To Trust, Perchance to Buy," printed on pp. 79–83 and outlined in the preceding section, is relatively easy to summarize because he states the conclusion of his research early in the article and develops the main idea by describing the different types of techniques. To give you an example of material that would require more analysis on your part, here is an article that was reprinted in an anthology of readings for criminal justice students. It is more difficult to summarize, partly because the author quotes and paraphrases people who hold differing opinions. The author does not announce a thesis at the start, and it is only through careful reading that we can identify the passages in which the author's opinions are expressed. Prepare to read the article using the pre-reading steps that we have suggested. Skim the article to see if you can identify the topic, the author's thesis or slant, and a pattern of development. Then read actively to check your preliminary picture.

HIGH-TECH HOUSE ARREST

Keenen Peck

Each day and night, the movements of hundreds of Americans are electronically monitored by local and Federal authorities. The snooping always penetrates the home; sometimes, it goes on at work as well. But unlike the targets of wiretapping and similar police surveillance, these subjects know they are being spied on. In fact, they volunteered.

For many of them, the alternative was serving time in jail or prison.

This is "electronic home detention," the latest rage in criminal corrections. Across the country, more and more individuals convicted of crimes are serving out their sentences at home, hooked up to government computers with ankle or wrist bracelet transmitters—"beepers" in the argot of the interested. About 100 jurisdictions use electronic monitoring, from Florida to New York, Wisconsin to California. Earlier this year, Federal officials jumped on the bandwagon and initiated a program to track some parolees by computer. The idea is spreading so fast that no one really knows just how many offenders are being watched this way.

It is clear, however, that electronic monitoring will continue to grow by leaps and bounds. Correctional agencies see the technology as a way to ease overcrowding in jails and prisons. Probation administrators regard electronic home detention as an effective, inexpensive method of supervising probationers. Offenders—or, at least, those who would otherwise be behind bars—welcome the beeper, considering house arrest better than the big house. And, predictably, a new industry of beeper manufacturers is working to spread the concept. In fact, the industry has already experienced its first scandal: A Florida judge was disciplined by judicial overseers for ordering offenders to wear beepers that he helped market.

Opposition to the beepers has been sparse. A few right-wing commentators have argued that beepers coddle criminals. A handful of police officials have expressed the reservation that potentially dangerous persons will be released into the community. Academic observers have questioned whether beepers serve any rehabilitative purpose. But civil libertarians seem to be split on the issue. At a national ACLU convention last summer, I took an unscientific, informal poll among some of the activists I met. Though many said beepers herald an Orwellian state of affairs,

---

Keenen Peck, a member of *The Progressive*'s Editorial Advisory Board, formerly chaired the Capital Area Chapter of the American Civil Liberties Union of Wisconsin.
Reprinted by permission from *The Progressive*, 409 E. Main Street, Madison, WI 53703.

others argued that beepers represent a humane alternative to institutional confinement.

Such ambivalence is understandable. One can hardly second-guess the prisoner who would rather surrender a modicum of privacy at home than lose all privacy, and possibly his life, in prison. At the same time, though, beepers appear beneficent only because our existing correctional system is so horrible. Beepers can be justified only because Americans have not embraced solutions to crime that go beyond isolating criminals in metal cells.

Moreover, beepers are believed to be used in situations where even this sorry rationale cannot be mustered. That is, they are sometimes used to monitor persons who would not have been sent to jail in the first place—persons who would have been placed on less intrusive forms of probation. More frightening is the possibility that beepers will one day be employed to keep tabs on us all. The technology itself invites such expansion.

With the beeper, the State can monitor its citizens in the last bastion of privacy, the home. Traditional probation, to be sure, entails a reduction in the offender's privacy at home. Last year, the U.S. Supreme Court went so far as to rule that probation agents may conduct warrantless searches of their clients' residences. But unlike old-fashioned probation, electronic monitoring empowers the government to control a population from *within* the halls of authority. That is a qualitative increase in police power.

A few years ago, polygraph examinations and drug tests appeared to be isolated incursions into the privacy of a handful of unfortunate individuals. Today, such probing is commonplace, at least in the private sector. We become inured to losing bits and pieces of ourselves to this or that greater good or technological imperative. The beeper blurs the line between freedom and imprisonment, and further erodes the sphere of self.

Objections like these are not immediately apparent because "electronic home detention" is actually a wide variety of programs and surveillance systems.

Beepers come in several shapes and sizes. A typical beeper resembles an oversize Dick Tracy wristwatch, but some are attached to the ankle. Some varieties send an intermittent electronic signal to a transmitter placed on the offender's home telephone, and that transmitter in turn relays data to police. Some beepers come with a portable transmitter, which the offender must plug in at work. In either event, the beeper alerts authorities if the wearer moves beyond a proscribed distance or approaches a forbidden location.

In New York, for example, a man named Barry Ryan had his probation revoked for traveling more than 100 feet from his home. According to the court in that case, his program was "designed so that on every occasion in which the defendant leaves the restricted area, in Ryan's case, 100 feet, and each time he returns to it, the exact times of his movements are recorded by the computer on a printout sheet. The printout states 'Valid' when the probationer's entry into or exit from the restricted area is made during an authorized time. When entry into or departure from the restricted area is made at a time when the defendant is required to remain at home, the computer printout states 'Violation.'"

Other beepers are less sophisticated. Instead of constantly tracking the offender, the beeper might do nothing more than emit an identifiable tone into the telephone when authorities call the wearer to see if he is where he is supposed to be.

The different beeper technologies are being used in disparate ways at many points in the criminal justice process. Some jurisdictions use them to watch pre-trial detainees; others use them to monitor persons sentenced to intensively supervised probation; and still others use them to track prisoners who were judged to be good risks and released before their prison sentences expired. In every program, participation is voluntary; no one has been forced to wear the high-tech shackle.

The greatest use of beeper technology has been in the probation context. "It's not as practical to use it for pre-trial because that's a fast-moving crowd, or should be," says Andy Hall, an associate at the Pretrial Services Resource Center, a nonprofit information clearinghouse in Washington, D.C. To the limited extent that electronic monitoring has, in fact, been used in the pre-trial setting, "it's been à la mode—for people who would otherwise have been released on recognizance, without supervision," adds Hall.

Of course, judges do not uniformly approve of beepers for those awaiting trial. In Pennsylvania, for example, an alleged embezzler was allowed to stay at home with a beeper but an accused drug dealer was denied similar treatment because, the judge said, home detention would not stop the latter defendant from selling drugs.

For those convicted of a crime and sentenced to electronic home detention, the punishment can be a boon or a bane depending on what would have happened in the absence of the beeper. If the judge would have sentenced the defendant to regular probation, then the beeper constitutes unfair punishment, for it restricts the offender's freedom more than typical conditions of probation (such as regular visits with a probation agent and the requirement of prior approval to travel out of the state). On the other hand, if the judge would have sentenced the defendant to jail, then the beeper affords more freedom because it allows the offender to continue part of his daily routine. The ACLU, among others, has expressed concern that beepers tempt judges to incarcerate offenders—albeit in their homes—who should be released into the community on traditional probation.

"It's not widening the net," counters Rolando del Carmen, professor of law and criminal justice at the Texas Criminal Justice Center at Sam Houston State University. Del Carmen was the co-author of a study on electronic monitoring for the National Institute of Justice. "Electronic monitoring provides a more structured environment for the probationer. It provides for better supervision and accomplishes a curfew situation."

Del Carmen maintains that judges can be prevented from widening the net. "You identify certain offenses where defendants are currently sent to jail, such as burglary, or where the penal code provides mandatorily that the defendant would have gone to prison. You want to hit that middle cohort instead of dipping down," he says.

But even if that problem can be avoided, another one may prove intractable: ensuring that rich and poor defendants have equal access to beeper probation.

Common sense suggests that judges are likely to sentence more middle-class offenders than poor offenders to home detention. First, the judge will conclude that a middle-class home is more rehabilitative than an environment of poverty and crime. Second, a working defendant poses a better risk than a defendant who is unemployed. Finally, the crimes for which electronic home detention is an option are usually minor offenses; felons in the prisons, a disproportionate number of whom are poor or belong to minorities, generally will not be eligible.

A Federal judge in New York made a similar observation with regard to alternative sentences in general. Writing in the *Howard Law Journal,* Henry Bramwell stated: "The poor and the minority defendant is usually one who has committed a violent crime, is without means, and has little or no recognition in his community. As a result, the middle-class defendant gets alternative sentencing or part-time imprisonment, usually without incarceration, and the poor and minority defendant gets a heavy jail term with incarceration. This certainly is not justice. Alternative sentencing and part-time imprisonment have strong class overtones."

"That is something we don't have control over," concedes del Carmen. "It is a socioeconomic problem." In the short term, he favors county subsidies for persons who cannot afford to pay the $7- to $22-per-day fee that authorities demand of electronic probationers.

Professor del Carmen is more optimistic about keeping the surveillance technology from spreading into other areas of life. He disapproves of using beepers to monitor, say, AIDS patients. "For people who are offenders, putting them on monitors is doing them a favor," he says. "There's not that justification in a civil context."

But the prospects for greater incursions into privacy are ominous. For example, video cameras, which del Carmen opposes, are already being used to monitor convicted drunk drivers in Annapolis, Maryland. The cameras are installed in the offenders' homes, though they are not always turned on. Instead, a jailer calls the offender once or twice a day and asks him to step in front of the camera, take a self-administered breath alcohol test, and display the results before the camera.

To be sure, a drunk driver is a criminal, unlike an AIDS patient. Nevertheless, the fact remains that beeper technology could be applied in settings outside of criminal justice if there were political pressure to do so. If the government can monitor pre trial detainees—who are presumed innocent under our system of law—some might say that it should also keep tabs on former mental patients, political agitators, or street people. Technologically, *1984* came and went years ago.

The U.S. Government has accumulated vast records about the citizenry in its 27,000 mainframe computers. The FBI alone maintains an index of almost ten million former offenders. (The index, known as the National

Crime Information Center, is legendary for its rampant errors.) Private industry, too, has assembled electronic dossiers on millions of workers and credit-card users.

Where today's computers can record the location of an offender, or measure the number of keystrokes a typist makes, tomorrow's will be able to ascertain the subject's mood and health. Nielsen Marketing Research foresees a sensor that can transmit a person's blood pressure, pulse, body temperature, and possible brain waves. "It could be implanted like a pierced earring, or under a tooth, or beneath a fingernail," a Nielsen employee told *Privacy Journal*.

And right around the corner are DNA files. Two companies, Lifecodes in California and Diagnostics in England, assist law-enforcement agencies in identifying suspects from tiny samples of blood, semen, or hair.

If an Orwellian world of intensive surveillance seems like the stuff of fantasy, consider the origins of the beeper itself: About five years ago, Jack Love, a judge in New Mexico, saw a Spiderman comic in which evildoers placed an electronic monitor on Spiderman to track his whereabouts. Love persuaded a friend to develop the idea as well as the gadgetry, and the rest is history.

The beeper simultaneously threatens privacy and promises to improve the lives of some convicted individuals. It is not the answer to prison overcrowding, however, because the nation's penal institutions are overcrowded by thousands, not hundreds. In addition, as more offenders are placed on beepers, the number of persons likely to get in trouble and end up behind bars—those likely to have their conditional freedom revoked—increases. Turning homes into jails is not the answer to jail overcrowding.

Nor is it the answer to crime. Beepers look good only against the backdrop of violent, fetid prisons. They nominally advance the enlightened idea of community-based corrections, but the lesser of two evils is still evil if the first is eliminated. The first evil in this instance is the prison system. In the words of the late James E. Doyle, a Federal judge in Wisconsin, "The institution of prison probably must end. In many respects it is as intolerable within the United States as was the institution of slavery, equally brutalizing to all involved, equally toxic to the social system, equally subversive of the brotherhood of man, even more costly by some standards, and probably less rational."

A real answer to crime must begin by addressing the correlation between poverty and law breaking; the prisoner population increases by about 4 per cent for every 1 per cent increase in unemployment. A real answer must also recognize that many types of behavior that clog our courts and prisons, particularly drug offenses, should be decriminalized.

Deep-rooted social problems cannot be cured by a better mousetrap. Even an electronic one.

Discussion

The title of the article and the first few paragraphs give us a clear idea of the topic: electronic monitoring of criminal offenders. However, we cannot be sure of the author's thesis until the end of the article when Peck implies that the new technology will not help much in solving the problems of crime and prison overcrowding. Skimming the article, we see that the opening sentences of paragraphs deal with the increased use of electronic monitoring, the types of monitors, the objections to their use, the relationship between this technology and other erosions of privacy.

As we read closely, we find that although some paragraphs contain objective information on the monitors and others contain quotes from advocates of their use, many of the paragraphs are devoted to examining the problems with their use and the potential for abuse. Read superficially, this article might give the impression of a report on the pros and cons of a new technology. We must pay close attention to the way information and opinions are introduced in order to notice that the article is really an argument against the promoters of electronic monitoring. The author quotes advocates of monitoring, but always goes on to refute their claims. For example, after quoting a law professor's claim that the use of monitors has not resulted in more convictions, the author states: "But even if that problem can be avoided, another one may prove intractable: ensuring that rich and poor defendants have equal access to beeper probation."

Furthermore, the author's reference to an "Orwellian state of affairs" in paragraph six and later to Orwell's novel, *1984*, is an indication of the author's slant. You may be familiar with either the novel or the movie version which depicts a society in which individuals have lost all personal rights to a government that has placed monitors everywhere. The author is identified as a former head of a chapter of the American Civil Liberties Union, an organization devoted to protecting the civil rights of individuals. If we were not familiar with either Orwell or the ACLU, we would have to check a reference book.

After a careful reading of the entire article, we are ready to sketch it. As we take notes or outline the article, we notice that over and over again the author keeps coming back to the problems with the use of electronic monitoring. We then have to decide how to reflect this pattern of development in a summary of the article. A list of the subtopics in the sequence in which they appear in the article might look like this:

increased electronic monitoring of criminal offenders
reasons for increase
little opposition
more serious problems
different types of monitors
uses of monitors: pre-trial, probation, early release

additional objections to monitors: "widening the net," discrimination against poor, use with "misfits"
connection with other types of government surveillance
not an answer to prison overcrowding or crime

If we pause to consider why the author presented the material in this fashion, we may recognize that a sense of audience was probably a major influence. Peck is writing for readers of a liberal magazine, yet he knew from conversations with people at an ACLU convention that many of them were sympathetic to the use of electronic monitors. Many people feel threatened by the amount of crime in our society. There has been a hardening of attitudes toward criminals, with the result that prisons are overcrowded. Meanwhile taxpayers are angry that they are being asked to pay for construction of more detention facilities. Liberals have long criticized the shortcomings of the prison system. All of these factors make the new technology of electronic monitoring seem like a great solution. The author wants to show the dangers of electronic monitoring, but is also trying to reflect the social attitudes that foster the expansion of government surveillance.

As we prepare to write a summary, we are also thinking of the audience and our purpose. In college, the audience will be an instructor or classmates, and the purpose will be to demonstrate understanding of the article. We cannot put our own opinions on a topic into a summary, nor is it appropriate to evaluate whether the author constructed a valid argument. Given those considerations, we may decide to slightly modify the order in which information is presented in the summary. Our primary goal is to condense the original material; consequently we will organize the summary according to the following outline:

Thesis: Although there has been little opposition to electronic monitoring of criminal offenders, this new technology can easily be abused.

   I. Increased use of monitors

      A. Types

      B. Uses

      C. Spread

   II. Reasons for increased use

   III. Problems and dangers of monitors

   IV. Other types of government surveillance

SAMPLE SUMMARY

Summary of ''High-Tech House Arrest'' by Keenen Peck, <u>The Progressive</u>, July 1988, pp. 26-28.

The major purpose of ''High-Tech House Arrest'' by Keenen Peck is to show the dangers of relying on electronic monitors to cope with the problems of crime and prison overcrowding. The monitors range from simple beepers to sophisticated systems which can alert the police if an offender moves beyond an approved area. The unobtrusive devices, about the size of a watch, are being used to keep track of people awaiting trial, criminals placed on probation, and those who receive an early release from prison. The exact number of people being monitored is not known, but the devices are being used in ''100 jurisdictions'' across the country.

The monitors, which make house arrest a feasible alternative to incarceration, have been promoted as ''effective,'' ''inexpensive,'' and ''humane.'' A few objections have been raised: ''beepers coddle criminals'' and dangerous criminals may be set loose in the community. The author, however, seems to think that the problem with electronic surveillance is the threat to civil liberties.

Peck explains that the monitors are part of an erosion of personal privacy. The courts may impose monitoring on offenders who in the past would have been given less stringent forms of probation. The privacy of the home has already been eliminated for people on probation because it is now legal to search them without a warrant. Monitors are a further extension of control by the police. The possibility that this technology could be used against non-criminals is supported by the example of lie detectors and drug tests, once used exclusively with criminals, but now used with ordinary citizens.

The objection that monitors have led to ''widening the net'' (sentencing would-be probationers to a more stringent house arrest) is countered by advocates such as Professor Rolando del Carmen, who researched the use of monitors for the National Institute of Justice. He maintains that judges can be guided to using the monitors only in cases where sentencing would have been mandatory.

Peck acknowledges that ''widening the net'' may be prevented, but that discrimination against the poor is a more difficult problem to solve. Middle-class criminals are more likely to receive electronic house arrest than are poor criminals who are sent to jail because their crimes are more often violent and their homes unstable. Even Professor del Carmen admits that this ''socioeconomic problem'' is one that the justice system faces.

Peck disagrees with Professor del Carmen about the possible use of monitors with non-criminals. Video cameras are now used in Maryland as part of alternative sentencing of drunk drivers. Peck believes that if social attitudes hardened, the technology could be used to keep track of AIDS patients, the mentally ill, the homeless, and other misfits. Peck cites other forms of government surveillance that have been fostered by technology: computer records of citizens maintained by government and industry, and DNA files.

In the final paragraphs, Peck argues that the huge numbers of prisoners packed into institutions will not be significantly reduced by monitors. In fact, monitors may lead to more overcrowding because officials are better able to spot violations by probationers. Peck does not believe that the solution to crime and overcrowded prisons is an electronic gadget but reduction in the poverty that breeds drug addiction and crime.

WRITING A COMPARISON/CONTRAST PAPER

As you read sources for your research paper, you will notice that some sources repeat ideas and information which you have already encountered. A new source may contain information that is different from what you have already read, but supports and elaborates upon earlier sources. Another possibility is that a new source may present information or opinions that contradict what you have already read. Sometimes writers will call your attention to the similarities or differences between their observations and interpretations, but this is not always the case. The ability to see similarities and differences between the writings of different authors is especially important in the research process. Almost all published research articles begin with a review of previous studies, comparing and contrasting the results and methods.

Many of your writing assignments in college are variations on the basic process of comparing and contrasting. You may be asked on an essay test to discuss the extent to which two economists agree on the impact of raising the minimum wage or to explain the difference between two interpretations of a poem. The wording of the assignment may suggest that the instructor expects that you will find more similarities (agreement) or differences, but to do a thorough job you should look for both and spell them out.

The purpose of a comparison/contrast paper may be

1. to show the similarities between things that seem different. For example, a paper might show that a conservative economist and a liberal share some basic assumptions.
2. to show differences between things that appear similar. For example, a student might show that feminists and fundamentalists oppose pornography for quite different reasons.
3. to evaluate one thing as better than another. For example, a writer might show that one plan for nuclear waste disposal is superior to another.

Steps in Writing A Comparison/Contrast Paper

1. Identify the common topic. Two authors may be writing about gun control, but are they both writing about control of hand guns, automatic rifles, or all guns?
2. Determine each author's thesis or slant on the subject.
3. Outline the points on which they agree. Do they cite the same facts, quote the same passages, refer to the same examples? Do they use similar materials in developing their ideas?
4. Outline the points of difference. Are the differences compatible or contradictory?

5. Decide whether there are more similarities or differences and write a thesis for your paper which sums up your perception.

More similarities: Although Pottle and Fernandez disagree on the exact steps that should be taken, both believe that the sources of acid rain have been adequately documented and that legislation is needed now.

More differences: Williams and Moore agree that during the 1980s the proportion of national wealth controlled by the top 1% in America increased, but Williams defends the economic policies of the Reagan years by focusing on the overall growth in the economy while Moore criticizes Reaganomics for deepening the split between rich and poor.

6. Decide on a pattern of organization for your essay that will reflect the emphasis in your thesis. There are two basic patterns for a comparison/contrast paper:

a. Discussion of source A, followed by a discussion of source B that repeatedly refers back to source A to highlight the similarities and differences. This is the **Block Pattern**.

b. Discussion of a point in source A and source B, followed by discussion of a second point in source A and source B, followed by discussion of a third (fourth, etc.) point in each source. This is the **Alternating Pattern**, and is often preferred by instructors because it fosters analysis rather than simple summary. The difficulty in using it is that you must keep signaling the reader as you move back and forth between two authors.

The pattern that you choose will depend on the extent to which the two sources overlap and on whether your instructor states a preference.

7. Provide enough paraphrases or quotations from each author to support the interpretations that you make.

8. Draft your paper with a reader in mind. Even if you are writing for an instructor, your paper should be understandable to someone who has not read your sources.

9. Revise your paper after getting feedback. Use the following checklist:

COMPARISON/CONTRAST PAPER CHECKLIST

_____	My introduction identifies the topic or issue that is common to both sources, identifies the sources, and gives the position taken by both sources.
_____	The thesis for my paper reflects my understanding of the amount of agreement or disagreement between the authors.
_____	My paper is organized according to the Block or Alternating Pattern. (Indicate which you have used.)
_____	I have provided sufficient signals and transitions.
_____	I have provided sufficient quotes and paraphrases.
_____	I have provided an evaluation of the sources if that was required by the assignment.

Application

Here is an example of a comparison/contrast paper, written for a sociology class. Students were asked to analyze the similarities and differences between two articles on legalizing drugs. The writer used the **Alternating Pattern** of organization. As you read it, note how the writer repeats the authors' names so that the reader will not get confused. Can you follow the student's discussion of the articles even though you have not read the original articles?

SAMPLE COMPARISON/CONTRAST PAPER

''Legalize Drugs? Not on Your Life'' by Charles B. Rangel

''Should Drugs Be Legal?'' by Tom Morgenthau

Illegal drugs pose numerous problems beyond serious health hazards to the users. The crimes committed to support drug habits have soared, straining the law enforcement and court systems. Drug trade has given rise to violent gangs whose shoot-outs have terrorized neighborhoods. As the economy sags, billions of dollars are spent to stop the flow of drugs into this country. And third world countries, such as Bolivia, find themselves caught between the desperation of peasants who can make money from growing coca and the U.S. government which wants them to accept military assistance for the war on drugs. In the face of these problems, a radical proposal has been made to legalize drugs. Inner-city mayors, including Baltimore's Kurt Schmoke, have joined affluent conservatives, such as former Secretary of State Schultz, in urging a new approach. Is there merit to their arguments? Charles Rangel of The New York Times and Tom Morgenthau of Newsweek say no.

The proposal to legalize drugs is a symptom that the nation has lost its will to fight for a better society, according to Rangel and Morgenthau. Rangel states that advocates of legalization are confessing "they're willing to abandon a war that we have not even begun to fight." Likewise, Morgenthau writes that the support for legalization "is a tacit acknowledgement that the war is being lost."

Both writers also agree that legalization will cause more problems than it will solve. Rangel poses a series of questions; for example, "How many people are projected to become addicts as a result of the introduction of cheaper, more readily available drugs sanctioned by government?" Morgenthau is more explicit; he presents many facts and figures to document the problems. On the question of whether legalization would increase the number of addicts, Morgenthau cites Dr. Robert DuPont, former director of the National Institute on Drug Abuse, whose figures project a grim future: 10 million people would become cocaine addicts, and 140 million would abuse drugs of one kind or another.

Although both writers reject the plan to legalize drugs, their articles are not identical. Rangel elaborates on the many practical problems that legalization would bring, aspects that proponents have not realistically considered. Will all drugs be made legal? How will the drugs be produced and sold? Will drugs be sold to minors and to workers involved in public safety, such as pilots and doctors? Morgenthau, on the other hand, spends more time detailing the arguments of legalization advocates. These advocates claim that the war on drugs is draining scarce tax dollars; it is turning the country into a police state; and it fosters crime and distorts foreign policy.

Morgenthau seems willing to concede that advocates of legalization have some solid arguments; however, the critical point for him is that legalization would surely lead to more addicts and, therefore, to more suffering and despair among the poor. Unlike Morgenthau, Rangel is unwilling to admit that legalization would result in less crime and violence. The poor, he argues, would continue to steal to support their addiction, and a black market would continue to exist.

Perhaps the major difference between the writers is in the solution that they see to the drug problem. Neither writer elaborates on a solution, but their concluding remarks reveal the gulf between them. Rangel takes a tough stand, urging ''a coordinated national battle plan that would include the deployment of military personnel and equipment to wipe out this foreign-based national security threat.'' In other words, Rangel sees the solution in terms of eliminating the supply of drugs. Morgenthau's final words refer to a ''a social order that provides abundant opportunities for self-destruction, but very few for hope.'' Clearly, Morgenthau is looking at the demand side of the problem. So long as conditions in the ghetto induce despair and anger, there will be a drug problem. The drug of choice may change from one decade to the next, and the source may shift from local concoctions to foreign markets, but people will continue to turn to drugs as an escape until society can persuade them that they have a stake in the future. Morgenthau's article reveals a deeper awareness of the root of our drug problem.

WRITING AN ACADEMIC ARGUMENT

In ordinary language, "argument" usually means "fight" or "quarrel," as in "He had an argument with his sister over who should get to use the family car." In academic language, however, "argument" means something that is not so personal: for example, "He had an argument with his TA over the candidate's qualifications for the Supreme Court nomination." An academic argument is about ideas. It is a position taken on an issue about which there is present or potential disagreement. The purpose of an academic argument is to support one of these positions in order to convince someone else or some other people that this position is better than an alternative position.

Here, for example, is the beginning of one of the readings in the Anthology:

> Last month animal-rights protesters challenged medical students at Yale University over the use of animals in medical research. As the confrontation made clear, the issue has neither faded away nor been resolved. Proponents of the practice usually cite the importance of animal research to the level of medical care Americans now enjoy. They claim that animal-rights activists take this medical care for granted and fail to show compassion for human suffering. But this position ignores the morality of the issue. It accepts the philosophy that the end—in this case, better human health—justifies the means—the infliction of suffering and premature death on animals. Few of us, upon reflection, would subscribe to such a philosophy. Is it enough, to justify experiments on living organisms, to show that they have proved successful and useful? Of course not.

Note how this passage identifies a controversy and establishes the authors' position. The rest of the reading explains and supports their position.

Any good academic argument has these two logical parts. First, it includes a claim asserting that something is true or a contrary claim that refutes an assertion. Second, it must include adequate evidence to back up the claim.

Most academic arguments fall into one of the following categories. The argument may be an assertion that something is true or a contrary argument that refutes an assertion.

1. *Definition:* For example, arguments to prove that the fetus is a human being are an important part of the debate on abortion; arguments to prove that animals share characteristics with humans are crucial to the animal rights debate; arguments to prove that hypnosis is not a special state of mind have been part of a debate in the field of psychology.

2. *Existence of a problem or opportunity:* For example, arguments to prove that global warming is taking place; arguments to prove that the level of education in the United States is inadequate to meet the challenge of international competition; arguments to show that a North American free trade zone, including Mexico and Canada, would benefit the U.S. economy. Arguments may also be made that something will become a problem or an opportunity.

3. *Cause of a problem or opportunity:* For example, arguments to show that certain chemicals are depleting the ozone layer in the earth's atmosphere; arguments to show that stereotypes of women continue to limit their career opportunities; arguments to prove that higher oil prices will create incentives for cleaner energy sources.

4. *Solution to a problem:* For example, arguments to prove that legalizing the use and sale of drugs would reduce crime; arguments to show that federally funded day care would lessen the difficulty that parents have in finding facilities for their preschoolers; arguments to prove that putting

employee representatives on pension fund boards would not improve the safety or performance of the funds.

Steps in Writing an Argument

1. Look over the information you have gathered so far and develop a thesis statement that you think you can support. You will have to decide how strong a position you want to take on your topic. Suppose you have been researching the problem of solid waste disposal. Perhaps you have come across enough information to allow you to argue that a tax should be placed on all items that cannot be recycled. If so, you can take a strong stand on this issue. On the other hand, if the information that you have suggests a more modest thesis, you should create a more limited thesis. For example, perhaps you can claim that Americans are finally facing the problem of solid waste disposal and taking steps to manage it properly.

2. Develop a thesis that is worth arguing. Some aspects of your topic may be so universally accepted that there is no point in developing an argument about them. For example, everyone probably agrees that child abuse is terrible and that it is a serious social problem. However, there are different opinions about how we should respond to this problem. Concentrate on an aspect of your topic where there is some disagreement among the experts and develop a position that you can support.

3. Consider the audience in developing your argument. The reality is that while you are in college, you are writing for an instructor, but some instructors will ask you to write with a specific audience in mind. For instance, a criminal justice instructor might ask you to address a position paper on the legalization of drugs to an audience of senior citizens. Or an instructor might give a general definition of the audience as skeptical. As you draft your paper, it is wise to test out your position on the instructor and ask if there are aspects that you have overlooked.

Outside the ivy walls, the nature of the audience that you are addressing is very important. You need to ask yourself: What do you know about the audience? Do you have anything in common with them? Does your audience share the same values and assumptions as you do? How much do they already know? For example, many psychologists already know that the use of hypnosis in police work poses certain dangers. However, a general audience might not be aware of the problem. For a less informed audience, then, your purpose might be to convince them that there is a problem. For an informed audience, you might develop an argument to support a solution to the problem.

4. List the support points for your thesis. Sometimes it helps to start writing freely without worrying about the order in which you will take up the points. After you have your ideas on paper, then you can sort them out and decide on the best sequence.

Suppose you had decided that the government should provide more incentives for the use of recycled paper. A list of your support points might look like this:

```
Paper is the largest category of waste.
Newspapers can be recycled.
The market for recycled paper is smaller than the supply.
A few states have passed laws requiring newspapers to print on
  recycled paper.
```

5. List all the objections that might be raised against your position and any information that does not support your thesis. You may have already discovered some objections in your reading, but it pays to talk to other people at this point. They may ask questions that you can't answer. If you cannot find answers before your paper is due, you can at least acknowledge briefly in your paper that there are some unanswered questions. Failure to indicate your awareness of facts or points that do not support your position will be a weakness in your argument.

A list of counterarguments on incentives for using recycled paper might look like this:

```
Paper could be burned in waste-to-energy incinerators.
Interfering with the free market will cause higher prices.
Greater use of recycled paper will hurt the wood pulp industry.
The quality of recycled paper is not good.
```

6. Look for weaknesses in the counterarguments or additional facts which will weaken the counterarguments. As you carefully assess the pros and cons, you may find yourself modifying or changing your position. That is fine. Your goal is to find a truly defensible position. A change in your position usually means that you are doing a thorough job of thinking through an issue.

7. Develop the organization of your paper. In the draft stages, you may find it easier to concentrate on the body of the paper first and to write the introduction later. As you revise your paper, keep in mind these guidelines for the introduction, body, and conclusion.

The Introduction: Depending on the length of your paper, the degree of controversy surrounding your position, and the audience you are addressing, your introduction may be a few sentences or several paragraphs. The objectives of an introduction are to:

1. Catch the reader's attention. You need to convince the reader that it will be worthwhile to spend time reading your paper. You can do this by
    a. using a startling example or case history;
    b. giving background on the issue;
    c. quoting an authority on the issue; or
    d. asking a series of questions.
2. Give a clear sense of the problem or issue that you will address.
3. Develop the reader's trust. You must present yourself as a reasonable, knowledgeable person. The quality of the information that you present in the introduction will influence the reader's opinion of you. You may also be able to establish a common ground with the reader

by acknowledging opposing viewpoints and the sincerity of them. Another technique is to praise the reader's interest in the topic.
4. State or imply your position. If your thesis is controversial and your audience is skeptical or hostile, you may not want to state your position. Instead, you may decide to let the force of your facts and reasoning lead the audience to the same conclusions that you have reached.

The Body: There are two basic patterns from which you can choose to develop your paper:

Pattern #1: Minimize objections to your position. If you have found a few counterarguments or facts that do not fit your position, mention them briefly early in the body of your paper. Then develop the arguments in support of your thesis. The danger of mentioning objections at the end of your paper is that the objections can seem more important if they are placed toward the end. Place the objections or counterarguments toward the end only if you have developed a strong refutation of them. A good example of the use of this pattern can be seen in the Anthology selection "Better Health Care Doesn't Justify Animal Research."

Pattern #2: Systematically refute objections to your position. If you are writing about a controversial issue and have been able to find answers to most of the objections that are raised to the position you are taking, the best pattern may be to build your paragraphs around a counterargument and your refutation of it. The sample argumentative paper that follows uses this pattern.

The Conclusion: End on a strong note. Save a compelling reason, fact, example, or quote for the end of your paper. If your paper is more than a few pages, it may be effective to summarize the arguments in favor of your position.

8. Acknowledge sources of information that you have used in the paper. Letting the reader know that you have used information from reliable sources adds weight to your argument. In a formal research paper you would follow one of the accepted systems of documentation, but in the argumentative paper you can use an informal method called a *running acknowledgment*. Using this method, you can include an author's name, the name of the publication or agency, or a person's qualifications.

Example: According to Thomas Wright, executive director of Rhode Island's Solid Waste Management Corporation, ''Recycling doesn't pay for itself.''

Example: Business Week reported that the glut of old newspapers available for recycling has driven down the price of new paper by 13% last year.

Example: Newspapers account for 10% to 18% of landfill volume, according to an article in The Atlantic.

Example: The facts presented in this paper come primarily from Editorial Research Reports, a publication prepared by Congressional Quarterly, Inc.

9. Revise your paper after it has been read by one or more people. The purpose of an argument is to convince other people, and without getting some feedback from other readers, it is difficult to tell how convincing your paper is. To help you get specific feedback, use the Argumentative Paper Checklist that follows.

ARGUMENTATIVE PAPER CHECKLIST

_____	Have I clearly introduced the problem or issue?
_____	Have I clearly stated my position?
_____	Have I provided a sufficient number of arguments to support my position?
_____	Have I mentioned the opposing arguments? Are there any that I have not considered?
_____	How have I dealt with the opposing arguments?
_____	Have I provided sufficient facts, examples, or case histories to support my position?
_____	Is additional evidence still needed?
_____	Are the connections between my ideas clear?
_____	Have I acknowledged informally the source of any facts or opinions that I have used?
_____	What are the strengths of my argument?
_____	What are its weaknesses?

SAMPLE ARGUMENTATIVE PAPER

Americans are becoming savvy about garbage. Faced with the closing of their local landfills, confronted with stories on the nightly news about the expense and difficulty of siting new dumps, and concerned about the environmental impact of incinerators, they have begun to pass regulations requiring that recyclable materials, such as glass and newspapers, be separated from other types of waste. The problem now is what to do with the recyclable trash, particularly newsprint. Within one year the price of old newspapers dropped from $25 a ton to $2 a ton in Rhode Island, a state that mandated recycling. Some communities must actually pay brokers to take the newsprint. In an effort to create a larger market for recycled paper, Connecticut and California now require that newspapers be printed on recycled paper.

Other states and the federal government should follow the lead of these two states and undertake an aggressive effort to promote the recycling of newspapers.

Many people think of plastics as the villains of the landfill because they do not decompose. What they may not know is that paper constitutes the largest single category of waste, almost 40%, and newspapers account for 10% to 18% of landfill volume, according to a recent news article. Contrary to popular belief, they do not decompose easily when they are buried. One landfill archaeologist has dug up papers that were forty years old and still readable. Furthermore, when they finally decompose, the inks cause a toxic runoff which can pollute water. Clearly, we are better off if we can keep newspapers out of the landfill.

As an alternative to dumping garbage, some communities have built high-temperature incinerators that produce energy from trash; however, these incinerators cost millions to build and pose pollution problems of their own. Even with pollution control devices, incineration produces dioxin which may cause cancer and which accumulates in human tissue, possibly leading to birth defects. At the very least, burning trash releases more carbon dioxide into the atmosphere, adding to the greenhouse effect.

The United States is just beginning to think seriously about recycling paper. Currently, we recycle about 10% of our old papers, compared with about 50% in Japan. Yet, judging from the drop in prices, we seem to have already saturated the existing market for used newspapers. According to Thomas Wright, executive director of Rhode Island's Solid Waste Management Corporation, ''Recycling doesn't pay for itself.'' The chairman of one of the country's largest trash collectors agrees: "The market will need a push in the short term." If communities want to keep newspapers out of the waste stream, the government must provide incentives to stimulate use of the recycled paper.

Some might object that legislation to require the use of recycled paper will lead to higher costs, but the opposite may be true. Business Week reported that the glut of old newspapers available for recycling has driven down the price of new paper by 13% last year. Using recycled newsprint may increase production costs because it breaks more easily when running through the presses. No firm figures have been developed to prove that this problem will hike costs significantly.

When California and Connecticut passed legislation requiring newspapers to use recycled newsprint, the publishers charged discrimination. Given the fact that newspapers create so much waste, it hardly seems unfair to require the papers to play a more active role in the recycling effort. Just one Sunday edition of the New York Times creates 8 million pounds of waste paper. However, it is true that there are other giants in the production of waste paper. Telephone directories and government documents are routinely produced and slated for early obsolescence. Junk mail piles up daily, along with the increasingly popular mail-order catalogs. Surely, there are ways to require these trash producers to print on recycled paper.

Any time the government intervenes in the market, there are economic repercussions, and they are likely to occur if legislation is passed to stimulate the use of recycled paper. One consequence, already noted earlier, is the drop in the price of virgin newsprint. However, companies that process wood pulp for paper might not have to cut jobs if they were encouraged to join the recycling venture.

A final benefit from stimulating the use of recycled paper would be that fewer trees would be cut. The difference is not likely to offset the enormous reduction of forests in tropical areas, but it would be a step in the right direction.

WRITING A REACTION PAPER

A reaction paper, critical analysis, or review presents your understanding of someone else's argument and your assessment of it. Your paper actually contains two arguments: a summary of the author's original argument and an argument that you construct to support your evaluation of the author's ideas. Your evaluation may be positive, negative, or a mixture of both, but it must include enough summary of the author's ideas so that your paper would be understandable to someone who had not read the original piece. You are probably familiar with the nature of a reaction paper just from reading the daily newspaper. Letters to the editor are often in response to an article that appeared in the paper. Similarly, movie and book reviews present evaluations of another person's ideas. In the academic world, scholars review one another's publications and respond to the articles printed in professional journals. Your research paper, if it is a thesis paper, will require you to evaluate the materials that you read. The practice in writing a reaction paper in response to the argument in one article will build the critical thinking skills that you need to write your research paper.

Steps in Writing a Reaction Paper

1. Follow the process of pre-reading and active reading to gain an understanding of the author's thesis and support. Remember that a thesis may be implied rather than stated directly. If you cannot find a direct statement of the author's position, then brainstorm for an assertion that would be proved or refuted by the information presented by the author.

2. Paraphrase the author's thesis and think up all the reasons and facts that would be necessary to prove such a thesis. Try to think independently of the author at this stage. For example, imagine an author who makes the assertion that antipoverty programs are doomed to failure because they cannot change the deeply rooted attitudes which cause people to be poor. What evidence would we expect before we would be convinced that the thesis was valid? First, we would expect some clear definition of terms: Is a program a failure if less than fifty percent of the participants succeed? What is the measuring stick for success and failure? Next, we would expect evidence that antipoverty programs have failed. We would also expect a fair consideration of all the possible reasons why the programs might have

failed: lack of community involvement, lack of follow-up, insufficient funding, lack of support services, bureaucratic difficulties. We would need definition and examples of the attitudes that supposedly cause poverty, along with evidence that these same attitudes do not exist among people who are not poor. Obviously, we would expect a great deal before we could conclude that the author has adequately defended the thesis.

3. Sketch the author's argument, noting whether key terms have been defined and whether the types of evidence and reasoning that you expect have been provided.

4. Assess the extent to which the author has provided adequate evidence. The standards for judging the adequacy of evidence vary greatly from one setting to another. For example, after hearing the unhappy story of one couple, the audience of a TV talk show may be quite convinced that open adoption, the practice of letting the birth mother select the adoptive parents, is a terrible idea. However, a more critical audience would want to know about other cases and the problems with closed adoption. Legislators or agency heads would want to collect much more evidence before ruling on adoption policies.

Evaluating Evidence and Reasoning

In the courts and in the academic world, strict standards have developed about what types of evidence are appropriate. Here are some of the standards for evaluating the adequacy of a writer's evidence:

Generalizations and claims should be supported by specific information: It is not enough for a writer to claim that "everyone knows" or "experiments prove" without substantiating the claim. Academic writers almost always refer to the specific research on which a generalization is based, just as a judge would refer to a specific case which set a precedent. In nonprofessional publications, the writers will not always substantiate their claims, so you have to maintain a skeptical attitude about whether the claim constitutes true knowledge or is just the opinion of the writer.

Isolated examples, whether real or hypothetical, cannot prove a claim: The exact number of examples that must be considered before a conclusion can be reached depends on the argument that the writer is making. For example, a writer claimed that people were foolish to think that their pension plans were safe because independent auditors were responsible for checking on how the funds were managed. To prove the claim, he cited the study conducted by the government agency that audits private pension plans. The study examined 62 plans whose managers had violated pension laws. The study showed that the independent auditors had failed to find the illegal transactions in 41 plans and that in 13 other plans violations had been found but never reported. In this instance, the number of examples was sufficient to convince some legislators that better enforcement was needed.

Evidence must be up-to-date and gathered by a reputable individual or agency: Some types of evidence never go out-of-date, but if a writer is arguing about a contemporary issue, the information should be recent and should have been gathered by someone who does not have a bias on the issue. A few years ago, the Surgeon General of the United States came to the conclusion that there was not sufficient evidence to show that women who had abortions suffered emotional problems as a consequence. He reached this conclusion because most of the studies were conducted by researchers who had a bias in favor of or against abortion.

Evidence which does not fit the author's thesis must be explained: Rarely do problems exist where the facts add up clearly and neatly to a clear-cut answer. There are always some facts, some cases, that just do not fit the pattern. A responsible researcher always points out the stray facts and tries to account for their divergence.

Alternate interpretations of the evidence must be considered: You have probably watched numerous mystery stories in which the detective, after collecting the evidence, sits in the office, pondering possible explanations. Confronted with raw facts or information, there is always more than one way that they can be interpreted. Finding the correct answer involves ruling out the less satisfactory solutions. The correct answer is the one that accounts for the most important or the greatest number of facts. When good writers are presenting the case to support a thesis, they usually give alternate interpretations and then explain why the alternate explanations are not as satisfactory as the thesis which they are proposing.

Analogies cannot be used to prove a claim: An analogy is a comparison between two or more items. Analogies are useful in explanations because they enable a writer to compare a new idea with one that the reader already understands. Comparing the narrator of a short story with the lens of a movie camera might help a student to understand point of view. Although analogies can illustrate a concept, they cannot prove an argument because no two cases are identical. The differences may be more important than the similarities. Of course, analogies can be a powerful persuasive device. When the government announced plans to build a dam that would have backed up water into a section of the Grand Canyon, conservationists ran an ad that asked: "Should we flood the Sistine Chapel to bring tourists closer to the ceiling?" The Sistine Chapel contains priceless art work, just as the Grand Canyon contains incomparable natural beauty. Advocates of the dam claimed the analogy was unfair, but conservationists won public support for their efforts to save the canyon.

5. Assess the author's reasoning about the evidence. Some of the common pitfalls are:

Failing to consider all possibilities when analyzing cause and effect: Many of the arguments that you will read attempt to prove either the cause or effect of something. The difficulty with analyzing cause and effect is that there are so many possibilities. For example, one writer claims that the low reading scores of students are caused by watching too much TV. Another writer claims that students are watching too much TV because schools do not get kids hooked on books. Which is the cause and which is the effect? With many issues it is difficult to tell. Consequently, we must always be alert to the danger of oversimplifying the cause of a problem. Likewise, a writer may oversimplify the solution by suggesting that unless we take a certain course of action, doom is certain. For example, advocates for English as an official language argue that unless everyone in the United States is required to learn English, we will lose a sense of national unity. What possibilities may they be overlooking?

Shifting the meaning of a key term: The writer's conclusion can be faulty if the meaning or use of an important term changes during the course of the discussion. For example, opponents of abortion sometimes begin an argument by stating that "abortion ends the life of the fetus" (which everyone agrees is the case), to claiming that "abortion is murder" (*murder* being a legal term which has a different meaning from *ending life*), to finally calling pro-choice advocates "baby killers" (a term that is quite different from the first one).

Inaccurately reporting the opposing viewpoint and refuting the inaccuracy: In the following paragraph, a writer who is arguing for the construction of a nuclear power plant begins by paraphrasing an objection to the plant, but then distorts the meaning of the objection. The result is that the writer does not refute the objection but an inaccurate version of it.

```
Critics of nuclear power plants claim that a serious accident
would be more devastating than an atom bomb. However, a nuclear power
plant cannot explode like a bomb. The reactors used in nuclear power
plants are fueled by small, scattered elements that are incapable of
combining to form the critical mass needed for an explosion of a
nuclear power plant.
```

The problem with the reasoning is that there is an important difference between saying that the *results* of an accident at a nuclear power plant would be worse than an atom bomb and claiming that a nuclear power plant can't *explode* like a bomb. The critics of nuclear plants never said that they would explode.

Hidden premise: If a writer fails to state the assumptions or generalizations on which an argument is based, it may be because everyone already agrees about it. However, sometimes a writer fails to state the basic premise of the argument because it is shaky. For example, some animal rights activists argue that animals should not be used for medical research because they should not be used for anything—zoos, pets, clothing, or food. Their premise, sometimes hidden because it is unpopular, is that humans have no special characteristics to distinguish them from the animals and therefore have no superior rights over animals.

Circular reasoning: This problem is equivalent to saying "Half a dozen is six, and six is half a dozen." In other words, the writer does not give evidence for the claim, but merely states it in different words. The reasoning goes round and round instead of progressing toward a proof of the claim.

Example:

```
Animal experimentation, also known as vivisection, is a cruel, bar-
baric procedure through which innocent animals are tortured in the
name of progress. Vivisection is a scam in the disguise of science. It
is immoral and unethical. At the root of vivisection are the innocent
animals which are uselessly tortured and killed. The fraudulence of
this so-called ''scientific'' procedure is obvious.
```

Discussion: This paragraph is saying that animal experimentation is wrong because it is wrong. To escape from the circular reasoning, the writer needs to produce evidence of its uselessness, examples of unnecessary cruelty, or an explanation of why it is unethical.

Failing to stick to the issue: Courtroom dramas always picture the lawyer leaping up to object that a question is irrelevant to the case. Likewise, a writer may bring in information or arguments that are not directly related to the issue being discussed. You must act as a judge to decide if the writer is getting off the track or is trying to discredit an opposing viewpoint. Sarcasm, ridicule, and name-calling can be effective devices to persuade an audience but are no substitute for discovering the truth of a matter.

6. Talk to others about the author's ideas. This will help you to refine your understanding and develop your response. Talking to others may give you different perspectives on the topic.

7. Try to find other books or articles on the same topic. This will broaden the base of information that you have to work with when you write your paper. Your paper should be more than just a series of your own opinion statements; you will need specific details to support your evaluation.

8. Consider a thesis contrary to the one presented by the author. Would there be any evidence or arguments to support the opposite point of view? If you are writing a reaction to a book or article on a controversial subject, your paper should reflect an awareness of both sides of the subject. Failure to do so implies that you have not understood the issue or thought carefully about it.

9. Develop a thesis for your paper which will express your evaluation. Usually you will discover that a piece of writing has some merits and some shortcomings. As you formulate your evaluation, make sure that you are taking a fair and balanced view of the author's work. If your evaluation is mixed, it is particularly important to phrase your thesis in a way that lets the reader know your position. You want to avoid confusing the reader by starting out on one note and ending on another. The body of your paper should have a consistent position which is stated early in the paper. Here are some examples:

Positive: William Wilson's The Truly Disadvantaged presents compelling evidence that the plight of the poor in the United States is caused by macroeconomic conditions far beyond their control.

Negative: Edward Banfield's The Unheavenly City Revisited fails to consider the basic economic facts of poverty and wrongly blames the victims for their lack of ambition.

Mixed: Although William Wilson's The Truly Disadvantaged presents compelling evidence of the economic forces that create poverty, he does not have any politically realistic ideas about how the problems will be solved.

10. Write a draft of the paper, including enough summary of the author's ideas so that your reaction will make sense. Provide signals to let the reader know when you are summarizing, such as "according to the author," "the author claims," or "the article explains." A sketch of the paper might look like this:

Introduction:	Identify author, title, and thesis of the book or article. State your evaluation.
Second paragraph:	Summarize one of the author's major points. Give your evaluation of it.
Third paragraph:	Summarize a second main point and give your evaluation.
Fourth paragraph:	Summarize and evaluate another point or bring in related information on the topic.
Conclusion:	Restate *your* reaction and summarize *your* points only in a long paper.

11. Revise your paper using the following checklist:

REACTION PAPER CHECKLIST

_____ The introduction identifies the author and title, the author's ideas, and states my reaction to them.

_____ The body paragraphs are developed to support my opinion of the author's ideas.

_____ I have provided sufficient summary of the author's ideas throughout the paper so that it can be understood by another person.

_____ I have provided sufficient signals to let the reader know when I am summarizing and when I am giving my own ideas.

_____ My paper reflects an understanding of both sides of the issue.

_____ I have maintained a consistent position throughout the paper.

_____ **Application**

Use the pre-reading and active reading strategies we have discussed to gain an understanding of the ideas presented in the following article. We will then examine the author's reasoning and use of evidence.

A NONBEARING ACCOUNT

Noel Perrin

Why Not Stem the Population Explosion by Paying Women Not to Have Babies?

Sometime in 1987 world population hit 5 billion. Sometime a little before 2000 it will hit 6 billion. Sometime around 2010 . . . Obviously growth like this can't continue indefinitely. We'll run out of parking space for all the cars. We'll run out of flight paths for all the airplanes. We'll eventually run out of essentials like food. A country like Nepal has already run out of firewood.

But how do you stop the relentless increase of humanity, currently proceeding at the rate of almost 2 million a week? Well, the most interesting idea I've heard is to do it with money. More specifically, bank accounts. One for every woman in the world. Forget the rest of the world for a minute: here is how the plan would work in the United States. Every girl, when she reached puberty, would notify her local population center. (These sunny offices had better be staffed entirely by women—well-paid ones, too.) At that moment a financial clock would start ticking.

If the girl went the next year without having a baby, she would get a government check for $500, placed in the bank account the center now opened for her. She could take it all out and spend it on angora sweaters, if she wanted. She could leave it in as the beginning of a fund for college. Whatever she liked. The next year, if she still hadn't had a baby, the government would increase the sum by a hundred, so that her second check would be for $600. The year after, $700. A young woman reaching the age of 20, and still not having had a child, would receive a check for around $1,200. No fortune, but worth having. Available without any discrimination of any kind. A Miss du Pont, an ordinary kid in Topeka, an intending nun, a teenage prostitute, all would get their checks.

Suppose the young woman *wants* a child, though. There's nothing to stop her, except a little financial self-interest. If at 21 she proceeded to have a baby, fine. Let's have a baby shower. The government payment, however, would abruptly drop to zero. But then, if she did not have another baby the next year, back would come a check for $500. If she went two

Perrin, who has written for *The New Yorker* and *New York* magazine, is professor of English at Dartmouth College.
Reprinted from *Newsweek*. Copyright © 1990 Newsweek.

years, she'd get $600, and so on up the modest pay ladder. A pleasant little extra income for the sex that has historically been underpaid.

Great Bargain

What would all this cost? In the case of women who never do have children, plenty. Start at 13 with a check for $500 and by the time you reached menopause at 53, the check would be $4,500. To that point, you would have received a total of almost $100,000. A lot of money. But still a bargain. A great bargain. The same hundred thousand is about half the cost of bringing up one abandoned child in New York City. It's less than a fifth the cost of bringing up one psychologically disturbed child in a group home in the District of Columbia. The total cost the first year would be about a billion dollars in payments to girls, maybe 2 or 3 billion to set up the centers. The total cost the fifth year would be around $10 billion. The cost wouldn't level off for about 40 years—and when it did, it would still be under what we now pay as welfare. And most of the money would flow back out immediately to stores or get turned over somewhat later to happy bursars at colleges.

Do I possibly exaggerate when I say that when the plan was in full operation, and every woman in the country between puberty and menopause receiving her check, the cost would still be less than that of the current welfare system? I don't think I do. Try looking in the "Statistical Abstract of the United States." The current figure is $770 billion a year—$298 billion in state and local money, $472 billion from the federal government. That table covers many things, including VA hospitals. So turn to a more modest table, the one called "Cash and Noncash Benefits for Persons With Limited Incomes." Here the total is $114 billion, all federal money.

Such a plan would be much harder to implement in, say, India, where most people don't have bank accounts and where the government would be hard pressed to find the funds. But it wouldn't be impossible. Such payment could be the first-ever democratic foreign aid—putting money directly in the hands of women, rather than in the pockets of businessmen and bureaucrats. Furthermore, India has already found ways to pay men to have vasectomies.

Of course there are problems with such a plan. Men will object to all this money going to women, money being power. There are bound to be accusations of racism, even though the offer would be voluntary, universal and totally color blind. There being no precedent (though there's plenty of precedent for the opposite case: governments paying women to *have* children), it would be hard to get started. The more stolid type of politician will call the plan impossible, utopian, dreamy, absurd.

But consider the alternatives. One, of course, is to go on exactly as we are—adding a billion people every few years until there is no more tropical forest, no more oxygen-carbon dioxide balance, no more space, and our world collapses in disaster. Another is nuclear war. A third (the likeliest, I expect) is mandatory birth control, starting one country at a time, with all the repression that implies. The repression is already there in China. And with the rigid immigration restrictions imposed by those countries that have started early against those that start late. Maybe even with population wars. How much more graceful to do it all with checks.

Discussion

1. What is the author's thesis? The question at the beginning of the article alerts us to Professor Perrin's main idea: the population explosion can be lessened by giving women money if they do not have children.

2. What evidence and reasoning would we expect for an adequate proof of the thesis? First, we would look for evidence that the growth in population will have dangerous consequences. If we are convinced of the need to control birth rates, we must carefully examine the plan Perrin proposes to achieve this goal. How would it work? How would it be funded? What evidence is there that it would work? What other plans might accomplish the same goal? Why would this plan be better? How would opposition to the plan be handled?

3. In sketching Perrin's article, we find that the first paragraph gives statistics on population growth and asserts that if increases continue at the present rate we will run out of resources. In the next few paragraphs, he introduces and describes a plan to stem the increase: from the moment they become capable of bearing children, women would receive a yearly check of an increasing amount as a bonus for not giving birth. Perrin explains that the plan would allow women the freedom to have children if they wished. They would simply forego the bonus for the year in which they had a child. He admits that the plan would be costly, but argues that it would be less than the cost of our current welfare structure. Although his explanation of the plan shows how it might work in the United States, Perrin also tries to demonstrate that it would work in poor countries such as India. Perrin briefly considers objections to the plan before concluding that it is better than all the alternatives.

In sketching Perrin's article, we see that he has covered most of the points that we anticipated. However, we must next look closely at the evidence and reasoning in the article.

4. Perrin presents figures on population growth. We could check the accuracy of the figures by consulting a reference book. All predictions about future growth are estimates, but there does seem to be consensus that the rate of increase in the world population has accelerated. What Perrin does not consider is the different rates of population growth throughout the world. Do all countries need to cut their population growth? Moreover, he makes a general claim that "we'll eventually run out of essentials like

food," but does not present any evidence except that Nepal has exhausted its supply of firewood. We would want to look for evidence that would confirm or refute this aspect of Perrin's argument.

Perrin presents figures on the cost of the proposed plan and then compares them with current spending on welfare programs. He claims that even if a woman received the maximum amount as a bonus for having had no children throughout her childbearing years, the cost would be less than "bringing up one psychologically disturbed child in a group home...." The hidden assumption here is that the plan will result in the birth of fewer children with problems. But will it? Will the reduction in the cost of caring for such children equal the total cost of such a program? Later, Perrin claims that the total cost of the program would be less than the $114 billion that the federal government now pays to poor people. Again, there is a hidden assumption that poor women will take advantage of the plan and limit the number of children that they have. He does not give an analysis of why poor women have children, nor of why poor nations tend to have higher birth rates than more affluent nations. Would the cash incentive that Perrin proposes be sufficient to offset the other forces that promote reproduction?

In considering how the plan might be implemented in third world countries like India, Perrin acknowledges the difficulties but offers as evidence of the plan's feasibility the fact that India has "found ways to pay men to have vasectomies." He does not present figures on what the plan would cost on a worldwide basis and how those figures compare with current levels of foreign aid.

5. When we examine the reasoning in Perrin's article, we find further problems. In addition to the lack of adequate evidence for some of his claims and the hidden assumptions, there is a great oversimplification of cause and effect. Given the complex problem that he is dealing with, offering a cash bonus seems deceptively simple. Population problems are likely to differ from one country to another and a country's cultural values would have to be taken into account in planning any program to reduce birth rates. He dismisses potential objections too quickly and indulges in a bit of rhetoric when he characterizes the potential opponents as "stolid." Perrin's conclusion that a cash incentive is preferable strikes us as unwarranted because he does not consider all the alternatives.

6. In talking to others about Perrin's article, we will encounter a mix of reactions. The very simplicity of his plan will appeal to some. Others may agree with his concern about unchecked population growth. Some will question whether politicians will ever tackle long-term problems when they can barely agree on a budget for the next year. As we engage in discussion with others, we will find views that we might not have considered and our own thinking about the author's ideas will deepen.

7. While searching for other material on the topic of population control, we found a reaction to Perrin's article: "Can We Buy Our Way Out of Overpopulation?" You will not always find something that relates so

directly to the material that your are evaluating, but you can consult *Book Review Digest* (see p. 48) or abstracts in various academic fields. As you read the following reaction to Perrin's article, note how the author summarizes Perrin's ideas so that someone who had not read Perrin's article would still be able to make sense of the reaction. Also, note how the writer signals the reader when she is summarizing Perrin's ideas. Examine the extent to which the writer agrees and disagrees with Perrin. Is it a positive, negative, or mixed evaluation of Perrin? Notice the additional information on the subject which the author introduces. A good reaction paper is one that goes beyond simply stating one's own opinions on the topic.

CAN WE BUY OUR WAY OUT OF OVERPOPULATION?

Marilyn Gardner

In most cultures, children have traditionally been regarded as valuable assets, even precious commodities. But if an idea put forth by a professor at Dartmouth College takes hold, *not* having children may come to be viewed as an even greater asset.

Noting that world population is growing at a frightening and intolerable rate—almost 2 million babies are born each week—Noel Perrin proposes a new form of birth control: money. If governments were to pay women not to have babies, he argues in Newsweek, they would help to avert a population crisis. The payments would also provide a "pleasant little extra income" for women, who have "historically been underpaid."

Professor Perrin's scenario goes like this: When a girl reached puberty, she would register at her "local population center." In the United States, he suggests, a first-year payment for not bearing a child might be $500. That sum would increase by $100 each year. If a woman gave birth, she would lose her payment that year, then begin again at the $500 level the following year. This pattern would continue throughout her childbearing years.

The idea is similar to two existing Planned Parenthood programs that pay teenage mothers to avoid another pregnancy. In Denver, a program that has been operating since 1985 pays $7 a week to girls who attend a weekly support group. In East Palo Alto, Calif., participants in a program called Teen Incentive receive $10 a week. Success rates are high, although leaders attribute this more to the effects of group discussions on birth control, childrearing, and college preparation than to the monetary rewards.

Giving teenagers this kind of economic incentive for a limited period of time may be useful in helping them set priorities: first get an education, then have a family. But paying women to avoid pregnancy over a reproductive lifetime seems nothing short of dehumanizing—a gesture as cooly calculated and brusquely efficient as paying farmers not to grow corn.

Money has frequently figured in government policies to encourage or discourage births. During the 1930s, Mussolini paid bonuses for babies, a practice critics then assumed to be a fascist technique that would never be applied in a democracy. More recently, the Ceausescu regime in Romania imposed economic sanctions against couples who did not bear children after two years of marriage. And China reportedly levels sanctions against couples who have more than one child.

Reprinted from *Christian Science Monitor.* Copyright © 1990 Christian Science Monitor. Reprinted by permission.

Whatever the motive, there is something humiliating to human dignity about tying childbearing (or not bearing) to a cash nexus.

It has become common in the United States to calculate the dollar cost of giving birth—an average of $4,334, according to the Health Insurance Association of America. Equally popular are figures estimating that it now costs $150,000 to raise a child to the age of 18.

Yet what happens to the perceived value of children when calculators start clicking in the opposite direction, figuring, as Perrin does, that a woman who bears no children could receive nearly $100,000 by the end of her childbearing years?

Life is in danger of being reduced to the terms of a corporate buyout.

Overpopulation remains a serious threat in many third world countries. The Population Crisis Committee, a Washington, D.C., think tank, estimates that world population, which now stands at 5.3 billion, will double in 39 years. But the numbers of overpopulation cannot be resolved by simply throwing other numbers at the problem—the figures on dollar bills that would reduce to a bribe what should be a choice.

It is ironic that Perrin, a professor, should so despair of the process of education. As the conditions of reproduction in the '90s become more and more complicated technologically and in political consequences, it seems imperative to bring more knowledge and more awareness to the choices rather than to fall into simplistic formulas like Perrin's. We can share in his genuine concern without accepting his trivializing proposal.

What a sad confusion, turning the bearing of life or the not bearing of life into a salaried business, and subjecting the deepest of human feelings to tinkering by economic incentive.

---

8. Having analyzed Perrin's article, talked to others about it, and read other ideas on the subject, we can easily see that other theses might be presented:

```
We should develop programs to provide better education and support
  for poor children;
Programs to lessen population increases are not needed at this time;
Programs to lessen population increases should be designed to match
  the needs and values of specific groups with high birth rates.
```

These are just a few examples of the many alternate positions that one might take on the topic of population control. The purpose of creating alternate theses is to discover our own position. After thoughtful consideration of the issue, where do we stand? Does Perrin's plan look like the best suggestion or is there another thesis that better expresses our position?

9. When we formulate a thesis for a reaction paper, we are trying to express our awareness of both the strengths and weaknesses of an author's ideas. Rarely will a work be completely without merit or without flaws.

We will usually be writing a mixed evaluation that leans either toward the positive or the negative. Our thesis statement should be phrased in such a way that the direction of our evaluation is apparent.

Example of a mixed evaluation of Perrin's article that leans toward the positive: Although there are some shortcomings in Perrin's article, the plan that he proposes is the most direct and practical solution to the threat of overpopulation.

Example of a mixed evaluation of Perrin's article that leans toward the negative: Although Perrin's concern for the environmental consequences of overpopulation is legitimate, his plan is impractical and based on a superficial analysis of the problem.

10. Some writers will find it easier to write a thesis after drafting a preliminary response. Whether you free write or brainstorm before developing your thesis depends on you. However, you must shape a thesis for your paper before you complete the final version. As you draft and revise the reaction paper, keep in mind the need to provide sufficient summary of the author's ideas. However, the emphasis in the reaction paper should be on explaining your evaluation and the reasons for your assessment.

SAMPLE REACTION PAPER

A Response to ''A Nonbearing Account''

In ''A Nonbearing Account,'' Professor Noel Perrin proposes that the way to cope with the problem of overpopulation is to give women a cash incentive not to have children. His proposal is that all women, once they reach puberty, would begin to receive a yearly bonus for not bearing a child. An initial payment of $500 would be increased by $100 for each year that the woman did not have a child. Women would still have the freedom to procreate but would lose the bonus for that year and would begin again at the $500 level. On the surface, the plan seems logical and fair, but Perrin fails to adequately analyze the complex problem that he is addressing.

Perrin's plan may appeal to some people who are concerned about environmental problems. He portrays a dire scenario of unchecked population growth, "adding a billion people every few years until there is no more tropical forest, no more oxygen-carbon dioxide balance, no more space, and our world collapses in disaster." Although experts disagree on just how many billion people our planet can support, not one claims that population growth can continue forever. Furthermore, no one disputes that the rate of population increase has accelerated to the point that the current 5.3 billion will double in about forty years. Clearly, we must address the population issue before we run out of time.

Perrin's plan at first looks like a direct solution. What could be more logical than to give women an incentive to limit or postpone childbearing? The plan also seems fair because individual women could still exercise the option to have children. It would not be forced on people whose religious or cultural values promote large families. Finally, the plan seems economical when compared to amounts that are currently spent on social programs. However, the lack of adequate evidence, the oversimplified analysis of the problem, and the unexamined assumptions behind Perrin's plan doom it to failure.

Perrin's figures on population growth do not tell the whole story. The fertility rate in the United States is 1.8, and net population is expected to level off by 2020. In fact, some economists are urging more liberal immigration laws as a way of increasing our work force and remaining competitive in the international market. The birth rate in most industrialized nations is comparable to that of the United States, which has led some to the conclusion that birth rates decline in societies that have a higher standard of living. Perhaps we should be devoting our financial resources to development in the third world. Perrin does not consider this alternative.

Perrin acknowledges that one of the objections to his plan will be that it is racist, and he counters that it is "voluntary, universal and totally color blind." Nevertheless, the plan is clearly aimed at the poor, and in this country, people of color are more likely to be poor. Perrin claims that the plan would be fair because it would not single out any one group. A "Miss du Pont" would be as eligible as a "teenage prostitute." But the fact is that a Miss du Pont does not need the cash incentive and if she did, a few thousand dollars would probably be inadequate. At the same time, the teenage prostitute's problems are not going to be overcome by a meager bonus. Chances are that the teenage prostitute has been a victim of abuse and is now a drug user. The combination of her self-destructive behaviors and emotional needs will lead the teenage prostitute to have children despite all the logic against it. Providing support to young girls who are at risk of becoming single parents is imperative, but Perrin's plan is not the answer.

The calculations that Perrin provides to support his claim that the plan would be a "great bargain" are questionable. He states that a woman who was paid under his plan during her entire childbearing years could receive up to $100,000, which is "about half the cost of bringing up one abandoned child in New York City." But Perrin is proposing to pay this bonus to all women, not just to the ones who might abandon their children. As already indicated, Perrin's plan probably will not reach its target. We would still have to pay out enormous sums to care for children who are born to women who cannot support them.

Admittedly, Perrin's plan is less repressive than the mandatory birth control programs that have been adopted by countries like China. And his plan is certainly more desirable than doing nothing at all. However, if we believe that unchecked population growth is a serious threat, then we should be committed to creating a broad program of services that will respect the complexity of the problem. Perrin's plan is just another expression of the desire for a simple solution to a difficult problem.

EXERCISES

Summary

1. Read "Why Worry about the Animals?" Make an outline of Elshtain's subdivided ideas.
2. Write a summary of Elshtain's article, checking your draft against the checklist on p. 131.

Comparison/Contrast

1. Use the strategies presented on pp. 142–143 to compare and contrast "Animal Rights" with "Am I Blue . . . ?"
2. Use the strategies presented on pp. 142–143 to compare and contrast "What's Wrong with Animal Rights?" with "The Facts about Animal Research."

Argument

Imagine that you have won a fur coat in a raffle. Would you accept it—either to wear yourself or, if you are a man, to give to a female relative to wear? List your reasons for your action (accepting the fur coat or not accepting it). Then list all the objections that might be raised against your position. Then write a short paper supporting your position on wearing fur. Organize your argument according to one of the two basic patterns explained on p. 150.

Evaluating Evidence

In "What's Wrong with Animal Rights?" Barbara Grizzuti Harrison evaluates the argument for animal rights and states that she thinks it "verges on lunacy." What are her reasons? Do you agree with her? Why?

Analogies

1. In "Am I Blue?" Alice Walker makes the analogy between Blue's experience and slavery. Evaluate the effectiveness of this analogy.
2. In "Animal Rights," Molly O'Neill quotes Julia Child: "Should I stop swatting flies? Should I invite mice into my kitchen and serve them lunch?" Explain how Julia Child is using her analogy to make an argumentative point and then evaluate its effectiveness.

Key Terms

1. According to critic Barbara Grizzuti Harrison, one animal activitist (Ingrid E. Newkirk) would give rights to "all those with faces." What is a face exactly? Most people would agree that a chimpanzee has a face, but what about a slug? Where do you draw the line? Does a cockroach have a face? Does a lobster?
2. Explain how the term "factory farming," for instance referring to the way veal calves are raised, works to communicate a negative attitude toward or criticism of the practice.

Reaction Paper

Draft a reaction paper on Dr. White's article, "The Facts about Animal Research." In your paper, assess both the evidence White presents and White's reasoning about this evidence. Then revise your paper using the checklist on pp. 159–160.

CHAPTER 7

Organizing Your Research

TAKING NOTES

Each writer's approach to taking notes is slightly different. The spectrum ranges from chaotic to highly disciplined. Some writers prefer to read extensively and take only occasional notes, which they use to help them relocate information that they want to quote or paraphrase. We are going to stress a more orderly recording process: note cards. The note card approach is used not only by academic researchers, but also by highly respected journalists, such as John McPhee. According to the editor of the *John McPhee Reader*, he takes extensive notes while interviewing people. Later, these notes are typed and read to spot any areas that need further research. After he has filled in the missing information, McPhee studies the complete set of notes to identify the subdivisions of his topic. He writes the labels of his subdivisions on index cards, "fans them out and begins to play a sort of writer's solitaire, studying the possibilities of order." Once he decides on a structure, he makes a folder for each subdivision. Then McPhee goes back to the typed notes, cuts them up, and sorts them into the appropriate folders. Each folder becomes the raw material for one section of his article.

Are Note Cards Necessary?

We don't blame students for believing that note cards are a fetish of English teachers. You probably know people who have written successful research papers without using note cards. They seem superfluous, and cumbersome;

they make a difficult task seem more complicated. However, our experience has convinced us that note cards have some important benefits and we would like you to try the system at least once. Then you will be free to decide for yourself whether to continue.

How Note Cards Will Help You

1. They will improve the content of your paper by making it less likely that you will rely on long quotes strung together by an occasional sentence of your own. The system we suggest requires you to strictly limit the amount of information on each card.

2. They will improve the organization of your paper by making it easier for you to integrate information from different sources. Unless you use note cards (or have already developed good organizational skills) you run the risk of writing a paper that is just a series of separate summaries. This is the most common flaw in undergraduate research papers.

There are two points to learn about note cards, a hard one and an easier one:

The easier one is what a note card looks like.
The hard one is deciding what information to take out of your reading and how to record it on a note card.

What a Note Card Looks Like

1. It looks like all your other note cards. That is, it is the same uniform size, not torn sheets of paper. Buy 5" × 8" index cards or make your own by recycling ordinary letter size paper (from the wastepaper basket perhaps?), folding it from top to bottom and cutting it in half to give you two note cards. This recycling is not only ecologically sound, but if the paper already has something written on the back you will not be tempted to write on two sides of a note card (which tends to complicate everything).

2. It has the same parts filled in as your other note cards. It uses the same pattern. The standard format for a note card includes this information:

Your borrowed information (your note). Put only one idea on each card.
An exact reference to the page(s) where you got this information. That magazine or book can be indicated by the author's name (if you are using only one source by that author) or, if there is no author, by the title. You can abbreviate this bibliographical information, too, because you already have a bibliography card somewhere else where you previously recorded all the important data and the complete details for each of your sources.
A subject label that you put at the top of the note card. Where do you get this subject label? You dream it up yourself by asking "What is this note I have just written down about?" The trick is to come up with a descriptive label that is as precise as possible without copying

out the whole noted idea again. You will need these subject labels later to group your note cards and sort them into piles. The process of creating labels becomes easier as you progress in your research. Gradually, you will begin to see how your topic is subdivided.

Example of the Pattern for a Note Card

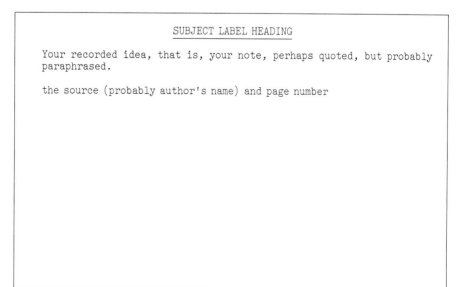

```
                    SUBJECT LABEL HEADING
Your recorded idea, that is, your note, perhaps quoted, but probably
paraphrased.

the source (probably author's name) and page number
```

Remember to put only one idea on each note card. Don't worry if that idea may be only one or two words. For example:

```
how many animals killed?

70 million annually


Rosenberger, p. 31
```

Stupid Note Cards

The technique for making stupid note cards is to treat note cards like little pieces of paper and copy long, continuous passages from your sources. This will completely defeat the purpose of note cards, which is to wean you from relying entirely on other people's ideas.

Adding Your Comments to Note Cards

The extra space on a note card can be very useful when you want to comment on an idea you are borrowing and recording.

Danger: Make sure you separate your own comments so that you don't mix them up with the information you have learned from your source. A convention like square brackets is a help, or you might want to use a specially colored pen.

```
the effect of protest?


Siegel says he doesn't ''know of any animal experiments that have
   been stopped''


[me-what about the ALF?]


Rosenberger, p. 31
```

We strongly encourage you to put your reactions on note cards as you record information. The little flashes that occur while you are reading frequently are forgotten unless you jot them down. Furthermore, we want to stress again that the purpose of the research is to help you answer an important question about your subject. Your goal is to formulate some conclusions about the subject and then to use the notes as a way of explaining and supporting your ideas.

What to Take Out of Your Reading and Put on a Note Card

You should make a note card for:

1. any main ideas that may be related to your research question or topic.
2. any particularly interesting supporting details. What does "interesting" mean here? Interesting to you. When you read a passage some details will stick in your mind because they connect to your own personal experience. Somebody else might not react the same way. Those details that you respond to are noteworthy.

You should also ask yourself why they strike you as particularly interesting. If you can bring these hidden reasons up to the surface, they may give you some direction about developing your own thesis on the subject.

As you can see, selecting information from your reading to record on a note card requires reading the source first as well as reconstructing an outline of the ideas in it so you can identify the parts you need.

At first, you will find yourself taking quite a few notes because the subject is new to you. However, as you read more and become more informed, and as you narrow your topic and it becomes more familiar, you will probably take fewer notes per reading. In any case, always make sure you put only one idea on each note card.

Review: Quoting and Paraphrasing

In general, you should paraphrase the original. That means you should boil it down and put it in your own words when you transfer the information from your reading to your note card. (See Chapter 4, pp. 86–88.)

You should quote only in a few special situations:

1. when the original is worded so elegantly, perfectly, memorably, powerfully, that you don't want to change its effect at all by messing with it.
2. when you just can't paraphrase it and do justice to the meaning, even though you have tried.
3. when the original is very provocative or unusual, and you want to borrow the prestige and authority of the original words to run defense for yourself, in case your reader may not agree with this point.

Remember that quoting means copying the exact words of the original and putting them inside double quotation marks.

Ellipsis

If it does not change the meaning at all, you can omit some words within the part you quote. You must indicate that you have discarded some of the author's words by replacing those words with a special punctuation mark called an ellipsis, which looks like three dots: (. . .). If the omission occurs within the sentence, put a space before and after each dot. If the omission occurs at the end of the sentence, add a fourth dot for the period.

AVOIDING PLAGIARISM

Three types of inadequate paraphrasing can constitute plagiarism. Study the example of an original passage and the inadequate paraphrases of it.

Original passage: (From "Biting Back. Animal Researchers, on the Offensive Against Increasingly Militant Activists," *L.A. Times*, 12 April 1990, sec. E, p. 1.)

> Three decades ago, when the animal rights movement was just reaching into public consciousness, its adherents airlifted wild burros marked for death from the Grand Canyon, stopped the clubbing of baby seals and took to the high seas to fend off whalers. Now they do that and much more, from staging anti-fur parades to operating a frog dissection hot line to burglarizing laboratories and torching a multimillion-dollar research facility. They have sent furriers into economic shock, forced the withdrawal of untold thousands of dollars from federally funded animal experiments and compelled a growing number of companies to stop using animals to test for the safety of cosmetics and household products.

Poor paraphrase #1: This version replaces individual words with synonyms, thereby suggesting that the student has not fully understood the material.

```
Thirty years back, while animal justice activity was merely extending
into community awareness, its supporters took savage donkeys destined
for extinction by air out of the Grand Canyon, prohibited the bashing
of infant seals and went on the oceans to ward off whaling ships. . . .
```

Poor paraphrase #2: The sentence order has been changed around, but the words are the same.

```
Airlifting of death-marked wild burros from the Grand Canyon, stop-
ping clubbed baby seals, and fending off whalers on the high seas,
were activities three decades ago of animal rights adherents. . . .
```

Poor paraphrase #3: The order is changed slightly and words omitted, but the vocabulary and sequence are essentially the same as the original.

```
When the animal movement was just starting to reach the public, wild
burros were airlifted to prevent their deaths, baby seals and whales
were saved. Today activists do much more. They torch research
```

facilities, force withdrawal of funds from animal experiments, and stop companies from using animals to test the safety of products.

Good paraphrase of the original passage:

Originally, animal rights activists seemed benign, if not sentimental. Today they have become deadly serious, militant, and dangerous.

SAMPLE NOTE CARDS

Direct Quotation

```
good quote--pro animals


''Animals are not handbags and hamburgers. They're living
   beings like ourselves.'' quote from Ingrid Newkirk, PETA
   nat'l director




Rosenberger, p. 31
```

Paraphrase

```
suffering = basis of animal rights


not ability to talk or think--according to Singer (influenced
   by philosopher Jeremy Bentham)




Rosenberger, p. 31
```

Combination of Paraphrase and Quotation

```
statistics--growing interest


7,000 animal welfare groups

''Congress has gotten more mail about animal research than about

   any other topic'' 100 to 1 against

PETA 250,000 members (largest group) People for the Ethical

   Treatment of Animals


Rosenberger, p. 31
```

A SET OF SAMPLE NOTE CARDS FOR ONE ARTICLE

There is no one perfect way to transfer information onto note cards. What one student chooses to select and record may be different from another student's choice. It depends on what this student has already read, recorded, and knows. What the student selects also depends on the purpose in reading the article and on the possibilities the student senses in the thesis as it develops. However, seeing what one student has done with one particular article can suggest ways for you to work with your sources.

Here is an article, "Whose Life Is It, Anyway?" with the student's underlining of important concepts. On one side you will find the thoughts that went through the student's head while reading the article. On the other side, you can see the note cards which record important information. Study this example. Ask yourself if you would think the same thoughts and make similar note cards. If not, what would you change? After all, this student's work is just one way of doing this assignment. There are other ways just as good.

WHOSE LIFE IS IT, ANYWAY?

Jack Rosenberger

I think I've read a different statistic somewhere. I'd better record this one. Who is right?

According to animal-rights activists, the suffering endured by laboratory animals in the United States is staggering—beyond human comprehension. <u>Seventy million animals</u>, they contend, are killed in this country's research labs every year.

how many animals killed?
70 million annually
Rosenberger, p. 31

I wonder if this is true? What animal rights groups is he talking about? How are they new? What are the old ones?

I like this quote. It makes the point well.

Traditional animal-welfare organizations, writes Australian philosophy professor Peter Singer, have emphasized "safe activities like collecting stray dogs and prosecuting individual acts of wanton cruelty." But the newer animal-rights groups have a much broader goal: They <u>aim to stop *all* animal experimentation</u>.

"Animal rights is not a matter of charity but of justice," says Tom Regan, author of *The Case for Animal Rights*. "<u>What's wrong with animal research is not that the cages are too small but that the animals are in cages at all</u>."

goal of ''newer animal-rights groups''
''to stop all animal experimentation''
[me--what groups is he referring to?]
Rosenberger, p. 31

''what's wrong with animal research''
''is not that the cages are too small but that the animals are in cages at all.'' Tom Regan quote from book <u>The Case for Animal Rights</u>
Rosenberger, p. 31

Somebody else I read changed their mind over meat eating—seems important.

If the movement has a <u>bible</u>, it's Singer's 1975 book, *Animal Liberation*. In it, he recounts his conversation with a fellow Oxford student at lunchtime one day in 1970: "I asked him why he <u>did not eat meat</u>, and he began to tell me about the conditions in which the animal whose body I was eating had lived." The answer changed Singer's life. "Although I had specialized in moral and social philosophy," he writes, "it had not occurred to me—any more

moment of revelation
lunch with vegetarian = the moment for Peter Singer, wrote <u>Animal Liberation</u> 1975, the activists' ''<u>bible</u>'' (Australian philosophy prof)
Rosenberger, p. 31

Reprinted from *New York*, January 15, 1990, pp. 31–32.

Definitions of terms are often important.

than it occurs to most people—that our relations with animals raised a serious moral issue."

Singer calls human beings' attitude toward other animals <u>speciesism</u>. He knows the word is awkward, "but I can think of no better term [for] a prejudice . . . toward the interests of members of one's own species and against those of members of other species." <u>In other words, all animals are equal</u>.

The italics here suggests an emphasis on something important.

Singer bases part of his argument on the utilitarian philosophy of <u>Jeremy Bentham</u>, who said, "The question is not 'Can they reason?' nor 'Can they talk?' but *'Can they suffer?'*" All animals, including mice and rats (which are used in most animal experiments), feel anger and fear, pleasure and pain, just like human beings.

What sort of rights does Singer have in mind? "Concern for the well-being of a child . . . ," he writes, "would require that we teach him to read; concern for the well-being of a pig may require no more than that we leave him alone with other pigs in a place where there is adequate food and room to run freely."

I've got enough examples of medical benefits. But a child's life is worth more than a rat's or a monkey's. Or worth something different, if not more.

<u>Concern for the well-being of a child, of course, is one of the most compelling arguments that those who use animals in research can make</u>. What the animal-rights advocates tend to leave out of their discussions is an acknowledgment of the <u>other side of the story</u>: the thousands of human lives saved, the human pain assuaged, as a result of experiments on animals. Health and Human Services Secretary Louis W. Sullivan has declared the <u>use of laboratory animals "crucial"</u> for research on life-threatening illnesses, including AIDS, cancer, and Alzheimer's disease. The benefits humanity has

```
''speciesism''

Singer's term for believing humans
  superior to animals


Rosenberger, p. 31
```

```
suffering=basis of animal rights

not ability to talk or think accord-
  ing to Singer (influenced by
  philosopher Jeremy Bentham)


Rosenberger, p. 31
```

```
benefits of research--
  ''speciesism''

Health and Human Services
  Secretary Louis W. Sullivan says
  animal research ''crucial'' for
  advances on human illnesses

[me-he's right. If it's
  speciesism, so what]

Rosenberger, p. 31
```

ORGANIZING YOUR RESEARCH   183

reaped from animal experiments include our understanding of the human nervous system; the development of insulin, antibiotics, and vaccines against hepatitis and polio; skin grafts; the transplantation of corneas and internal organs; and the development of open-heart surgery and other advanced surgical techniques. A mother of a child whose life has been saved by these discoveries can make a case as heart-rending as any animal-rights advocate's. But, of course, Singer would call that speciesism—the assumption that a child's life is worth more than a rat's or a monkey's.

{ Some more good statistics here. I feel comfortable with figures. }

There are some 7,000 groups in the United States concerned with the plight of animals, and their cause—once viewed as oddball—is winning more and more converts. In the year after the Humane Farming Association initiated its advertising campaign against cruelty to calves being raised for veal, the group's strength rose from 22,000 to 45,000 members. Indeed, animal-rights activists have put their case so persuasively that for the past few years Congress has gotten more mail about animal research than about any other topic. (The letters have run 100 to 1 against the use of animals in experiments.)

And the movement has claimed some tangible victories. By June of last year, several large cosmetics companies, including Avon and Revlon, had agreed to stop—and Mary Kay cosmetics had declared a moratorium on—animal testing. (The companies don't acknowledge, though, that pressure from the activists led them to these decisions). And People for the Ethical Treatment of Animals (PETA), the nation's largest animal-rights group, which has 250,000 members, believes

---

statistics--growing interest

7,000 animal welfare groups
''congress has gotten more mail about animal research than about any other topic'' 100 to 1 against PETA 250,000 members (largest group) People for the Ethical Treatment of Animals

Rosenberger, p. 31

its efforts were responsible for persuading toy companies like Mattel and Tonka to stop animal testing.

Even so, the number of animals killed in laboratories every year has hardly lessened. Therefore, to get the media attention that forces change, activists are using confrontational tactics. PETA members have demonstrated outside researchers' houses on Halloween, bombarded the Gillette Company with calls protesting its animal-testing policy, and picketed the American International Fur Fair in Las Vegas. PETA also publicizes the activities of the Animal Liberation Front, which since 1979 has broken into research institutions 24 times, "liberated" more than 3,000 animals, and caused nearly $4 million worth of damage. PETA sells videotapes "consisting of actual footage of conditions in laboratories," says Carol L. Burnett, a spokeswoman. "A picture is worth a thousand words, and the tapes show exactly what we say."

The hard-core activists divide their lives into two halves: Life Before Animal Rights and Life Now. Steve Siegel, 40, director of Trans-Species Unlimited's New York regional office (a windowless lower Broadway room about the size of a studio apartment), was a fund-raiser, wrote fiction and poetry, and worked part-time as a high-school teacher in New York public schools before he joined the group as full-time director. He calls himself "a fairly intelligent and well-read person." But, he says, "I don't know where I was the first 35 years of my life. I mean, I didn't know what was going on in labs."

What opened his eyes was a viewing of *The Animals Film*, a British documentary with a shocking segment about a burn experiment whose subject is a live pig. "The animal is fully

---

Margin note (left): This ALF organization is interesting. I think I read something in the campus newspaper about them.

Margin note (left): I'm glad the author gave this example of Steve Siegel. Makes it seem more real somehow, maybe because he was a high school teacher.

Note card (right):

militant organization

increasing violence, e.g., ALF
Animal Liberation Front
''liberated'' thousands of
animals, destroyed lab equipment,
much damage

Rosenberger, p. 32

Note card (right):

example of an activist

Steve Siegel NY 40 yrs. old
ex-h s teacher
director of Trans-Species
 Unlimited
saw British documentary film
 about burned pigs
''gruesome experiments''
no painkillers

Rosenberger, p. 32

conscious and squealing throughout the whole thing," says Siegel. He learned, much to his surprise, that <u>gruesome experiments</u> like the film's burn-research scenes are common. (Anne St. Laurent, of United Action for Animals, says her organization has collected hundreds of recent research papers about burn experiments, and though the animals were anesthetized during the experiments, "only a few papers mention giving painkillers after they wake up.")

> The emphasis seems important.

Like PETA, Trans-Species is employing the <u>activists' newest technique</u> —challenging the *scientific merit* of a researcher's work. Three years ago, the group managed to derail <u>Cornell University</u> researcher Michiko Okamoto's studies of <u>barbiturate addiction in cats</u>. First Trans-Species turned for advice to the Medical Research Modernization Committee, a group of health professionals (half of them doctors) highly critical of current animal-testing standards; when the committee said it did not consider Okamoto's research critically relevant to human patients, Trans-Species went to the public. Its relentless picketing, demonstrations, and letter-writing campaigns generated such pressure (the National Institute on Drug Abuse—NIDA—got 10,000 letters and postcards and 75 to 80 congressional-office inquiries about the matter) that Okamoto—who had been using cats in her research for fourteen years—gave up and returned her grant to NIDA.

> One example—the Cornell one—is enough. I don't need this one about NYU.
>
> But if most of the lab animals are rats and mice, why does the author use these examples of cats and monkeys?

Now Trans-Species is targeting Ronald Wood, a researcher at New York University Medical Center who is using <u>macaque monkeys</u> in researching crack addiction and the effects of inhaling an ingredient used in glue and paint-thinner. Is Wood a reasonable target? Not according to Charles

---

activists' newest technique

''challenging the scientific merit'' of the research
e.g., Cornell scientist's work on barbiturate addiction in cats stopped by Trans-Species Unlimited

Rosenberger, p. 32

Schuster, NIDA's director. "Wood's research is one of the very few projects we support that study the behaviors of animals self-administering inhalants," he says. "The proper question is not why we're supporting Dr. Wood but how we can get other scientists to study this problem as well."

Ironically, Trans-Species' success against Okamoto may prove to be the strongest barrier to its triumph at <u>NYU</u>, for that victory <u>woke up the biomedical community</u>. NYU has held <u>three press conferences stressing the legitimacy of its research on animals</u>; the last, held this past April, included leading officials of federal health agencies, New York State medical schools, and a patient-advocacy group.

"After we won at Cornell," Siegel says, "I thought animal researchers would take a look around and start cleaning house on their own. But <u>I don't know of any animal experiments that have been stopped</u>."

"Animals have a need to breathe, not to feel pain, and to experience enjoyment in life," says PETA's national director, Ingrid Newkirk. "We have very selfishly denied animals those needs for our own whims and peripheral interests. <u>Animals are not handbags and hamburgers. They're living beings like ourselves</u>."

I was wondering what the researchers were doing about it.

This sounds like a contradiction. What about the ALF?

I really like this qoute.

---

researchers fighting back

e.g., NYU press conferences

Rosenberger, p. 32

---

the effect of protest?

Siegel says he doesn't ''know of any animal experiments that have been stopped''

[me-what about the ALF?]

Rosenberger, p. 32

---

good quote-pro animals

''Animals are not handbags and hamburgers. They're living beings like ourselves.'' quote from Ingrid Newkirk PETA nat'l director

Rosenberger, p. 32

REVISING YOUR NOTE CARDS

At this stage you should have a disorganized heap of note cards. One temptation is to keep on making note cards forever in order to put off this next step. This temptation is understandable because you often know that there is some excellent book or magazine article on your subject that you are waiting for someone to return to the library or to be sent through interlibrary loan. However, after you have read or made note cards on a reasonable number of sources you just have to say to yourself, "OK, that's it. On to the next step." The problem then becomes what to do with this mess of note cards. The first thing to do is to go back and look at your cards, one by one. It doesn't matter in what order. The purpose of this step is to make sure that only one idea or set of facts is recorded on each note card. If necessary, rewrite some of your note cards (you don't need to consult the original source). For example, what could be improved in this note card? How many note cards are needed for these different ideas?

```
statistics--growing interest

7,000 animal welfare groups
''Congress has gotten more mail about animal research than about any other
   topic'' 100 to 1 against
PETA 250,000 members (largest group) People for the Ethical Treatment
   of Animals


Rosenberger, p. 31
```

Although there is no perfect answer to the question, more than one is needed. The information about congressional mail might be put on a second card under the heading "Impact" or "Lobbying."

Also make sure that the subject headings you have put at the top of each note card accurately label the idea recorded. The heading on the following note card is too general. What heading would give a better idea of the information?

```
animal rights

   increasing violence, e.g., ALF, Animal Liberation Front, ''liberated''
      thousands of animals, destroyed lab equipment, much damage


   Rosenberger, p. 32
```

A phrase such as "militant groups" or "increasing violence" would be a more descriptive heading.

The purpose of revising your note cards is to facilitate the sorting of your cards into related groups.

WORKING TOWARD A PROVISIONAL OUTLINE

Your next step is to design a road map or blueprint to describe the arrangement of information in your paper, particularly main points that you wish to stress and the order in which you intend to introduce them. If you have not read the section on outlining on pages 128–129, we suggest that you do so now. Remember that an outline or logical skeleton of a piece of writing does two things:

1. It shows the relationship of ideas—main ideas and their supporting details. Symbols indicate how these ideas are related to each other (I, II, III, or 1, 2, 3, 4, 5, or a, b).
2. It shows the order of these ideas.

This outlined order of main points in any paper is determined by three pressures: the author, the reader, and the information.

1. The *author*'s main interest is the thesis. This is the central idea to be announced and showcased. From the author's point of view, this thesis is the most important part of the paper. The author therefore faces the temptation to simply keep repeating the thesis. Since the author already believes it as self-evident, supporting evidence and explanation is less important for the author. An entry in a journal is an example of writing determined only by this kind of pressure.

2. The *reader* usually approaches the paper skeptically, looking for something important for understanding. The reader wants the paper's points to all follow clearly one from another, and the evidence to add up to something significant and convincing. The reader doesn't want to feel that time was wasted reading something useless, confused, or confusing.

3. *Information* is what the paper is about. In some papers, this information can be personal: it can be about the author, as in a statement of intent. In yet other papers it can be about one or two readings—for example, a summary, reaction paper, or comparison paper. However, in research papers the information is primarily the note card data about events, leaders, definitions, statistics, organizations, places, problems, and other issues which exist outside the author and reader, and which the author has extracted from many sources.

When you work on designing a provisional outline for a research paper you must mesh these three aspects. Because it is a *research* paper, however, its organization is especially determined—and limited—by the research, that is, by your note cards. The information on your note cards alone, however, will not automatically support your thesis. This information needs to be introduced, interpreted, and connected to your thesis. We accordingly want to recommend two strategies for organizing an outline. The first depends on sorting your note cards into piles according to their subject label headings. The second depends on arranging these groups to anticipate your reader's needs.

Grouping Note Cards

As you revise your note cards and possibly replace some subject heading labels with others, you will become more familiar with your researched information. At this point you will be in a good position to start shuffling these cards into piles of related information. For example, a student researching the topic of animal experimentation had piles of note cards grouped according to the following headings:

```
statistics
organizations
animal rights activists
philosophy
kinds of animals
Peter Singer
researchers' rationale
medical benefits
vegetarianism
speciesism
ALF
```

As the student looked at these piles of note cards, several things came to mind: First, some of the piles seemed to go together, logically. For example, speciesism, vegetarianism, and philosophy seemed to go together as reasons for concern about animals.

Second, some piles overlapped, like organizations and animal rights activists.

Third, some piles looked like they should be split up and merged with others. Information about statistics could fit in organizations or in medical benefits.

Fourth, some cards seemed to fit equally well in several different piles. Peter Singer could go in philosophy or animal rights activists.

At this point, just do the best you can, shuffling, rearranging, and experimenting with different groups. This process is not merely a mechanical outlining exercise. It will also be automatically helping you in another important way—it will help you decide what you want to say about all this information. In other words, it will be helping you clarify your own thesis. It may also force you to go back to the library to fill in obvious gaps.

As you experiment with various groupings, consider which groups seem like main headings that include other groups as subdivided parts. For instance, `organizations` includes `animal rights activists` as well as other kinds of activists like some members of the medical community, and `animal rights activists` includes the ALF as well as others.

In any case, there usually is no one perfect way of arranging note cards and grouping them in piles. You just have to experiment and try out different versions to find one you like best.

Anticipating Your Reader's Needs

You may say at this point, "OK, my groups of note cards represent main ideas, and they include enough subdivisions of supporting evidence, but what order do I put them in? When I turn these groups into a formal outline, which will be number I and what will follow it?"

Think of the reader. What would be the clearest order for the reader of your paper? You want the reader to understand and be convinced. So, arrange the order of your groups of ideas with the reader in mind. What does the reader need to know first? Perhaps it is a definition to establish the terms within which the argument will be developed. Perhaps it would be a startling example to grab the reader's attention. Perhaps it would be several statistics to establish the scope of the problem under investigation. Ask yourself, accordingly, what order will be most helpful for the reader? Do it that way.

At this point there really is no substitute for rehearsing with a real potential reader. If your class does not provide such an opportunity with peer editing groups or writing workshop teams, then ask someone you know to help. This person can be a family member, roommate, sorority sister, or someone you take a coffee break with at work. Tell—or preferably show in writing—what your thesis is. Say, "This is what I'm writing a paper about and this is what I believe." Then ask the person what questions come immediately to mind, and write them down. For example, a psychology student was investigating the relationship between gender and mental illness, and suggested this thesis:

```
Sociocultural differences, as well as biological differences,
   influence men and women to become afflicted with different types of
   mental illness.
```

Her potential reader came up with these questions:

```
What do you mean by ''sociocultural differences''?
Are all biological differences influential? Which biological differ-
   ences are most influential?
What ''biological differences'' are you talking about anyway?
Which are more important: sociocultural or biological differences?
What types of mental illness are you talking about?
```

What is it about socialization that influences men and women to become mentally ill?
What is socialization?
If you talk about socialization in connection with girls and boys, how does it affect men and women?

As a result of thinking about these questions, this student realized that most of her paper would have to deal with sociocultural differences, because biological differences, such as hormones, are mostly speculation and she had found no conclusive evidence about them. She also realized from her rehearsal with a potential reader that her paper would have to go into considerable detail about sociocultural differences: what socialization is, how boys and girls learn different sex-role behavior, and how this learning might involve different kinds of stress leading to different kinds of mental illness. She also had a clearer idea of the order of these topics that would make most sense to her reader.

MAKING THE OUTLINE

An outline has two purposes: it helps you to discover the logical connection between parts of your paper and it helps a reader follow your reasoning. A written outline gives the reader an X ray of the logical skeleton of your paper. It shows how all the parts are related to your thesis. The process of sorting, grouping, and labeling your note cards leads directly to the construction of a provisional outline. After you draft your paper, you may find that trying to outline it will help with revising the organization.

Some instructors require a formal outline as a step toward the finished paper, while others require an outline as part of the paper. If you have to prepare a formal outline, keep these basic principles in mind:

1. Related ideas are lined up in columns and given a comparable symbol. Major points are indicated with Roman numerals; support points are indicated with capital letters; details related to the support points are indicated with Arabic numbers. Further subdivision can be indicated with lowercase letters. Study the sample outline to see how the ideas move from major to minor points as you move from Roman numerals to lowercase letters.

2. The symbols indicate the subdivision of ideas into their component parts. Not all major points will be subdivided. Likewise, all points do not have the same amount of subdivision. However, if you begin to subdivide a particular idea, you must have at least two points to list. If you have only one, then you have an example or an explanation, but not a proper subdivision. Notice that in the sample outline, some ideas labeled with a Roman numeral or a capital letter are subdivided and others are not.

3. The thesis is always stated at the beginning. It is not a subdivision, so no letters or numbers are placed before it.

4. There are two types of formal outline: the sentence outline and the topic outline. If you use the topic outline, you must use parallel structure (express the ideas in the same grammatical pattern).

SAMPLE SENTENCE OUTLINE

Thesis: The health benefits advertised for breakfast cereals have been exaggerated.

  I. Production removes nutrients and adds harmful ingredients.
  II. Health claims began with birth of cereal industry.
     A. Breakfast cereals were introduced by Kellogg and Post.
     B. Early ads claimed varied benefits.
  III. Recent ads claim cancer and cholesterol reduction.
     A. Bran was supposed to reduce cancer.
        1. 1984 study suggested link.
        2. New cereals were developed.
        3. Research did not substantiate claims.
     B. Bran was supposed to reduce cholesterol.
        1. Studies cast doubt on oat bran.
        2. Rice bran was introduced.
        3. Studies questioned effectiveness of rice bran.
     C. Psyllium was touted as cholesterol reducer.
        1. Restrictions were placed on laxative ads.
        2. Advertisers skirted restrictions.
  IV. F.D.A. shares blame for confusion.
  V. Consumers must practice moderation.

SAMPLE TOPIC OUTLINE

Thesis: The health benefits advertised for breakfast cereals have been exaggerated.

    I. Effects of processing cereal
   II. Beginning of claims
       A. Introduction by Kellogg and Post
       B. Varied claims
  III. Recent claims
       A. Effect of bran on cancer
           1. 1984 study
           2. New cereals
           3. Lack of substantiating research
       B. Effect of bran on cholesterol
           1. Oat bran
           2. Rice bran
           3. Lack of substantiating research
       C. Effect of psyllium on cholesterol
           1. Restrictions on laxative ads
           2. Avoidance of restrictions
   IV. F.D.A.'s role
    V. Advice to consumers

EXERCISES

I. Provide headings for the following note cards:

---

pro-animal groups usually ignore the compelling reasons for
   experimentation--to save human life, e.g., children

Rosenberger, p. 31

```
        in one year, Humane Farming Association membership rose from 22,000 to

            45,000 after anti-veal campaign


        Rosenberger, p. 31
```

II. Find information to make note cards with the following headings. The article begins on p. 79.

Use direct quotation.

```
        results of Moine's 1981 research
```

Use paraphrase.

> storytelling by salespeople

Use a combination of paraphrase and direct quotation.

> influential techniques used by salespeople

    III. Make a set of note cards based on an article you will use for your research paper.
        A. Make at least ten cards.
        B. Limit the information on each card to a few facts about one idea.
        C. Label each card with a subject heading at the top.
        D. Indicate the source and page number at the bottom of the card.
    IV. Outlining Exercises
        A. The following sentences are in the correct order for an outline. Insert the proper symbols to indicate the relationship between ideas.

Thesis: There is considerable controversy over the Pass/Fail grading system.

_____ The Pass/Fail system differs from the letter grade system.
_____ It has only two options.
_____ It ignores the concept of a curve.
_____ Critics of the Pass/Fail concept claim it has many disadvantages.
_____ It lessens student's incentive.
_____ It removes the reward-punishment system from the teacher.
_____ It denies the competitiveness of life.
_____ Pass/Fail grading shelters students from facing their limitations.
_____ Advocates of Pass/Fail grading stress its advantages.
_____ The academic pressure on students is reduced.
_____ Better learning takes place under stress-free conditions.
_____ Students do not fear to try new areas.
_____ Teachers are forced to make classes more interesting.

B. Arrange the following statements into outline form, using the proper symbols. The statements are *not* in the correct order, but the thesis is provided. We have numbered them for identification purposes only.

Thesis: Buying a car is a major step and should be carefully thought out.

(1) A used car may be a better deal than a new car.
(2) There are different ways to finance the purchase.
(3) Many car dealers provide financing plans.
(4) First, one must decide whether to buy a new or used car.
(5) New cars are usually guaranteed for longer periods of time than used cars.
(6) Used cars are much cheaper.
(7) There are certain advantages to a new car.
(8) The best way to finance the purchase of a car is to save the money ahead of time.
(9) Reputable used car dealers will guarantee the car for at least thirty days.
(10) Personal loans from a bank are another method of financing.
(11) A new car provides personal satisfaction.
(12) The classified ads often contain good buys on used cars.
(13) There is a greater range of choices if you are purchasing a new car.

C. From the statements below, choose one that will best serve as a thesis. Then arrange the remaining statements into an outline that shows the relationship between ideas. The statements are *not* in correct order. Again we have numbered these statements for identification purposes only.

(1) Cars are a drain on our energy resources.
(2) The amount of traffic can be regulated through improved mass transit, car pools, and gasoline taxes.
(3) Steps can be taken to solve many of the problems caused by the use of private cars, thereby ensuring a continuation of their true usefulness.
(4) There are justified complaints against the widespread use of private cars.
(5) Cars contribute to pollution.
(6) Remedies can be found for most of the complaints.
(7) Private cars still have many benefits.
(8) Cars are needed for quick transportation in case of emergencies.
(9) Safety features would help to reduce death and injury.
(10) Cars are needed for vacations when people do not want to follow a schedule.
(11) Cars are largely responsible for traffic congestion.
(12) Pollution control devices are now being perfected.
(13) Cars are a major source of death and injury.

D. Organize the following statements into outline form. There is no thesis statement included in the list. After you have made an outline, write your own thesis statement to fit the information.

(1) Soap operas provide a substitute family for many lonely people.
(2) Twenty million viewers watch the soaps.
(3) The soap operas are technically sophisticated in their production aspects.
(4) The sets on soap operas tend to be very monotonous.
(5) The plots are full of suspense, a tried and true device for hooking the audience.
(6) The viewers come from all walks of life, from homemakers to federal judges.
(7) Soap operas are a popular pastime.
(8) The problems with soaps are due to limited budgets and the serial form.
(9) There are several reasons for the popularity of soap operas.
(10) Viewers develop a strong allegiance to actors who stay with a role for many years.
(11) Each segment tends to repeat a good deal of what happened in previous episodes.
(12) The soaps are thematically relevant to contemporary problems, such as drug abuse.

E. Find at least four mistakes in the following topic outline.
   I. Thesis: The problems of overpopulation

      II. Causes of overpopulation

         A. Medical advances

            1. lower infant mortality rate

            2. longer life span

            3. control of fatal diseases

         B. Resistance to birth control

            1. religious reasons

         C. In countries without social services, parents want large families as a guarantee of protection in their old age, and to help them by working and contributing to the family income.

      III. Dealing with overpopulation

         A. Find means of birth control that are acceptable to religious opponents.

         B. Provide incentives for sterilization and limitation of family size.

         C. Governments should not restrict abortions.

V. Choose one of the readings in the Anthology that appeals to you and make a set of note cards.

VI. Identifying plagiarism and incorrect quotation: Compare the original passage with the paraphrase and determine whether the paraphrase would constitute plagiarism. Also indicate places where the original has not been quoted correctly.

   A. **Original:** The new animal-welfare activists are drawing attention in part because of the tactics they espouse. Many preach and practice civil disobedience, violating laws against, say, breaking and entering. Some have been known to resort to violence against property and—on a few occasions—against humans.

   Paraphrase: The recent animal rights advocates are getting noticed because many are violating laws and resorting to violence, usually against property, but sometimes against humans.

B. **Original:** Politically, the new abolitionists, as many animal-welfare activists call themselves, eschew sentimentalism in favor of a tough-minded, insistent claim that animals, too, have rights, and that violating those rights constitutes oppression. It follows that animals must be liberated—and since they cannot liberate themselves in the face of overwhelming human hegemony, they require the help of liberators much as slaves did in the last century.

Paraphrase: Modeling themselves on the abolitionists who helped in the fight against slavery, modern animal rights advocates take a tough stand. They believe that animals have rights, ''that violating those rights constitutes oppression,'' and that humans should help to liberate them.

C. **Original:** Those wonderful chimpanzees that have been taught to speak to us through sign-language also arouse concern. If the funding ends or a researcher loses interest, they are sometimes turned over to the less-than-tender mercies of laboratory researchers to be addicted to cocaine, infected with a virus, or subjected to some other terrible fate. Eugene Linden describes, in his study *Silent Partners,* chimps desperately trying to convey their pain and fear and sadness to uncomprehending experimenters.

Paraphrase: Concern also exists for the chimpanzees that can speak to us through sign language. Sometimes when funding ends, they are turned over to labs where researchers subject them to some terrible fate. Stories have been told of these ''chimps trying to convey their pain and fear to the uncomprehending experimenters.''

D. **Original:** For some animal protectionists, the case against hunting is open and shut. They argue that the vast majority of the estimated 170 million animals shot to death in any given year are killed for blood sport, not for food, and that the offspring of these slaughtered creatures are left to die of exposure or starvation. Defenders of blood sports see them as a skill and a tradition, a lingering relic of America's great frontier past. Others—from nineteenth-century feminists to Norman Mailer of *Why Are We in Vietnam?*—link the national mania for hunting with a deeper thirst for violence.

Paraphrase: Defenders of hunting view it as a tradition, an important part of ''America's great past,'' but animal protectors think hunting comes from a thirst for violence. They point out that most of the animals killed by hunters are not for food and that the offspring are left to die.

E. **Original:** We must consider our meat-eating habits as well. Meat-eating is one of the most volatile, because most personal, of all animal-welfare questions. Meat-eaters do not consider themselves immoral, though hard-core vegetarians find meat-eating repugnant—the consumption of corpses. Such feminist theorists as Carol Adams insist that there is a connection between the butchering of animals and the historic maltreatment of women. Certainly, there is a politics of meat that belongs on the agenda along with other animal-welfare issues.

Paraphrase: One of the hottest aspects of the animal rights debate is eating meat. ''Hard-core vegetarians'' think it is immoral, and at least one feminist has argued that there is a link between slaughtering animals and mistreating women.

F. **Original:** For years, industry has determined the toxicity of floor wax and detergents by injecting various substances into the stomachs of beagles, rabbits, and calves, producing vomiting, convulsions, respiratory illness, and paralysis. The so-called LD (lethal dose) 50 test ends only when half the animals in a test group have died. No anesthesia or pain killers are administered.

Paraphrase: For some time now, the toxicity of products such as floor wax and detergents was determined by injecting substances into the stomachs of animals. This made them vomit, have convulsions, and other illnesses. No pain killers were given and half the animals died.

Original passages come from "Why Worry about the Animals?" See Anthology for complete article.

Worksheet 10 _____ **TAKING NOTES**

Name _____ Date _____

Directions: Pick an important paragraph from one article, or from one chapter in a book, that you intend to use for your research paper.

1. Write a note card in the space below *quoting* your paragraph, or a good part of it verbatim. Conform to proper note card format: indicate the source, the page number(s), and an appropriate subject heading.

2. Write a note card in the space below *paraphrasing* the same paragraph you quoted above.

3. Write a note card in the space below combining a paraphrase of, and a quotation from, your paragraph.

Worksheet 11 _____ **PROVISIONAL OUTLINE**

Name _____   Date _____

Topic _____

1. Your thesis statement (central idea):

2. Outline of major ideas and minor supporting details for your paper. (Sequence of ideas and balanced relationship of ideas.)

CHAPTER 8

Drafting and Revising Your Paper

DRAFTS

The step-by-step approach in this book may give you the misleading impression that writing a research paper is a tidy, if not a totally mechanical, process. True, these techniques are the ones that most writers rely on to produce research papers. However, they are only guidelines to a process that is at times frustrating, creative, and messy. As guidelines, they can help by giving you direction, but, as you know from your work so far, you must be prepared to make constant adjustments as you proceed: adjusting your own curiosity and interest to fit a manageable topic; adjusting your topic to fit the material you find; adjusting your thesis statement to the evidence in your sources; adjusting your outline to your note cards, and your note cards to your outline. At this stage you will need to adjust the sentences and paragraphs that you start composing on paper to the ideas you have in your head and to the ways that you would like them to appear and sound to a reader. This means getting something down on paper that is necessarily going to be less than perfect, and then revising it, often several times. In this rough draft stage you will find yourself changing words, rearranging sentences, adding some parts, and throwing out others.

Several principles govern the choices you make as you revise your drafts. First, remember how you kept your reader in mind when you designed a provisional outline for your paper. So, too, your audience's expectations will affect your style and word choice. A research paper is, of course, an academic assignment, and academic disciplines tend to have their own writing conventions, rather like etiquette. This means that you have to recognize these expectations and adjust your own writing so that it is appropriate and conforms to them. This principle is particularly true of word choice and tone. The social sciences, for instance, aim at objectivity and detachment. Social scientists favor the passive voice to eliminate the intrusive presence of a researcher: They favor neutral descriptive words. Notice the deliberately clinical tone of the sample paper on hypnosis for a psychology class.

A second principle that will affect the drafting of your paper is your own sense of style. It is your paper after all; it is what you want to say. Note in the sample paper on redress for Japanese Americans how Kevin, a Japanese American, communicates his own emotional involvement. We can hear his personal voice explain the feelings of the people involved. What is appropriate in one paper would not be appropriate in the other.

Third, if you are writing a thesis paper rather than a report, you must pay attention to the development of a good argument. Your job is to convince your reader that your thesis (the conclusion you reached about your subject) is sensible. You accomplish this goal by presenting your reasons and backing them up with information and ideas that you discovered in your research. The greatest danger at this point is to just write out facts and opinions that were expressed by other writers.

One of the most important skills in writing a research paper is being able to lead into and away from the facts and ideas that you have obtained from other writers. We will show you a number of patterns for doing this, but right now we want to give a warning: NEVER QUOTE OR PARAPHRASE WITHOUT PROVIDING A CONTEXT. In other words, do not throw undigested chunks of data at the reader. You must always say something about the borrowed facts and ideas.

In addition, you want to make each of your ideas clear to the reader. To do this you need to separate your main points from each other, which you do with paragraphs. You also need to provide logical bridges between ideas by providing transitions (special words and phrases within and between paragraphs) that show how these ideas are connected to one another and to your thesis. Introductions and conclusions require special kinds of paragraphs, which we will describe at the end of this chapter.

This chapter deals with these techniques:

1. constructing paragraphs
2. incorporating sources
3. providing transitions
4. developing an introduction, conclusion, and title

CONSTRUCTING PARAGRAPHS

A rough draft or even several rough drafts are necessary before you type the final version. At the rough draft stage your job is to fit together your material in paragraph form, making fine adjustments and adding comments to show the reader how your ideas fit together.

Paragraph Structure

Paragraphs are logical units, composed of sentences, and set off from each other by an indented beginning. They are typically composed of a "topic sentence" that communicates the paragraph's main point, and other sentences that back up the main point with supporting detail. Paragraphs are the building blocks of essays, just as sentences are the building blocks of paragraphs.

Good writers and good readers always approach a piece of writing expecting a certain structure. You should keep this sense of structure in mind when you approach a reading assignment, or a writing assignment like your rough draft.

To help you, here is a chart for people who like charts, and an analogy for those who prefer that kind of description.

AN ESSAY (OR A CHAPTER)	A PARAGRAPH	A SENTENCE
is composed of a thesis statement and main ideas	is composed of a topic sentence and sentences of supporting details	is composed of subject and verb and other modifying words

In this chart, notice that an essay (or chapter) is made up of two logical parts: a thesis and main ideas. So, too, a paragraph is like a miniature essay, and its two parts (the topic sentence and the sentences of supporting details) have the same relationship to each other as the two parts in an essay have. A sentence also is made up of its two essential parts: (1) its subject and verb, and (2) the other words in the sentence that develop the subject and verb. All these logical units—sentence, paragraph, and essay—have the same logical shape or structure of their parts. Their parts fit together in the same way; they are symmetrical.

AN ANALOGY (OR COMPARISON). Many of you know how Russian dolls sometimes come cleverly packed one inside the other. So, too, sentences are packed inside paragraphs, and have the same shape and the same division into parts. Paragraphs are packed into essays. (And essays, or chapters, are packed inside books.)

To get back to you writing your rough draft of the research paper, you already have an outline telling you the order in which you are going to take up the main ideas. Depending on how long your paper is, and how detailed your outline is, you can often expect to spend one paragraph on each major idea or each major subdivision.

How many sentences should there be in a paragraph? There is no easy way to tell. There should be at least two, though. If you want to write a one-sentence paragraph, watch out; there may be something wrong. That one sentence would be either a main point ("topic sentence") without any supporting details, or it would be a supporting detail just floating around, not connected to any point. Occasionally a writer will use a one-sentence paragraph as a means of highlighting an idea. However, if one-sentence paragraphs were used frequently, they would lose this special effect. If you find yourself writing a paragraph of more than, say, ten sentences or so, you probably need to split them up into smaller logical units (like the Russian dolls).

A TYPICAL PARAGRAPH. The paragraph we have annotated is *not* the only kind of paragraph in a research paper. Paragraphs in research papers take many different shapes, as a glance at any of the sample papers will show. However, here is one basic and essential structure, and you must master it in order to assemble the components of your argument. The point is that evidence does not speak for itself.

Remember that a paragraph is usually composed of a topic sentence that makes a generalization, and sentences of supporting details to illustrate that generalization. That sounds like two kinds of information, but in a research paper it really involves three kinds of information. In addition you need a commentary to explain the connection. Supporting details are not usually self-explanatory. Remember, evidence does not speak for itself; you must speak for it. So, this third step—a commentary—is necessary to connect the first two.

Any of these three components (a generalization, supporting details, commentary) can be your observations or they can be chosen by you from your sources to speak on your behalf.

Here is a typical example. Note the three kinds of information:

Topic sentence	Dual career couples have less time to spend with their children.
More specific version of topic sentence	Work demands particularly affect the mother because she is the traditional caretaker. Lamb (1982) contends that ''as women are becoming
Supporting evidence borrowed from source to prove the point	increasingly successful and more committed to work, childrearing becomes a less central, less defining activity of parenthood, especially for women'' (46). This is not to say that women are not
Commentary explaining the significance of the borrowed information	concerned about childrearing, but merely that it is no longer their central defining role. As a result, couples are now willing to rely on other institutions to perform duties traditionally performed at home.

To repeat, not all paragraphs have this shape. Depending on how much evidence you think necessary, you might want to reserve a whole paragraph for support: a collection of compelling sentences borrowed from one or more sources. Or you might want to reserve a whole paragraph for your commentary alone, connecting and interpreting borrowed evidence inserted earlier in the paper.

The point is that many students omit the third step—the commentary. They assume that the borrowed information—quotation or paraphrase—is self-evident. It usually is not. What is required additionally is your commentary: your explanation, interpretation, connection, or whatever.

INCORPORATING AND ACKNOWLEDGING SOURCES

According to the outline you made, you know that you will be weaving certain borrowed facts and ideas into your paper at particular places and in particular pararaphs. But how exactly do you go about weaving them in?

You have a choice, which boils down basically to one of four possibilities, all correct:

1. *A simple quotation.* You simply quote the borrowed data, documenting the quotation, of course.

Example:

```
The reality is that ''less than 2% of cats and dogs from pounds go
to research.''
```

In this case you rely entirely on a parenthesis or a footnote to indicate where you got this information. (Documentation will be explained in detail in Chapter 9.)

2. *A quotation with a running acknowledgment.* Here you quote your borrowed data, but you introduce it with "a running acknowledgment" that indicates in the text of your paper where you got the idea.

Example:

```
A spokesperson for a student organization called CFAAR (Coalition for
Animals and Animal Rights) claims that ''less than 2% of cats and dogs
from pounds go to research. Those who do are screened to be sure that
none were pets.''
```

In your running acknowledgment you can include not only the author's name but also qualifications and, if you like, the title of the source where the information comes from.

3. *A simple paraphrase.* Here you just paraphrase the borrowed data, with no running acknowledgment, relying on the documentation alone to indicate the source:

Example:

```
Very few pound animals are used for research, and they are not pets.
```

4. *A paraphrase with a running acknowledgment.*
Example:

    According to the CFAAR (Coalition for Animals and Animal Rights), very few pound animals are used for research, and they are not pets.

How Do You Choose among These Four Options?

Sometimes it helps the reader to judge your argument better and faster if you provide a running acknowledgment, indicating the quality of your borrowed data (the expert's qualifications, the title of the source). At other times a running acknowledgment just gets in the way. Think of your reader.

Be prepared to experiment as you compose your rough draft. Devise some running acknowledgments, and then read the result. Perhaps you like it? If so, leave it in.

A hint: Most college students do not use enough running acknowledgments.

Some Phrases to Use for Running Acknowledgments

Here is a sentence illustrating a running acknowledgment:

    Jerod M. Loeb, Ph.D., director of the Division of Biomedical Sciences for the American Medical Association, states that ''Virtually every advance in medicine has directly or indirectly depended on experiments that utilized animals.''

Instead of "Jerod M. Loeb states" you could write:

    Jerod M. Loeb
        argues that
        points out
        concludes
        warns that
        notes
        refers to
        proposes
        believes
        makes the case for
        analyzes
        observes that
        reports
        agrees (disagrees)
        discusses
        adds
        writes
        states
        explains that

Or, you could start off with something like:

```
In the words of Jerod M. Loeb,
As Jerod M. Loeb observes,
According to Jerod M. Loeb,
As Jerod M. Loeb assesses the issue,
Claims Jerod M. Loeb,
```

Placing Running Acknowledgments in a Sentence

You have three choices, all of which are correct:

1. You can begin the sentence with the phrase for the running acknowledgment:

Jerod M. Loeb, Ph.D., director of the Division of Biomedical Sciences for the American Medical Association, states that ''Virtually every advance in medicine has directly or indirectly depended on experiments that utilized animals.''

2. You can insert the running acknowledgment phrase in the middle of the quotation, enclosed within commas:

''Virtually every advance in medicine,'' according to Jerod M. Loeb, Ph.D., director of the Division of Biomedical Sciences for the American Medical Association, ''has directly or indirectly depended on experiments that utilized animals.''

3. You can place the running acknowledgment at the end of the sentence:

''Virtually every advance in medicine has directly or indirectly depended on experiments that utilized animals,'' claims Jerod M. Loeb, Ph.D., director of the Division of Biomedical Sciences for the American Medical Association.

To sum up, here is a series of examples showing how the same idea, taken off the following note card, could be incorporated into a research paper.

```
good quote--pro-animals


''Animals are not handbags and hamburgers. They're living beings
like ourselves.'' quote from Ingrid Newkirk,
PETA nat'l director


Rosenberger, p. 32
```

    1. *A quotation:*

Animal rights activists maintain that animals have rights just like people. ''Animals are not handbags and hamburgers. They're living beings like ourselves.''

    2. *A quotation with some words omitted (ellipsis):*

Animal rights activists maintain that animals have rights, too, just like people. ''Animals are not handbags and hamburgers. They're living beings. . . . ''

    3. *A quotation with running acknowledgment:*

Animal rights activists maintain that animals have rights, too, just like people. According to Ingrid Newkirk, national director of PETA (People for the Ethical Treatment of Animals), ''Animals are not handbags and hamburgers. They're living beings like ourselves.''

    4. *A paraphrase:*

Animal rights activists maintain that animals have rights, too, just like people. Animals are not personal property for us to eat and wear as we wish.

5. *A paraphrase with a running acknowledgment:*

Animal rights activists maintain that animals have rights, too, just like people. According to Ingrid Newkirk, national director of PETA (People for the Ethical Treatment of Animals), animals are not personal property for us to eat and wear as we wish.

Punctuating Quotations

Exact words of the original are put within double quotation marks:

Some researchers complain that ''well intentioned legislation based on emotion rather than empirical arguments can negatively impact scientific inquiry.''

If the exact words of the original contain a built-in quotation, double quotation marks go around the whole excerpt you borrow from the original, and single quotation marks now go around the original's built-in quotation:

They point out that the Department of Agriculture now requires ''standards for physical environments that promote the 'psychological well-being' of laboratory primates.''

Periods and commas go inside quotation marks.
Colons and semicolons go outside quotation marks.
Question marks go inside or outside quotation marks, depending on whether the whole sentence is a question, or only the quoted part.

She asked, ''How many people saw the eclipse of the sun?''

Did he actually promise, ''There will be a party at my house after the final exam''?

Footnote numbers go outside the quotation marks.
To punctuate quotations that you introduce into your sentence, you can use a comma, a colon, or nothing at all.
A running acknowledgment phrase requires a comma:

According to Ingrid Newkirk, ''Animals are not handbags or hamburgers. They're living beings like ourselves.''

A running acknowledgment sentence requires a colon:

Ingrid Newkirk argues that animals have rights: ''Animals are not handbags and hamburgers. They are living beings like ourselves.''

Nothing is required when you blend the quotation into your own sentence:

```
Ingrid Newkirk believes that we shouldn't think of animals as
''handbags and hamburgers. They are living beings like ourselves.''
```

Block Form for Long Quotations

A quotation that is longer than three lines is handled differently. It has no quotation marks and it is indented as a block. See the sample papers for illustrations.

Weaving In Documentation

Regardless of whatever stylistic choices you may make, you will always have to identify the sources of borrowed information. The two basic systems (note and parenthesis) are explained in detail in Chapter 9. At this point we merely want to explain how they affect the way you draft sentences in your paper.

The *note* system is relatively easy to follow at the draft stage. Simply insert the appropriate number, raised as a superscript, after the borrowed information:

```
Ingrid Newkirk believes that we shouldn't think of animals as ''hand-
bags and hamburgers. They are living beings like ourselves.''[7]
```

The *parenthesis* system, however, requires some calculation if you want to make your paper as readable as possible. This means that you shouldn't clutter it up with long parenthetical interruptions. Therefore, as much as possible try to weave into your own sentences the information that would otherwise go into parentheses. Notice the differences and their different effects in the following sets of sentences:

Example, MLA system:

```
Animal activists believe that animals aren't ''handbags and hamburgers.
They are living beings like ourselves'' (Ingrid Newkirk qtd. in
Rosenberger 32).

Animal activists, like Ingrid Newkirk, believe that animals aren't
''handbags and hamburgers. They are living beings like ourselves''
(qtd. in Rosenberger 32).
```

Rosenberger concludes with the words of animal activist, Ingrid Newkirk: ''Animals are not handbags and hamburgers. They are living beings like ourselves'' (32).

Rosenberger deals in depth with the subject of animal activists.

   Example, APA system:

''Those opposed to research with animals have seldom stood on principle and instructed their physicians not to use the results of biomedical research on animals when it would benefit their loved ones or themselves'' (Kaplan, 1988, p. 242).

John Kaplan (1988) points out that ''Those opposed to research with animals have seldom stood on principle and instructed their physicians not to use the results of biomedical research on animals when it would benefit their loved ones or themselves'' (p. 242).

John Kaplan points out in his 1988 article in Science that ''Those opposed to research with animals have seldom stood on principle and instructed their physicians not to use the results of biomedical research on animals when it would benefit their loved ones or themselves'' (p. 242).

John Kaplan's 1988 article in Science criticizes animal activists.

PROVIDING TRANSITIONS AND SIGNAL WORDS

You know how the ideas fit together in your research paper because they are your ideas. You have been working with them carefully—reading, taking notes, making an outline, and so on. However, your reader doesn't have this benefit. The reader won't know how your ideas are connected unless you include signals, like traffic lights, indicating the flow of your argument. These words and phrases that you insert into your sentences and paragraphs are called "transitional expressions." Your sentences and paragraphs may be grammatically correct without them, but adding them will improve the clarity of your paper tremendously. Most college students do not use enough of these expressions. Using them is not difficult. It is only a matter of using the right ones, and remembering to use them in the first place.

Here, for example, is a grammatically correct paragraph without enough transitional expressions:

> Expense is a major limitation in the conduct of primate research. A rhesus monkey costs from $600 to $2000 to purchase, and several hundred dollars annually to maintain. Studies requiring large numbers of primates are rarely feasible. The supply of many species of primates is limited. Most of the commonly used monkeys and apes are obtained from domestic breeding programs. The low reproduction rates (as compared to rodents) and long developmental period limit supply and elevate costs. Space for housing and care of the animals is a consideration, with substantial space and expensive materials required.

Now here is the paragraph as it was originally written in *Science,* with all its transitional expressions:

> Expense is a major limitation in the conduct of primate research. For example, a rhesus monkey costs from $600 to $2000 to purchase, and several hundred dollars annually to maintain. Consequently, studies requiring large numbers of primates are rarely feasible. In addition to cost factors, the supply of many species of primates is limited. Indeed, most of the commonly used monkeys and apes are obtained from domestic breeding programs. Nonetheless, the low reproduction rates (as compared to rodents, for example) and long developmental period limit supply and elevate costs. Space for housing and care of the animals is also a consideration with substantial space and expensive materials required.

Frederick A. King et al., "Limitations and Constraints in the Use of Primates," Science, *10 June 1988, 1481.*

Quick List of Transitional Expressions and Signal Words

What exactly has been added? Go back and underline the additions.

Transitional expressions or signal words show the logical order and relationship of ideas. Here are the most common kinds of logical relationship expressed by transitional expressions, and some of the words for them. You can probably add some more synonyms for each category yourself:

1. **Indicating order in time:** first, second, third, next, last, finally, then, subsequently, ultimately.
2. **Adding something:** and, in addition, moreover, additionally, also, too, furthermore, not to mention, besides.

3. **Contrasting two somethings:** but, however, nonetheless, on the other hand, yet, conversely, on the contrary.
4. **Drawing a conclusion:** therefore, consequently, in conclusion, to conclude, summing up, accordingly, evidently.
5. **Emphasizing something:** indeed, surely, in fact, it is clear that, certainly, in particular, to repeat.
6. **Bringing in an example:** for example, namely, to illustrate, for instance.

Other Transitional Devices

Besides using these special words and phrases by inserting them into your rough draft, there are three other noteworthy techniques of providing connections to help your reader follow your argument.

1. Using these words that automatically refer back to a previous idea: *this, that, these, such.*

Examples:

This illustrates how well intentioned legislation based on emotional rather than empirical arguments can negatively impact scientific inquiry.

These similarities in the biological mechanisms of humans and primates underlie the value of **these** animals for medical research.

Such studies, by qualified scientists, are needed before primate research laboratories are required to build costly facilities (King 1481).

2. Using loose synonyms (including pronouns) for words in preceding sentences. Synonyms are equivalents referring to the same thing or person.

Examples:

Most **scientists,** at first, thought that what separates us from the other animals is that human beings use tools. So **ethnologists** went out into the field and returned with innumerable examples of tool use in animals.

ethnologist = scientist

If the **killing** is done behind closed doors, if the government says **it** must be done, or if some man or woman in a white coat assures us that **it's** for our benefit, we ignore our own ethical good sense and allow **it** to happen.

killing = it

Ingrid Newkirk, quoted in "Just Like Us," Harper's Magazine, August 1989, 45–46.

3. Using the same words can connect the ideas in sentences with an echo effect.

Example:

I believe that animals have **rights.** This is not to say that animals have the same **rights** that we do, but the reasons that lead us to accord certain **rights** to human beings are equally applicable to animals.

Gary Francione, quoted in "Just Like Us," Harper's Magazine, August 1989, 44.

PREPARING AN ABSTRACT

Some academic disciplines prefer an abstract, or summary of your paper, rather than an outline at the beginning of your paper. You can make an abstract of your paper by converting your outline into paragraph form or by using the techniques of summarizing that were discussed in Chapter 4 (see pp. 88–91). The abstract should be a true summary of the key ideas and arguments in your paper, not just another version of your introductory paragraph. The abstract should be placed after your title page. Here is an example of an abstract. It comes from the sample paper on hypnosis (pp. 285–297).

Abstract

An analysis of the research on the essence of hypnosis suggests that the debate between state and non-state theorists is a problem of terminology, stemming from different orientations. Barber's research demonstrates that a special hypnotic state cannot be identified on the basis of physiological changes. Furthermore, he shows that most of the traits associated with the hypnotic state can be produced through a process of involved imagining. Barber is criticized for arguing against a position never espoused by state researchers, for paying insufficient attention to the subjective experience of hypnotism, and for flaws in his research design. Edmonston argues that hypnosis is basically a state of relaxation; however, he is unable to fit alert hypnosis into his model. The debate over terminology has practical implications because hypnosis has long been recognized as a powerful and potentially dangerous procedure.

THE INTRODUCTION

An introduction usually consists of one paragraph, occasionally several paragraphs, and has three basic functions.

First, it should inform the reader by identifying the thesis. After reading your introduction, the reader should know what your paper is about and what your slant on the topic is.

Second, it should provoke the reader's interest or justify the whole undertaking by providing a rationale of its importance. You don't want the reader to respond "So what?" or "Who cares?" to your thesis. Anticipate that possible response and reassure the reader that investigating this topic will be worthwhile.

Third, it should set up some expectations in the reader by previewing what is to come. Give the reader a bird's-eye impression of what is in the paper. After finishing your introduction, the reader should be ready to attend to your first main point and have a sense of where that fits into your developing argument.

You can consider various specific stylistic possibilities as you draft your introduction:

1. Ask a question or a series of questions to focus your reader's attention on the subject.
2. Use a particularly powerful quotation from your reading.
3. Use dramatic facts or examples.
4. Give a short anecdote, an illustrative personal story.

Here are examples of two good introductions. The first is less formal than the second, but note how each introduction fulfills its three major functions.

Question used to provoke interest	1. Breakfast cereals present a myriad of choices and a multitude of claims to promote good health, but is there a ''grain'' of truth to their promises? Appparently consumers think so because the industry
Statement of importance	has yearly sales approaching 6.6 billion dollars (Freundlich 114). Consumers have allowed themselves to be mesmerized by boasts of improved
Use of examples is a preview.	health and fitness and have paid little attention to the actual facts. Tony the Tiger may think cereals are ''G-G-Great!'' but as one TV commercial inadvertently hints, the promises are empty. When the character asks,
Thesis	''What are you eating?'' the reply is telling: ''Nut-N-Honey.'' As these examples suggest, breakfast cereals offer entertaining advertising, but the claims for their health benefits have been exaggerated.

Statement of importance	2. Right-handedness is something that most of us take for granted as the ''normal'' way to do things, but a substantial number of the population, approximately 10%, are left-handed, a rate consistent across cultures and stable since pre-historic times (Springer & Deutsch, 1985). Although the presence of left-handedness is well
Preview of paper's major parts	documented, nearly 200 years of speculation has not produced an accepted theory of the cause. Genetic and pathogenic theories have received the most attention and are the most plausible. Genetic models suggest different gene or allele combinations may determine handedness. Pathogenic models theorize that brain trauma causes individuals to switch from their natural handedness to the opposite hand. Still other researchers maintain that handedness is completely
Thesis	determined by the environment. On their own, none of these theories can accurately explain handedness, but a combination of the genetic and pathogenic modes provides the most complete explanation.

The Do Nots

1. Do not beat around the bush. Give the reader a clear idea of your topic and your slant on the subject. Weak introductions are a product of not knowing where you want to go with your subject.

2. Avoid a bare announcement of your topic, such as This paper will analyze the different theories about the cause of left-handedness.

3. Do not make obvious statements, such as Conservation is a very important topic now that everyone is interested in ecology. How can you tell if something is too obvious? Well, you can try it out on your friends and classmates.

4. Do not use quotations that have become clichés, such as The way to a man's heart is through his stomach.

5. Do not rely on the title or outline to provide information. The introduction should be capable logically of standing by itself so the reader knows what is going on (the topic and your slant on it).

6. Do not begin with a definition unless you really need one. For example, a paper on euthanasia would have to begin by distinguishing between "active" and "passive" euthanasia. A paper on the hospice movement would have to explain what a hospice is. But don't fall into this old

rut: Webster's Dictionary defines zoning as ''dividing a city into sections reserved for different purposes.'' This definition isn't necessary; it just gets in the way because everybody already knows what zoning is.

THE CONCLUSION

The purpose of a conclusion is to give a note of finality to your paper. You can do this by:

1. restating your thesis in slightly different words.
2. summing up your main points.
3. giving a final example or quote that drives home your thesis.
4. stating the implications or importance of the research you have done.
5. advising what the reader can do as a response to the information you have presented.

Here is an example of a concluding paragraph that states the *implications* of the research:

> There are practical implications to this seemingly esoteric debate about the nature of hypnosis. For instance, professional and governmental guidelines recognize the potential for the misuse of hypnosis. The government requires that special steps be followed in experiments on hypnosis, and professional societies prohibit the training of lay people as hypnotists. One potential problem is that a person can sidestep these guidelines by renaming the process. Likewise, if a client objects to therapy which involves hypnosis, but agrees to relaxation procedures that create the same level of suggestibility as hypnosis, this raises another ethical problem. In light of these clinical problems, it is important that research continue into the nature of hypnosis.

Here is an example of a concluding paragraph that *advises* the reader:

> Meanwhile, the consumer continues to shop the cereal aisles, looking for the most healthful products. Given the fact that current research cannot fully substantiate the claims of cereal advertisers, the soundest advice seems to be to concentrate on alternative sources

of fiber. Fruits, vegetables, whole grains, dried peas, beans, and lentils offer proteins, vitamins, and minerals with less fat and sugar than anything that Kellogg, Post, or General Mills currently has on the shelf. The old maxim still holds: Moderation, variety, and balance in one's diet promote the best health possible.

THE TITLE

Let's consider the title. What can a title do?

1. Define the topic.
2. State or imply the thesis.
3. Create interest.

A title should *not*:

1. be a bare question unless it is a reference your reader can easily associate with something else, like What Is the Sound of One Paw Clapping? Your job is not only to spark your reader's curiosity; it is also to make a point about the subject, which the title should express. For example, instead of the question How Safe is Airline Travel? your title should reflect your thesis: Airlines: Still the Safest Way to Travel. Remember the primary purpose of a title is to inform the reader.
2. be so cute or so funny in the title that you confuse your reader. Junk Food for Thought in a philosophy paper, or Montezuma's Revenge for an American History paper on the Mexican War, are kinds of titles to avoid. On the other hand, good titles often involve a bit of word play, for example, Bored of Education: The Rural Education Crisis in America.

A phrase is better than a complete sentence. A title is one place for sentence fragments. If you feel your title, for instance, The Sinking Ark, is not enough, add a second half after a colon.

> The Sinking Ark: Endangered Species
>
> Airlines: Still the Safest Way to Travel

Notice the correct punctuation for titles. Your title is never put within quotation marks, underlined, or capitalized in full. Don't put a period at the end.

> Redress: From the Congressional Floor to the Hearts of the Japanese-Americans

YOUR ROUGH DRAFT

Now you are ready to draft a rough version of your own research paper. Begin by building up paragraphs, in the same order as the ideas in your outline. Weave your sources into your writing, with or without running acknowledgments, and provide transitions between ideas in your sentences and paragraphs. After you have developed the body of your paper, work on an introduction and conclusion.

USING A LISTENER

The readability of a piece of writing is closely related to its success and value. If a listener can understand and follow the presentation of your ideas as you read them aloud, you can then feel reassured that your writing is effective. The worksheets at the end of this chapter will give you a structure to use for peer evaluation and self-assessment.

REVISING

We want to make a distinction between *revising* and *editing* your paper. By revising, we mean making substantive changes in the content or organization of your paper; editing refers to correcting mistakes in the spelling, grammar, documentation, or formatting of your paper. We advise you to edit only after you have finished revising.

Adding Material

After you have received some feedback on your rough draft, you will have an idea about whether you have left some questions in a reader's mind. If so, your most important task is to insert information or explanations. In the process of assembling material from different sources, we often leave gaps in our writing. We can usually fill those in once another reader makes us aware of their existence.

A slightly different problem may be that we have failed to cover a particular aspect of our topic. Sometimes this omission can only be spotted by someone who is more knowledgeable than we are, such as an instructor. If this is the case, revision may require going back to our sources to look for more information or even hunting up additional sources.

Deleting Material

Cutting can be more difficult than adding because we sometimes fall in love with an example or a phrase, but we must not waste the reader's time with any unnecessary material. A critical eye led to cutting a sentence from the following paragraph of a paper on breakfast cereals:

> Gradually the cereal industry moderated its medicinal claims, and the rule of thumb became avoid remedial boasts. This claim lasted until 1984 when the National Cancer Institute announced ''a high-fiber, low-fat diet may reduce the risk of some types of cancer'' (Samuelson 49). The rallying word was fiber and with it came a new market potential for bran. Fiber refers to the walls of the plant cell which have an exterior coating of bran. Astute marketers at Kellogg Company adopted the NCI findings in their advertising for ''All-Bran'' cereal. Soon <u>the health claims mushroomed</u>, and products containing corn, wheat, oat, rice, or barley bran flooded the market. Today, at least twenty-five varieties of bran/fiber cereals fill the supermarket shelves. [Advertising claims now included everything from lower risks of cancer, cholesterol reductions, lower chances of heart disease, to the old stand-by ''eases constipation''] (''Cereal: Breakfast Food or Nutritional Supplement'' 646).
>
> Although grain cereals provide fiber, <u>their promise to reduce cancer may ring hollow</u>...

Cut. I've already said the claims mushroomed. In the next paragraph, I discuss one of the major claims.

Rearranging the Parts

As we indicated in the previous chapter, an outline is a good way to check the organization of your paper. When the student outlined the paper on breakfast cereal, it was apparent that he had mixed together information about different health claims and needed to move parts of paragraphs. Part of his outline of the rough draft looked like this:

    IV. Fiber hits the market and medicinal boasts mushroom.

    V. Research refutes health claims.

    VI. Psyllium arrives.

    VII. Proctor and Gamble treads a fine line.

VIII. Rice Bran arrives.

IX. Research casts doubts.

After revision, an outline of the same section looked like this:

III. Recent ads claim cancer and cholesterol reduction.

A. Bran was supposed to reduce cancer.

B. Rice Bran was supposed to reduce cholesterol.

C. Psyllium was touted as a cholesterol reducer.

Sometimes it is the parts of a sentence that need rearranging to provide a better transition from one idea to the next. In the following instance, the parts of a sentence were reversed to provide a more logical sequence:

Move fiber content to front of sentence to parallel sequence in first sentence. Moving sentence elements will provide better transition to the next sentence.

Although grain cereals provide fiber, their promise to reduce cancer may ring hollow. Research studies contradict one another and the actual fiber content of many cereals is less than two grams per one ounce serving and ("Cereal: Breakfast Food or Nutritional Supplement" 642). Research on fiber is not definitive, according to Dr. David Klurfeld...

Clarifying Ideas

As a result of your familiarity with your topic, you may write sentences which are perfectly clear to you but a bit puzzling to a reader. For example, the following sentence is somewhat confusing:

Manufacturers enrich their products with supplements, overloading cereal and the human body with goodness.

After rereading the source, the writer made this revision:

Manufacturers enrich their products with supplements, but the additions have little relevance to the consumer's dietary needs.

EXERCISES

A. Indicate whether each of the following sentences incorporates its source as (1) a simple quotation, (2) a simple paraphrase, (3) a quotation with a running acknowledgment, (4) a paraphrase with a running acknowledgment.

1. Secretary of Health and Human Services Frederick Goodwin complained recently that complying with new Federal regulations on the use-or abuse-of animals will drain off some 17 percent of the research funds appropriated to the National Institutes of Health.

2. ''But the real cost is that there will be less research,'' says Carol Scheman of the Association of American Universities, ''and when research is slowed, people die.''

3. ''People don't realize that they are being steam rollered. They may not recognize what is happening until a lot of damage has been done.''

4. There is no need to replicate many studies because they are irrelevant and we know the results in advance anyway.

B. Look at "Animal Rights" by Molly O'Neill (pp. 310–313). Find an example for each of the options listed above. Then consider her use of running acknowledgments, particularly her reliance on "he said," "she said." What alternatives would you recommend to Ms. O'Neill?

C. *Transitions*
Read "Why Worry about the Animals?" (pp. 302–309) and find particularly good examples of transitional expressions. Try to find one example for each of the six categories listed on pp. 216–217 (adding, contrasting, etc.) Then find examples of the other kinds of transitional devices, listed on pp. 217–218 (this, synonyms, repetition).

D. *Abstract*
Write a one-paragraph abstract of "Why Worry about the Animals?" or "Facts about Animal Research."

E. *Title*
1. Assess each title in the Anthology in light of the guidelines about titles on p. 222.
2. What subtitle after a colon would you recommend to Molly O'Neill for her article on "Animal Rights"?

Worksheet 12 _____ **PEER EVALUATION**

Name _____ Date _____

Peer Evaluator: _____

Read your paper and complete the worksheet by asking the peer evaluator to answer these questions. You can both refer back to the paper as you complete the worksheet.

- A. Introduction
    1. Did the opening capture your interest?
    2. What is my thesis?

    3. Could the thesis be worded more clearly?
    4. Should it be stated earlier or later than the point at which I introduce it? Where?

    5. Do I adequately prepare you to expect a certain structure in my argument?

- B. Support
    1. What details (such as: examples, statistics, case histories, definitions) have I given to support the main idea?

    2. Were all my details connected to the main idea?
    3. Should I give more supporting details? Or fewer?

- C. Transitions
    1. Did the order of points seem logical?
    2. Did you get lost anywhere? Where?

    3. Should I include more transitional expressions? Where?

- D. General
    1. What parts were most effective?

    2. Did I ever seem to be trying to impress you, rather than communicating my ideas? Where?

    3. Do I need to provide more definitions of terms? Which?

    4. Did I use too many short, jerky sentences, or too many long, complicated ones?

E. Conclusion
 1. Did my conclusion answer the questions that came to mind as you listened to my paper?
 2. Is there anything about the end of my paper that leaves you up in the air?

Worksheet 13 _____ **SELF-EVALUATION OF DRAFT**

Name _____ Date _____

Title _____

1. What have you done to catch the reader's interest?

2. Where is your thesis statement located?

3. What steps have you taken to develop or support the thesis? (List details, examples, case histories, definitions.)

4. Do you think you have enough supporting information?

5. Are there any aspects of the paper that do not satisfy you? List any problems on which you need advice.

CHAPTER 9

Documenting Your Sources

THE PURPOSE OF DOCUMENTATION

You will be using information and ideas from several sources when you write your research paper. Readers want to know where the information comes from, so you must follow a recognized system of indicating where you got your information. When you use someone's ideas or words, there is a moral requirement for you to acknowledge that you have borrowed the material. Failure to do so constitutes plagiarism and can result in serious consequences. In a recent presidential campaign, one candidate lost public confidence when it was shown that he had used another person's words as his own. Honest students sometimes run the risk of unintentional plagiarism when they repeat a memorable phrase without being aware that they read it somewhere. Careful note-taking is the solution to this problem. Paraphrase your sources in your own words as you take notes. Whenever you do copy the author's exact words, be sure to use quotation marks and indicate the precise page number.

In addition to the ethical requirement to document your sources, there is a practical reason to indicate where your information came from. Documentation makes your paper more convincing. It lets the reader know that you have read a variety of sources and carefully recorded the information. Backing up your ideas with information and opinions of knowledgeable people adds a note of authority to your paper.

WHAT NEEDS DOCUMENTING?

The rule goes: "Document every bit of borrowed information (idea or fact) that would not be obvious to someone familiar with the topic." But how do you apply this rule? When you start researching a topic, you know very little about it, and every bit of information seems as if it will need documentation. Does that mean, then, that you would have to document every sentence in your paper? No, because the rule continues: "Document every bit of borrowed information that is original to that source." An idea may be new to you but not to a lot of other people. As you continue to read, you will realize that there is a body of information that is common knowledge to those in the field. If it is common knowledge, you don't need to document it even though you discovered it by reading, not through your own observation. On the other hand, if the information is someone's original idea or newly displayed fact, then it is that person's property; that person created it and is entitled to be identified with it. If you don't acknowledge the creator of the idea, you are technically stealing it.

Consider the first part of this rule: "Document information that is not obvious to someone familiar with the topic." A student who began researching the nutritional value of breakfast cereals, for instance, did not know that bran referred to the exterior coat of the grain seed and that fiber was found in the walls of the cell. As he continued to read, he found other sources that explained the same information. Consequently, in his paper, he did not have to document the source in which he first found the explanation of these terms.

Now consider the second part of the rule: "Document specific information original to a source." For example, where exactly Columbus landed in the New World is now being debated. Everyone knows Columbus was trying to find a route to India and that he made a landfall in 1492. This information would not be documented. Neither would the information that there is a controversy be documented because it is obvious. But the idea that Columbus landed on Hispaniola, as opposed to some other location like Watling Island, would be attributed to some source, as would be the reasons for that choice. To take the example of the student researching the nutritional value of breakfast cereals, only one of his sources mentioned that the first cereal marketed by J. H. Kellogg in 1878 was called "Granula." Consequently, when he used this fact in his paper, he decided to document the source.

To determine if something is general knowledge or obvious, remember the process whereby knowledge is generated and distributed in print. Information usually appears first in newspapers and magazines, whether they are magazines for the general public or scholarly journals. Here results of new studies and new interpretations of existing information are reported. These ideas are read by others who process this information over time, synthesizing it with other information, and produce more articles and books. The information continues to be read, integrated with other ideas, reinterpreted, diluted, and reshaped in the process, gaining a wider audience at each stage. Ultimately if this information is interesting and useful to enough people it will become general knowledge and will find its way into encyclopedias and textbooks. By the time it emerges in textbooks it is no longer controversial and the original author's private property; it belongs to everyone as common knowledge and does not need documentation.

If you are in doubt about whether to document something, it is usually better to do so. Your instructor is likely to be more tolerant of too much documentation than not enough.

METHODS OF DOCUMENTATION: AN OVERVIEW

To the dismay of students, there is not just one way of indicating where information was found. The method varies from one course to another; and even within the same field of study, there are changes from time to time. You should always check with your instructor about the preferred method and ask for the department guidelines. At this stage of your career, you should become familiar with the basic systems. Once you have decided on a major field of study, you should purchase a copy of the style manual for that field. A comprehensive list of the style manuals for all fields was compiled by John Bruce Howell in *Style Manuals of the English-Speaking World* (Phoenix: Oryx, 1983).

All methods of documentation consist of two parts:

1. A *textual reference*. In your paragraph, you briefly indicate that there is a source. Depending on which method you use, the reference can be woven into your sentence structure, placed in parentheses, or indicated with a number.

2. A *list of sources* (a bibliography) at the end of your paper. The list gives all the information that a reader would need to locate the source you have used, but the textual reference provides just enough information so that the reader can find the full citation in the list of sources. The list is called **Works Cited** in the MLA and Note systems; it is called **References** in the APA system.

Although there are several methods, they are variations of two basic systems: the note system and the parenthesis system. As you scan the examples below, you will see the essential differences and many of the small variations in punctuation, capitalization, and sequence of information.

1. *The note system* (footnotes or endnotes) uses a raised number (superscript) within the text to indicate that information has been taken from a source. Footnotes (at the bottom of the page) or endnotes (at the back of the paper) are then used to give the reader information about the source. An alphabetized list of sources, called Works Cited, is given at the end of your paper. The note system is used in philosophy, religion, art, dance, music, theater, and often in history and political science.

The note system that we illustrate is taken from Kate L. Turabian's *A Manual for Writers of Term Papers, Theses, and Dissertations,* 5th ed., rev. and exp., Bonnie Birtwistle Honigsblum, Chicago: Univerity of Chicago Press, 1987.

Example:
Textual Reference:

Each box of cereal lists its ingredients by descending weight in product makeup, which means breakfast may well be a bowl of sugar.[1]

Footnote or endnote:

[1] John Carey, ''Now I've Read the Label, What's in the Package?'' Business Week 9 October 1989, 133.

This full citation would be given only when you used the source for the first time in your paper. If you used information from the same source at another point in your paper, you would use a short form. You have two choices: 1. Use the author's last name and the page number; 2. Use Ibid. (a Latin abbreviation that means "the same source and the same page.") Ibid. can be used if you are using the same source as the one identified immediately before. If you are using the same source, but a different page, add the page number.

[5]Carey, 133.

[6]Gerus, p. 31.

[7]Ibid.

[8]Ibid., p. 33.

Works Cited (list at the end of your paper):

Carey, John. ''Now I've Read the Label, What's in the Package?'' Business Week 9 October 1989, 133.

The sample paper on Redress in Chapter 10 uses the note system.

2. *The parenthesis system* uses parentheses within the text to give enough information so that the reader can locate the citation in the list of sources. This system eliminates the need to duplicate information in both a note and a list of sources. Consequently, the parenthesis system is favored by most academic departments. There are two examples of the parenthesis system in Chapter 10: the paper on breakfast cereals uses the MLA system and the paper on hypnosis uses the APA system.

The *APA (American Psychological Association) System* requires a textual reference that identifies the author (or brief title if no author is given) and date. This system makes sense in any field where the date of

the research is important. It is used exactly or with slight variation in many of the social sciences (Sociology, Economics, Geography, Anthropology, Archaeology, Linguistics, Law), some applied sciences (Social Work, Child Development and Family Relations, Education, Home Economics, Law Enforcement/Criminal Justice, Sports and Leisure Studies, Business), and some of the sciences (Botany, Zoology, Geology). The APA System is illustrated in the sample paper on hypnosis. Our source for this system is the *Publication Manual of the American Psychological Association*, 3rd ed., rev. 1984.
Example:
Textual reference:

```
Each box of cereal lists its ingredients by descending weight in

product makeup, which means breakfast may well be a bowl of sugar

(Carey, 1989).
```

```
References (list at the end of your paper):

Carey, J. (1989, October 9). Now I've read the label, what's in the
     package? Business Week, p. 133.
```

The *MLA (Modern Language Association) System* requires a textual reference that identifies the *author* (or short title if no author is given) and *page(s)* on which the information was found. It is used in Literature, Languages, and sometimes in Political Science, Education, and History. The MLA System is illustrated in the sample paper on breakfast cereals. Our source for this system is Joseph Gibaldi and Walter S. Achtert's *MLA Handbook for Writers of Research Papers*, 3rd ed., New York: The Modern Language Association of America, 1988.
Example:
Textual reference:

```
Each box of cereal lists its ingredients by descending weight in

product makeup, which means breakfast may well be a bowl of sugar

(Carey 137).
```

```
Works Cited (list at the end of your paper):

Carey, John ''Now I've Read the Label, What's in the Package?''
     Business Week 9 Oct. 1989: 133.
```

The *Number System* is a variation of the parenthesis system. The textual reference is a *number* placed in parenthesis or superscript (raised one-half line). The number corresponds to a source in the list of references. The same number is used every time that particular source is cited. The list can be arranged alphabetically or according to the order in which sources were first cited in the paper. This system is used in Biology, Chemistry, Computer Science, Engineering, Mathematics, Health Sciences, and Physics.

Example:
Textual reference:

Each box of cereal lists its ingredients by descending weight in product makeup, which means breakfast may well be a bowl of sugar (1).

References (list at the end of your paper):

1. Carey, J. Now I've read the label, what's in the package? Business Week 22: 133, Oct. 9, 1989.

Use of Computers/Word Processors

The increasing sophistication of word processing programs has lessened the tedium of typing footnotes and source lists. Many programs have features which automatically number the notes and alphabetize the source list. For example, the *Norton Textra Writer* provides the option of using the APA, MLA, or endnote system. When you are listing your sources, Textra provides a split screen so that you can call up models of the correct format for books, articles, etc. It also automatically formats the entry with the proper indentations. Not all programs are geared to writing research papers. If you are working with a program that sets tabs and margins by a ruler rather than by spaces, you will have to adapt the guidelines given in this book.

Regardless of what program you use, you can start to enter your sources once you begin to take notes. You are then able to store the information in a separate file which you can add to and edit as you go along.

COMPARATIVE MODELS: NOTE, MLA, AND APA

Now that you have an overview of the basic systems of documentation, you can use the following models to help you set up the documentation in your paper. For each specific kind of source, you will find a set illustrating variations in the different systems. Each set begins with two entries illustrating the note system: a note example (N) to use for footnotes or endnotes, and then a corresponding entry (WC). Use this form for the Works Cited page. The third entry (MLA) illustrates the parenthesis and the Works Cited page for the MLA system, and the last entry (APA) illustrates the parenthesis and the Reference page for the APA system.

Books

A BOOK WITH ONE AUTHOR

N

 [1]Michael Allen Fox, <u>The Case for Animal Experimentation: An Evolutionary and Ethical Perspective</u> (Berkeley: University of California Press, 1986), x.

WC

Fox, Michael Allen. <u>The Case for Animal Experimentation: An Evolutionary and Ethical Perspective</u>. Berkeley: University of California Press, 1986.

MLA (Fox x)

Fox, Michael Allen. <u>The Case for Animal Experimentation: An Evolutionary and Ethical Perspective</u>. Berkeley: U of California P, 1986.

APA (Fox, 1986, p. x)

Fox, M. A. (1986). <u>The case for animal experimentation: An evolutionary and ethical perspective</u>. Berkeley: University of California Press

A BOOK WITH TWO (OR THREE) AUTHORS

N

 [2]Edward G. Fairholme and Wellesley Pain, <u>A Century of Work for Animals: The History of the RSPCA</u> (London: J. Murray, 1924), 21.

WC

Fairholme, Edward G. and Wellesley Pain. <u>A Century of Work for Animals: The History of the RSPCA</u>. London: J. Murray, 1924.

MLA (Fairholme and Pain 21)

Fairholme, Edward G. and Wellesley Pain. <u>A Century of Work for Animals: The History of the RSPCA</u>. London: J. Murray, 1924.

APA (Fairholme & Pain, 1924, p. 21)

Fairholme, E. G., & Pain, W. (1924). <u>A century of work for animals: The history of the RSPCA</u>. London: J. Murray.

A BOOK WITH MORE THAN THREE AUTHORS

N

 [3]W. R. Hendee and others, <u>Use of Animals in Biomedical Research. The Challenge and Responsibility</u> (Chicago, IL: American Medical Association, 1988), 76.

WC

Hendee, W. R., and others. <u>Use of Animals in Biomedical Research. The Challenge and Responsibility</u>. Chicago, IL: American Medical Association, 1988.

MLA (Hendee et al. 76)

Hendee, W. R., et al. <u>Use of Animals in Biomedical Research. The Challenge and Responsibility</u>. Chicago, IL: American Medical Association, 1988.

APA (Hendee et al., 1988, p. 76)
Hendee, W. R., Loeb, J. M., Schwarz, M. R., & Smith, S. J. (1988). *Use of animals in biomedical research. The challenge and responsibility*. Chicago: American Medical Association.

AN ANONYMOUS BOOK

N

⁴*Wildlife and Sporting Paintings* (New York: Kennedy Galleries, 1979), 10.

WC

Wildlife and Sporting Paintings. New York: Kennedy Galleries, 1979.

MLA (*Wildlife and Sporting Paintings* 10)
Wildlife and Sporting Paintings. New York: Kennedy Galleries, 1979.

APA (*Wildlife and Sporting Paintings*, 1979, p. 10)
Wildlife and sporting paintings. (1979). New York: Kennedy Galleries.

A BOOK EDITED BY ONE PERSON

N

⁵Tom Regan, ed., *Animal Sacrifices: Religious Perspectives on Use of Animals in Science* (Philadelphia: Temple University Press, 1986), ix.

WC

Regan, Tom, ed. *Animal Sacrifices: Religious Perspectives on Use of Animals in Science*. Philadelphia: Temple University Press, 1986.

MLA (Regan ix)
Regan, Tom, ed. *Animal Sacrifices: Religious Perspectives on Use of Animals in Science*. Philadelphia: Temple U P, 1986.

APA (Regan, 1986, p. ix)
Regan, T. (Ed.). (1986). *Animal sacrifices: Religious perspectives on use of animals in science*. Philadelphia: Temple University Press.

A BOOK EDITED BY TWO (OR THREE) PEOPLE

N

⁶Stanley and Roslind Godlovitch and John Harris, eds., *Animals, Men, and Morals: An Enquiry into the Maltreatment of Non-Humans* (New York: Taplinger, 1972), xxiii-xxiv.

WC

Godlovitch, Stanley and Roslind, and John Harris, eds. *Animals, Men, and Morals: An Enquiry into the Maltreatment of Non-Humans*. New York: Taplinger, 1972.

MLA (Godlovitch, Godlovitch and Harris xxiii-xxiv)
Godlovitch, Stanley, Roslind Godlovitch, and John Harris, eds. *Animals, Men and Morals: An Enquiry into the Maltreatment of Non-Humans*. New York: Taplinger, 1972.

APA (Godlovitch, Godlovitch, & Harris, 1972, pp. xxiii-xxiv)
Godlovitch, S., Godlovitch, R., & Harris, J. (Eds.). 1972. <u>Animals, men and morals: An enquiry into the maltreatment of non-humans</u>. New York: Taplinger.

SOMEBODY ELSE'S BOOK EDITED BY ONE PERSON

N

⁷Theodore Roosevelt, <u>Wilderness Writing</u>, ed. Paul Schullery (Salt Lake City: Peregrine Smith Books, 1986), 117.

WC

Roosevelt, Theodore. <u>Wilderness Writing</u>. Ed. Paul Schullery. Salt Lake City: Peregrine Smith Books, 1986.

MLA (Roosevelt 117)

Roosevelt, Theodore. <u>Wilderness Writing</u>. Ed. Paul Schullery. Salt Lake City: Peregrine Smith, 1986.

APA (Roosevelt, 1986, p. 117)

Roosevelt, T. (1986). <u>Wilderness writing</u> (P. Schullery, Ed.). Salt Lake City: Peregrine Smith Books.

A REVISED OR SUBSEQUENT EDITION OF A BOOK

N

⁸Raymond F. Dasmann, <u>Wildlife Biology</u>, 2nd ed. (New York: Wiley, 1981), 82.

WC

Dasmann, Raymond F. <u>Wildlife Biology</u>, 2nd ed. New York: Wiley, 1981.

MLA (Dasmann 82)

Dasmann, Raymond F. <u>Wildlife Biology</u>, 2nd ed. New York: Wiley, 1981.

APA (Dasmann, 1981, p. 82)

Dasmann, R. F. (1981). <u>Wildlife biology</u> (2nd ed.). New York: Wiley.

A BOOK THAT IS A VOLUME IN A SERIES BY DIFFERENT AUTHORS

N

⁹R. O. Hunt, <u>Nonhuman Primate Models for Human Diseases</u>, vol. 4: <u>Recent Advances in Primatology</u>, eds. D. J. Chivers and E. H. R. Ford (New York: Academic Press, 1978), 117.

WC

Hunt, R. O. <u>Nonhuman Primate Models for Human Diseases</u>. Vol. 4: <u>Recent Advances in Primatology</u>. Eds. D. J. Chivers and E. H. R. Ford. New York: Academic Press, 1978.

MLA (Hunt 117)

Hunt, R. O. <u>Nonhuman Primate Models for Human Diseases</u>. New York: Academic Press, 1978. Vol. 4 of <u>Recent Advances in Primatology</u>. Eds. D. J. Chivers and E. H. R. Ford. 4 vols.

240 DOCUMENTING YOUR SOURCES

APA (Hunt, 1978, p. 117)
Hunt, R. O. (1978). Nonhuman primate models for human diseases (D. J. Chivers & E. H. R. Ford, Eds. Recent advances in primatology, Vol. 4). New York: Academic Press.

A TRANSLATION OF A BOOK

N
   [10]Pol Chantraine, The Living Ice: The Story of the Seals and the Men Who Hunt Them in the Gulf of St. Lawrence, translated by David Lobdell (Toronto: McClelland and Stewart, 1980), 3.

WC
Chantraine, Pol. The Living Ice: The Story of the Seals and the Men Who Hunt Them in the Gulf of St. Lawrence. Translated by David Lobdell. Toronto: McClelland and Stewart, 1983.

MLA (Chantraine 3)
Chantraine, Pol. The Living Ice: The Story of the Seals and the Men Who Hunt Them in the Gulf of St. Lawrence. Trans. David Lobdell. Toronto: McClelland and Stewart, 1983.

APA (Chantraine, 1983, p. 3)
Chantraine, P. (1983). The living ice: The story of the seals and the men who hunt them in the Gulf of St. Lawrence (D. Lobdell, Trans.). Toronto: McClelland and Stewart.

A BOOK WITH A CORPORATE AUTHOR

N
   [11]International Conference on the Biology of Whales, The Whale Problem: A Status Report (Cambridge, MA: Harvard University Press, 1974), 17.

WC
International Conference on the Biology of Whales. The Whale Problem: A Status Report. Cambridge, MA: Harvard University Press, 1974.

MLA (International Conference on the Biology of Whales 17)
International Conference on the Biology of Whales. The Whale Problem: A Status Report. Cambrige, MA: Harvard U P, 1974.

APA (International Conference on the Biology of Whales, 1974, p. 17)
International Conference on the Biology of Whales. (1974). The whale problem: A status report. Cambridge, MA: Harvard University Press.

A REPRINTED BOOK

N
   [12]Charles Darwin, Diary of the Voyage of H. M. S. Beagle (1845, reprinted ed., New York: Kraus, 1969), 79.

WC
Darwin, Charles. Diary of the Voyage of H. M. S. Beagle. 1845; reprinted ed., New York: Kraus, 1969.

MLA (Darwin 79)
Darwin, Charles. <u>Diary of the Voyage of H. M. S. Beagle</u>. 1845. New York: Kraus, 1969.

APA (Darwin, 1845/1969, p. 79)
Darwin, C. (1969). <u>Diary of the voyage of H. M. S. Beagle</u>. New York: Kraus. (Original work published 1845)

A POEM, SHORT STORY, ESSAY, OR CHAPTER IN A BOOK BY THE SAME AUTHOR

N

[13]Vicki Hearne, "What Is It about the Frog," <u>In the Absence of Horses</u> (Princeton, NJ: Princeton University Press, 1983), 16-17.

WC

Hearne, Vicki. "What Is It about the Frog." <u>In the Absence of Horses</u>. Princeton, NJ: Princeton University Press, 1983.

MLA (Hearne 16)
Hearne, Vicki. "What Is It about the Frog." <u>In the Absence of Horses</u>. Princeton, NJ: Princeton U P, 1983.

APA (Hearne, 1983, p. 16)
Hearne, V. (1983). What is it about the frog. In V. Hearne <u>In the absence of horses</u> (pp. 16-17). Princeton, NJ: Princeton University Press.

A POEM, SHORT STORY, ESSAY, OR CHAPTER IN A BOOK COLLECTION OF DIFFERENT AUTHORS

N

[14]Gavan Daws, "'Animal Liberation' as Crime: The Hawaii Dolphin Case," in <u>Ethics and Animals</u>, eds. Harlan B. Miller and William H. Williams (Clifton, NJ: Humana Press, 1983), 362.

WC

Daws, Gavan. "'Animal Liberation' as Crime: The Hawaii Dolphin Case." In <u>Ethics and Animals</u>, eds. Harlan B. Miller and William H. Williams, 361-371. Clifton, NJ: Humana Press, 1983.

MLA (Daws 362)
Daws, Gavan. "'Animal Liberation' as Crime: The Hawaii Dolphin Case." <u>Ethics and Animals</u>. Eds. H. B. Miller and W. H. Williams. Clifton, NJ: Humana Press, 1983. 361-371.

APA (Daws, 1983, p. 362)
Daws, G. (1983) "Animal liberation" as crime: The Hawaii dolphin case. In H. B. Miller & W. H. Williams (Eds.), <u>Ethics and animals</u> (pp. 361-371). Clifton, NJ: Humana Press.

A REVIEW OF A BOOK

N

[15]Peter Singer, "Unkind to Animals," review of <u>Animal Liberators: Research and Morality</u>, by Susan Sperling, <u>New York Review of Books</u> 2 February 1989, 36.

WC

Singer, Peter. ''Unkind to Animals.'' Review of <u>Animal Liberators: Research and Morality</u>, by Susan Sperling. In <u>New York Review of Books</u>, 2 February 1989, 36-38.

MLA (Singer 37)

Singer, Peter. ''Unkind to Animals.'' Rev. of <u>Animal Liberators: Research and Morality</u>, by Susan Sperling. <u>New York Review of Books</u> 2 Feb. 1989: 36-38.

APA (Singer, 1989, p. 37)

Singer, P. (1989, February 2). Unkind to animals [Review of <u>Animal liberators: Research and morality</u>]. <u>New York Review of Books</u>, <u>36</u>, 36-38.

A GOVERNMENT PUBLICATION

N

[16]U.S. Congress, Office of Technology Assessment, <u>Alternatives to Animal Use in Research, Testing, and Education</u> (Washington, DC: Government Printing Office, 1986), 34.

WC

U.S. Congress, Office of Technology Assessment. <u>Alternatives to Animal Use in Research, Testing, and Education</u>. Washington, DC: Government Printing Office, 1986.

MLA (U.S. Cong. 34)

United States. Cong. Office of Technology Assessment. <u>Alternatives to Animal Use in Research, Testing, and Education</u>. Washington, DC: Government Printing Office, 1986.

APA (Office of Technology Assessment, 1986, p. 34)

Office of Technology Assessment. (1986). <u>Alternatives to animal use in research, testing, and education</u>. Washington, DC: U.S. Government Printing Office.

A PAMPHLET (FOLLOW FORMAT FOR A BOOK AS MUCH AS YOU CAN)

N

[17]<u>Are You Willing to be the Guinea Pig Instead</u>, handout. (Los Angeles: CFAAR [Coalition for Animals and Animal Research], 1989).

WC

<u>Are You Willing to be the Guinea Pig Instead</u>. Handout. Los Angeles: CFAAR [Coalition for Animals and Animal Research], 1989.

MLA (Are You Willing)

<u>Are You Willing to be the Guinea Pig Instead</u>. Handout. Los Angeles: CFAAR [Coalition for Animals and Animal Research], 1989.

APA (<u>Are You Willing to be the Guinea Pig Instead</u>)

<u>Are you willing to be the guinea pig instead</u> [handout]. Los Angeles: CFAAR (Coalition for Animals and Animal Research).

Periodicals

AN ARTICLE FROM A SCHOLARLY JOURNAL*

N

[19]C. Dumas, ''Cognitive Development in Kittens,'' Journal of Comparative Psychology 103 (June 1989): 192.

WC

Dumas, C. ''Cognitive Development in Kittens,'' Journal of Comparative Psychology 103 (June 1989): 191-200.

MLA (Dumas 192)

Dumas, C. ''Cognitive Development in Kittens.'' Journal of Comparative Psychology 103 (June 1989): 191-200.

APA (Dumas, 1989, p. 192)

Dumas, C. (1989). Cognitive development in kittens. Journal of Comparative Psychology, 103, 191-200.

AN ARTICLE FROM A GENERAL INTEREST MAGAZINE*

N

[20]N. C. Comfort, ''Can You Love Animals and Kill Them?'' Utne Reader, September-October 1989, 46.

WC

Comfort, N. C. ''Can You Love Animals and Kill Them?'' Utne Reader, September-October 1989, 46-7.

MLA (Comfort 46)

Comfort, N. C. ''Can You Love Animals and Kill Them?'' Utne Reader Sept.-Oct. 1989: 46-47.

APA (Comfort, 1989, p. 46)

Comfort, N. C. (1989, September-December). Can you love animals and kill them? Utne Reader, pp. 46-47.

AN ANONYMOUS MAGAZINE ARTICLE

N

[21]''Transgenic Animals: Direct Delivery,'' Economist, 1 July 1989, 70.

WC

''Transgenic Animals: Direct Delivery.'' Economist, 1 July 1989, 70-71.

MLA (''Transgenic Animals'' 70)

''Transgenic Animals: Direct Delivery.'' Economist 1 July 1989: 70-71.

APA (''Transgenic Animals,'' 1989, p. 70)

Transgenic animals: Direct delivery. (1 July 1989). Economist, pp. 70-71.

---

*Scholarly journals usually appear four times a year and have volume numbers. General interest magazines are the kind you find in a doctor's waiting room. General interest magazines appear weekly or monthly. Although they may have a volume number, they are identified by the date, not the volume number.

AN ARTICLE FROM A NEWSPAPER

N

²²Elizabeth Venant and David Treadwell, ''Biting Back: Animal Researchers, Industries Go on Offensive against Increasingly Militant Activists,'' Los Angeles Times, 12 April 1990, sec. E, pp. 12-13.

WC

Venant, Elizabeth and David Treadwell. ''Biting Back: Animal Researchers, Industries Go on Offensive against Increasingly Militant Activists.'' Los Angeles Times, 12 April 1990, sec. E, pp. 12-13.

MLA (Venant and Treadwell 12-13)

Venant, Elizabeth and David Treadwell. ''Biting Back: Animal Researchers, Industries Go on Offensive against Increasingly Militant Activists.'' Los Angeles Times 12 April 1990: sec. E: 12-13.

APA (Venant & Treadwell, 1990, pp. 12-13)

Venant, E., & Treadwell, D. (1990, April 12). Biting back: Animal researchers, industries go on offensive against increasingly militant activists. The Los Angeles Times, sec. E, pp. 12-13.

Encyclopedias

AN ARTICLE IN A GENERAL ENCYCLOPEDIA (THAT IS, ONE THAT IS FREQUENTLY UPDATED), AUTHOR NAMED

N

²³Encyclopedia Americana, 1989 ed., s.v. ''Animal Experimentation,'' by John C. Rose, M.D.

WC

Encyclopedia Americana, 1989 ed. S.v. ''Animal Experimentation,'' by John C. Rose, M.D.

MLA (Rose)

Rose, John C., M.D. ''Animal Experimentation.'' Encyclopedia Americana, 1989 ed.

APA (Rose, 1989)

Rose, J. Animal experimentation. Encyclopedia americana, 1989 ed.

AN ARTICLE IN A SPECIALIZED REFERENCE WORK (ONE NOT FREQUENTLY UPDATED)

N

²⁴Raymond J. Corsini, ed. Encyclopedia of Psychology (New York: Wiley, 1984), s.v. ''Bonding and Attachment,'' by Robert W. Zaslow.

WC

Corsini, Raymond J., ed. Encyclopedia of Psychology. New York: Wiley, 1984. S.v. ''Bonding and Attachment,'' by Robert W. Zaslow.

MLA (Zaslow)
Zaslow, Robert W. ''Bonding and Attachment.'' Encyclopedia of
    Psychology. Ed. Raymond J. Corsini. New York: Wiley, 1984.

APA (Zaslow, 1984)
Zaslow, R. W. (1984). Bonding and attachment. In R. J. Corsini (Ed.),
    Encyclopedia of psychology (pp. 160-162). New York: Wiley.

AN ANONYMOUS ARTICLE IN AN ENCYCLOPEDIA

N
       [25]Encyclopaedia Britannica: Micropedia, 1985 ed., v.s.
''Hypnosis.''

WC
Encyclopaedia Britannica: Micropedia, 1985 ed. S. v. ''Hypnosis.''

MLA (''Hypnosis'')
''Hypnosis.'' Encyclopaedia Britannica: Micropedia, 1985 ed.

APA (''Hypnosis,'' 1985)
Hypnosis. Encyclopaedia britannica: Micropedia, 1985 ed.

Other Sources

A LECTURE

N
       [26]Professor Bob Hamilton, lecture, Geography 10, Los Angeles,
CA, 23 October 1990.

WC
Hamilton, Bob. Lecture, Geography 10. Los Angeles, CA. 23 October 1990.

MLA (Hamilton)
Hamilton, Bob. Lecture. Geography 10. UCLA, Los Angeles, CA. 23
    October 1990.

APA (Hamilton, 1990)
Hamilton, B. (1990, October 23). [Lecture for Geography 10].

AN INTERVIEW

N
       [27]Garrett Hardin, interview by author, Santa Barbara, CA, 16
February 1989.

WC
Hardin, Garrett. Interview by author. Santa Barbara, CA. 16 February
    1989.

MLA (Hardin)
Hardin, Garrett. Personal Interview. Santa Barbara, CA, 16 Feb. 1989.

APA: **Source identified in text of paper only, not in References:**
Professor Garrett Hardin (personal communication, February 16, 1989)
suggested that . . .

A FILM

N

²⁸Blade Runner, with Harrison Ford, Warner Bros., 1982.

WC

Blade Runner. With Harrison Ford. Warner Bros. 1982.

MLA (Blade Runner)

Blade Runner. Dir. Ridley Scott. With Harrison Ford. Warner Bros. 1982.

APA (Blade Runner, 1982)

Scott, R. (Director) & Ford, H. (Actor). (1982). Blade runner [Film]. Los Angeles, CA: Warner Bros.

A LIVE PERFORMANCE (CONCERT OR PLAY)—BEGIN WITH THE MOST IMPORTANT PERSON (CONDUCTOR, PERFORMER, AUTHOR, COMPOSER, DIRECTOR, ETC.)

N

²⁹Arthur Miller, The Crucible, Los Angeles Theater Center, Los Angeles, CA, 13 October 1990.

WC

Miller, Arthur. The Crucible. Los Angeles Theater Center, Los Angeles, CA, 13 October 1990.

MLA (Miller)

Miller, Arthur. The Crucible. Dir. Bill Bushnell. Los Angeles Theater Center, Los Angeles, CA. 13 Oct. 1990.

APA: Source identified in text of paper only, not in References:

The October 13th stage performance of The Crucible at the Los Angeles Theater Center, clearly demonstrated Arthur Miller's understanding of . . .

A RECORDING

N

³⁰Josafat Roel and David Lewiston, jacket notes for Fiestas of Peru. Music of the High Andes, Nonesuch Records Explorer Series H-72045.

WC

Roel, Josafat and David Lewiston. Jacket notes for Fiestas of Peru. Music of the High Andes. Nonesuch Records Explorer Series H-72045.

MLA (Roel and Lewiston)

Roel, Josafat and David Lewiston. Jacket notes. Fiestas of Peru. Music of the High Andes. Nonesuch Explorer Ser., H-72045, 1972.

APA (Roel & Lewiston, 1972)

Roel, J., & Lewiston, D. (1972). Fiestas of Peru. Music of the High Andes [Jacket notes for audiorecording No. H-72045]. New York: Nonesuch Records Explorer Series.

A RADIO OR TELEVISION PROGRAM

N

³¹PBS, ''The Decade of Destruction,'' *Frontline*, 18 September 1990.

WC

PBS, ''The Decade of Destruction.'' *Frontline*, 18 September 1990.

MLA (''The Decade of Destruction'')

''The Decade of Destruction.'' *Frontline*. New York: PBS. KCET, Los Angeles. 18 Sept. 1990.

APA (''The Decade of Destruction,'' 1990)

Frontline. (1990, September 18). Los Angeles: PBS-TV.

A COMPUTER PROGRAM

N

³²Pro-Cite (Ann Arbor, MI: Personal Bibliographic Software, Inc.).

WC

Pro-Cite. Personal Bibliographic Software, Inc., Ann Arbor, MI.

MLA (Pro-Cite)

Pro-Cite. Computer software. Personal Bibliographic Software, 1988.

APA (Pro-Cite, 1988)

Pro-Cite [Computer program]. (1988). Ann Arbor, MI: Personal Bibliographic Software.

A WORK OF ART

N

³³Emanuel Gottlieb Leutze, *Washington Crossing the Delaware*, oil on canvas, 1851, Metropolitan Museum of Art, New York.

WC

Leutze, Emanuel Gottlieb. *Washington Crossing the Delaware*. Oil on canvas. 1851. Metropolitan Museum of Art, New York.

MLA (Leutze)

Leutze, Emanuel Gottlieb. *Washington Crossing the Delaware*. Metropolitan Museum of Art, New York.

APA (Leutze, 1851)

Leutze, E. G. (1851). *Washington Crossing the Delaware* [Art work]. New York: Metropolitan Museum of Art.

A LETTER

N

³⁴Garrett Hardin to the author, 8 August 1983.

WC

Hardin, Garrett, to the author, 8 August 1983.

MLA (Hardin)
Hardin, Garrett. Letter to the author. 8 August 1983.

APA: Source identified in text of paper only, not in References:
Biologists generally agree (G. Hardin, personal communication, February 16, 1983) that...

The preceding models illustrate those most commonly needed in undergraduate papers. For more examples we refer you to the following guides:

NOTE:
Turabian, Kate L. *A Manual for Writers of Term Papers, Theses and Dissertations*, 5th ed. Ed. Bonnie Birtwistle Honigsblum. Chicago: University of Chicago Press, 1987.

MLA:
Gibaldi, Joseph, and Walter S. Achtert. *MLA Handbook for Writers of Research Papers*, 3rd ed. New York: Modern Language Association of America, 1988.

APA:
American Psychological Association. (1983). *Publication Manual of the American Psychological Association* (3rd ed.). Washington, DC: American Psychological Association.

Abbreviations

Here are the most common abbreviations used in the three major systems (Note, MLA, APA). Plurals are indicated within parentheses; for example, chap(s). means chapter = chap. and chapters = chaps.

TERM	NOTE	MLA	APA
chapter	chap(s).	ch(s).	chap.
part	pt(s).	pt(s).	Pt.
volume	vol(s).	vol(s).	Vol.
page	p. (pp.)	p. (pp.)	p. (pp.)
edition	ed.	ed.	ed.
editor(s)	ed(s).	Ed(s).	Ed(s).
revised edition			rev. ed.
section	sec(s).	sec(s).	
translated by	trans.	trans.	Trans.
number	no(s).	no(s).	No.
no date	n.d.	n.d.	
no place	n.p.	N.p.	
no publisher	n.p.	n.p.	
and others		et al.	et al.
directed by		dir.	
quoted		qtd.	
University Press		UP	

FORMATTING A FINAL DRAFT: NOTE SYSTEM

Arranging and Citing Sources

1. Number your textual references—either footnotes or endnotes—consecutively throughout the paper.

2. You only need to indicate where you found information, not where the writer you read got it. If your source quotes a point you want to make, indicate it like this:

>   [16]Quoted by Frankie L. Trull, ''Animal Research is Critical to Continued Progress in Human Health,'' USA Today March 1988, 54.

3. Ibid.—What It Is and When to Use It. Ibid. is an abbreviation of a Latin word that means "in the same place." It is used in footnotes as a shortcut. If you want to footnote information from a source that you have identified immediately before in a footnote, then you can use this abbreviation. You can only use Ibid. if no other information comes in between Ibid. and your previous footnote to this source. Ibid. means the same source and the same page. If you want to refer to the same source but a different page, add the different page number.

Example:

>   [19]Singer, 87.
>
>   [20]Zak, 69.
>
>   [21]Ibid.
>
>   [22]Ibid., 70.

4. Sometimes you can avoid sprinkling many numbers throughout a passage in your paper by an appropriate running acknowledgment and subsequent single textual reference. Instead of using three textual references like this:

Equal rights for animals have been claimed by Peter Singer,[7] Tom Regan,[8] and John Passmore,[9] to mention only a few.

do this:

Several distinguised philosophers[7] have claimed equal rights for animals.

Then identify Singer, Regan, and Passmore in one note:

>   [7]Peter Singer, The Expanding Circle: Ethics and Sociobiology (New York: Farrar, Straus and Giroux, 1981) and Practical Ethics (Cambridge UK and New York: Cambridge University Press, 1979); Tom Regan, The Case for Animal Rights (Berkeley: University of California

Press, 1986); John Passmore, Man's Responsibility for Nature: Ecological Problems and Western Traditions (New York: Scribner's, 1974).

5. If you have two or more sources by the same author, in the Works Cited section give the author's name only in the first entry, arranged alphabetically. For a second entry, or more, type eight hyphens and a period. Continue as usual with the title and publication data.

Singer, Peter. The Expanding Circle: Ethics and Sociobiology.
    New York: Farrar, Straus and Giroux, 1981.

--------. Practical Ethics. Cambridge UK and New York: Cambridge University Press, 1979.

Typing Guidelines—Note System

1. Double-space the text of your paper, but single-space notes and block quotations.

2. Type or print on one side only of white, unruled paper. Do not use the type of paper that smudges easily. Make sure that the type is dark enough to be easily readable. If you are using a word processor, separate the pages and trim the margins.

3. Leave one-inch margins on the top, bottom, and right margin of each page. Leave a one and one-half margin on the left side.

4. A separate title page is required. Place your name, your instructor's name, the course name and number, and the date on separate lines, and center them on the page. Do not number the title page.

5. An outline or table of contents should follow the title page. Do not number this page.

6. Repeat the title of your paper and center it at the top of the first page of your text. Place the number of the first page in the bottom center.

7. Number all the other pages at the top right (except on any page with a heading, e.g., Notes, if you use endnotes, or Appendix, or Works Cited; in which case, place the number in the bottom center). Do not use an abbreviation (p.) or any punctuation with the number.

8. Indent the beginning of each paragraph six spaces. Indent block quotations four spaces.

9. If you are using footnotes, separate them from the text of your paper by typing an unbroken line for twenty spaces from the left margin. Endnotes are placed on a separate page after the body of your paper. Indent the beginning of each footnote six spaces. The footnote number should be raised one-half line. Don't put a period or space after the number. Single-space within footnotes, but double-space between each note.

10. Any content notes should be numbered consecutively throughout your paper. Place the content notes on a separate page, titled Notes, inserted before the Works Cited section.

11. Graphs, charts, tables, and any other illustrative material should be placed in an Appendix. At the top of each item, place a number and title (e.g., Graph 1. Workers Enrolled in Pension Plans). Refer to the number or title in your paragraph so that it is clear to the reader why you are including this material. The source of the material should be indicated below the illustration. The Appendix is inserted just before the Works Cited section.

12. The list of sources comes last in your paper. Title it Works Cited. Each entry should begin at the left margin. Indent subsequent lines five spaces. Single-space within the entry, but double-space between entries.

13. Proofread carefully and correct any errors in ink.

FORMATTING A FINAL DRAFT: PARENTHESIS SYSTEM, MLA

Arranging and Citing Sources

1. Information within parentheses includes author's name and page number (Hart 22) unless the author is named in the sentence.

2. The first time you name an author in one of your sentences, provide the full name:

```
Kathleen Hart describes one of the better known, genetically produced
monsters, the Beltsville pig, as ''bowlegged, cross-eyed, arthritic,
and barely able to stand up'' (22).
```

Subsequently, refer to the author by surname only.

3. It is often a good idea to frame the information you cite by providing additional information about the author's credentials:

```
Hart quotes Adelle Douglas, director of the Washington DC office of
the American Humane Association, who explains that ''the point . . . is
that you're intentionally passing on those genes, transferring the
suffering from generation to generation'' (22).
```

4. Place the parenthesis as near as possible to the information it cites where a pause would naturally occur, usually at the end of the sentence.

5. If you are borrowing information from two or more sources by the same author, then the name and page alone would not be enough. In this case, you must add a brief title:

```
Women and blacks, like animals today, were once deprived of rights
(Singer, Expanding Circle 3).
```

6. If there is no author, then use the title within parentheses to identify the source. The title can be shortened:

A California high school student who claimed that a class exercise in frog dissection violated her religious freedom lost her case when the judge said that ''to push the issue further would border on the absurd'' (''Frog Suit Croaks'' 458).

Note the punctuation within the parentheses:

name of author(s) + space + page number(s)

If you need to add the title, too, then:

name of author(s) + comma + space + title + space + page number(s)

Typing Guidelines—Parenthesis System, MLA

1. Double-space the entire paper—headings, text, list of sources, and block quotations.
2. Type or print on one side only of white, unruled paper. Do not use the type of paper that smudges easily. Make sure that the type is dark enough to be easily readable. If you are using a word processor, separate the pages and trim the margins.
3. Leave one-inch margins on the sides, top, and bottom of each page.
4. A separate title page is not required. Place your name, your instructor's name, the course name and number, and the date on separate lines, flush with the left margin, at the top of your first page.
5. Indent paragraphs five spaces. Indent block quotations ten spaces.
6. Place your last name, a space, and the number for each page one-half inch from the upper right corner and flush with the right margin. Number the pages consecutively throughout the entire paper, including the Works Cited section.
7. Graphs, charts, tables, and any other illustrative material should be placed near the paragraph to which it relates in your paper. At the top, place a number and title (e.g., Graph 1. Workers Enrolled in Pension Plans). Refer to the number or title in your paragraph so that it is clear to the reader why you are inserting this material. The source of the material should be indicated below the illustration.
 Some instructors may prefer to have all illustrations placed in an Appendix. Check with your instructor. The Appendix is inserted after the body of your paper and before the Works Cited section.
8. Any content notes should be numbered consecutively throughout your paper. Place the content notes on a separate page, titled Notes, inserted before the Works Cited section.
9. The list of sources comes last in your paper. Title it Works Cited.
10. Proofread carefully and correct any errors in ink.

FORMATTING A FINAL DRAFT: PARENTHESIS SYSTEM, APA

Arranging and Citing Sources

1. Information within parentheses includes author's name, date, and page number (Kaplan, 1988, p. 839) unless the author and date are identified elsewhere in the sentence. Consider these two examples:

>One supporter pointed out that ''the researchers, constrained by concern for the privacy of patients and the dictates of good taste, have hesitated to show the photographs of human burn victims or of quadriplegics to offset the pathetic pictures of the animals used in the research'' (Kaplan, 1988, p. 839).

>Kaplan (1988) pointed out that ''the researchers, constrained by concern for the privacy of patients and the dictates of good taste, have hesitated to show the photographs of human burn victims or of quadriplegics to offset the pathetic pictures of the animals used in the research'' (p. 839).

2. Within your sentence, place the date information within parentheses as close after the author's name as you can. Note these possible alternatives:

>Kaplan (1988) pointed out . . .

>In a recent defense of animal experimentation (Kaplan, 1988), photographs . . .

>In 1988, Kaplan defended animal experimentation by . . .

3. Always cite both names every time you acknowledge borrowing from a source with two authors: (Adamson & Sieber, 1983).

4. If the work has more than two authors, cite their surnames completely the first time, and then cite only the first author's surname, followed by "et al." and the year.

First: (Romski, White, Miller, & Rumbaugh, 1984)

Later: (Romski et al., 1984)

5. When you want to credit several sources with the same information, separate the entries by semicolons and arrange them in the same order as in the References section: (Regan, 1983; Singer, 1989)

6. When you cite several sources by the same author, list the earliest publication first. Use lowercase letters (a, b, c) to distinguish works published in the same year.

Hilgard, E. R. (1973). The domain of hypnosis: With some comments on alternative paradigms. American Psychologist, 28, 972-981.

Hilgard, E. R. (1979a). Divided consciousness in hypnosis: The implications of the hidden observer. Journal of Abnormal Psychology, 84, 196-208.

Hilgard, E. R. (1979b). Hypnosis and ego development. American Journal of Clinical Hypnosis, 15, 211-223.

Typing Guidelines—Parenthesis System, APA

1. Double-space the entire paper—title page, abstract, headings, text, list of sources, and block quotations.

2. Type or print on one side only of white, unruled paper. Do not use the type of paper that smudges easily. Make sure that the type is dark enough to be easily readable. If you are using a word processor, separate the pages and trim the margins.

3. Leave one and one-half inch margins on the sides, top, and bottom of each page.

4. A separate title page is required. The title of the paper, your name, the name and number of the course, and the date should be centered and double-spaced in the middle of the page. In the top right corner, place the key words of your title. Place the page number below the brief title and flush with the right margin.

5. A separate page is required for the abstract, a one-paragraph summary of your paper. Do not indent the paragraph.

6. Place your brief title and, below it, the number for each page flush with the right margin. Number the pages consecutively throughout the entire paper, including the title page, abstract, and References section.

7. Indent the beginning of each paragraph five spaces. Indent block quotations five spaces. If the quote is longer than one paragraph, indent the beginning of subsequent paragraphs an additional five spaces.

8. Graphs, charts, tables, and any other illustrative material should be placed near the paragraph to which they relate in your paper. At the top, place a number and title (e.g., Graph 1. Workers Enrolled in Pension Plans). Refer to the number or title in your paragraph so that it is clear to the reader why you are inserting this material. Place any explanatory notes below the table or illustration. Also indicate the source of the material if you did not create it yourself.

Some instructors may prefer to have all illustrations placed in an Appendix. Check with your instructor. The Appendix is inserted after References and Footnotes.

9. Any content notes should be numbered consecutively throughout your paper. Place the content notes on a separate page, titled Footnotes, and insert after the References.

10. The list of sources comes last in your paper. Title it References.

11. Proofread carefully and correct any errors in ink.

NUMBER SYSTEM: A VARIATION OF THE PARENTHESIS SYSTEM

Some sciences prefer a variation of the parenthesis system that uses a number to refer to the source being cited. Here is an example of a few paragraphs from the beginning of an article in *The American Journal of Maternal/Child Nursing*:

Children affected by prenatal abuse of alcohol, illegal drugs, and drugs available at pharmacies or groceries are a growing concern of nurses. Professional literature describes maternal substance abuse and the damage evident in neonates at birth (1-3). Limited information, however, is available that reflects in-depth study of affected neonates as they progress to infancy and toddlerhood. (See *MCN*, Jan./Feb. 1989, pp. 44–46.)

Probably the most commonly used teratogenic substance is alcohol (1). Because the placenta affords no protection to the fetus from alcohol, the ethanol concentration in the mother's blood reaches the fetus essentially unaltered. The impact of alcohol on the fetus, however, may be greater than it is on the mother because of the higher ratio of fetal blood alcohol to body weight, and inefficient fetal liver and renal ethanol clearance. Alcohol and its first metabolite, acetaldehyde, probably impair nutrient and oxygen transport to the fetus, and thereby inhibit protein synthesis and cellular growth (2).

The most severe effect of maternal alcohol ingestion—fetal alcohol syndrome (FAS)—is characterized by cranial and midface dysmorphia, central nervous system dysfunction, and poor prenatal and postnatal growth (evident in weight, height, and head circumference, and organ systems development). The most characteristic dysmorphic facial features are short palpebral fissures; broad, low nasal bridge; short, upturned nose; and flattened philtrum and thin upper lip (2). Related features frequently include microcephaly with associated mental deficit, epicanthic folds, strabismus, ptosis, and micrognathia. Mothers who have more than five drinks daily or who go on binges risk having a baby with fetal alcohol syndrome.

(Numbers refer to sources listed at end of the article.)

Free, T., Russell, F., Mills, B., & Hathaway, D. A descriptive study of infants and toddlers exposed prenatally to substance abuse. *The American Journal of Maternal/Child Nursing* 15:245–49, July/August 1990.

The numbers in parentheses refer to sources on a page of References at the end of the article. As is true with the other variations of the parenthesis system, you can insert the author's name, a specific page reference, or both.

Example: Author's name inserted: `(Bolsen, 1)`
Page reference inserted: `(1, p. 1543)`
Both: `(Bolsen, 1, p. 1543)`

There are two ways to number the list of references at the end of your paper. One possibility is to alphabetize the list and number each entry. The number corresponding to the source is then inserted in your paper. A second possibility, which is used in most of the medical journals, is to number each source as you use it. The list of references for the article from the *American Journal of Maternal/Child Nursing* is shown below. Notice that each entry contains the author's name (inverted and all capitalized), the title of the article (only the first word is capitalized), the name of the journal (abbreviations are used, and the title is italicized or underlined), volume number, and inclusive pages, the date.

REFERENCES

List of sources is arranged numerically, rather than alphabetically.

1. STREISSGUTH, A. P., AND LADUE, R. A. Psychological and behavioral effects in children prenatally exposed to alcohol. *Alcohol Health Res. World* 10:6–12, Fall 1985.
2. PETRAKIS, P. L. *Alcohol and Birth Defects: The Fetal Alcohol Syndrome and Related Disorders* (DHHS Publ. No. (ADM) 87-1531). Rockville, MD: U.S. Department of Health and Human Services, 1987.
3. DOBERCZAK, T. M., AND OTHERS. Impact of maternal drug dependency on birth weight and head circumference of offspring. *Am.J.Dis.Child.* 141:1163–1167, Nov. 1987.
4. SMITH, D. W. The fetal alcohol syndrome. *Hosp.Pract.* 14:121–128, Oct. 1979.
5. McCARTHY, P. A. Fetal alcohol syndrome and other alcohol-related birth defects. *Nurse Pract.* 8:33–37, Jan. 1983.
6. STEPHENS, C. J. The fetal alcohol syndrome: cause for concern. *MCN* 6:251–256. July–Aug. 1981.
7. ERB, L., AND ANDRESEN, B. D. Hyperactivity: a possible consequence of maternal alcohol consumption. *Pediatr.Nurs.* 7:30–33, 51 July–Aug. 1981.
8. STREISSGUTH, A. P., AND OTHERS. Natural history of the fetal alcohol syndrome: a 10-year follow-up of eleven patients. *Lancet* 2:85–92, July 13, 1985.
9. DAY, N. L., AND OTHERS. Measurement of substance use during pregnancy: methodological issues. *Natl.Inst.Drug Abuse, Res. Monogr. Ser.* 59:36–47, 1985.
10. SMITH, J. E. The dangers of prenatal cocaine use. *MCN* 13:174–179, May–June 1988.
11. ABEL, E. L. Effects of prenatal exposure to cannabinoids. *Natl.Inst. Drug Abuse Res. Monogr. Ser.* 59:20–35, 1985.
12. HAYES, J. S., AND OTHERS. Newborn outcomes with maternal marijuana use in Jamaican women. *Pediatr.Nurs.* 14:107–110, Mar.–Apr. 1988.
13. TENNES. K., AND OTHERS. Marijuana: prenatal and postnatal exposure in the human. *Natl.Inst.Drug Abuse Res.Monogr.Ser.* 59:48–60, 1985.
14. FRIED, P. A. Postnatal consequences of maternal marijuana use. *Natl.Inst.Drug Abuse Res.Monogr.Ser.* 59:61–72, 1985.
15. HINGSON, R., AND OTHERS. Effects of maternal drinking and marijuana use on fetal growth and development. *Pediatrics* 70:539–546, Oct. 1982.

16. CHASNOFF, I. J., AND OTHERS. Cocaine use in pregnancy. *N.Engl.J.Med.* 313:666–669, Sept. 12, 1985.
17. ORO, A. S., AND DIXON, S. D. Perinatal cocaine and methamphetamine exposure: maternal and neonatal correlates. *J.Pediatr.* 111:571–577, Oct. 1987.
18. HEINS, M., AND SEIDEN, A. M. Parenting and the pediatrician. *Am.J.Dis.Child.* 141:1188–1192, Nov. 1987.
19. HOWARD, B. Single parenting in America. *Early Childh. Update* 5:1, Winter 1989.

SUMMARY OF MAJOR SYSTEMS OF DOCUMENTATION

Here are the same two sentences extracted from the middle of a research paper illustrating four different systems:

Note System

Animal experimentation is becoming more expensive. ''For example, a rhesus monkey costs from $600 to $1200 to purchase, and several hundred dollars annually to maintain.''[15]

[15]Frederick A. King and others, ''Limitations and Constraints in the Use of Primates,'' <u>Science</u> 10 June 1988, 1481.

MLA System

Animal experimentation is becoming more expensive. ''For example, a rhesus monkey costs from $600 to $1200 to purchase, and several hundred dollars annually to maintain'' (King et al. 1481).

APA System

Animal experimentation is becoming more expensive. ''For example, a rhesus monkey costs from $600 to $1200 to purchase, and several hundred dollars annually to maintain'' (King et al., 1988, p. 1481).

Number System

Animal experimentation is becoming more expensive. ''For example, a rhesus monkey costs from $600 to $1200 to purchase, and several hundred dollars annually to maintain'' (15).

Here is this borrowed source documented in four corresponding bibliographical citations:

Note System

Works Cited

King, Frederick A., and others. ''Limitations and Constraints in the Use of Primates.'' Science, 10 June 1988, 1475-1482.

MLA System

Works Cited

King, Frederick A., et al. ''Limitations and Constraints in the Use of Primates.'' Science: 10 June 1988, 1475-1482.

APA System

References

King, F. A., Yarbrough, C., Anderson, D. C., Gordon, T.P., & Gould, K. G. (1988). Limitations and constraints in the use of primates. Science, 240, 1475-1482.

Number System

REFERENCES

15. KING, F.A., AND OTHERS. Limitations and constraints in the use of primates. Science 240:1475-1482, 1988.

EXERCISES

A. Here are several sentences from the middle of a research paper. Documentation is omitted for the purposes of this exercise. The reference is to John Passmore's book titled *Man's Responsibility for Nature: Ecological Problems and Western Traditions*. It was published in 1974 in New York by Scribner's.

DOCUMENTING YOUR SOURCES 259

> John Passmore makes an important distinction between conservation and preservation. According to him, preservationists want to save something, like endangered species, from damage or extinction; conservationists want to save it for later use.

_____ **Footnote System**

1. Insert the textual reference in this passage. It is note number 11.
2. Make up a first note to citation number 11.
3. Make up an immediately following subsequent note. It is note number 12.
4. Make up a subsequent note to this citation. It is note number 23.
5. Make up a Works Cited entry for this citation.

_____ **MLA System**

1. Insert correct parenthetical information in the passage to identify the source.
2. Make up a Works Cited entry for this citation.

_____ **APA System**

1. Insert correct parenthetical information in the passage to identify the source.
2. Make up a References entry for this citation.

_____ **Number System**

1. Insert a numbered reference to this source. It is number 11.
2. Make up a REFERENCES entry for this citation.

B. Make a bibliography according to one of the three major systems (Note, MLA, APA) for the readings in the Anthology.

Worksheet 14 _____ **DOCUMENTATION**

Name _____ Date _____

List the sources you have used for your paper, using either the note format or the parenthesis format.

The following final checklist is for you to fill in before you hand in your research paper.

FINAL CHECKLIST

_____ The paper is organized to support my thesis.
_____ The thesis reflects my insight on the topic I researched.
_____ The paper is based on the best information available on the topic.
_____ I used the required number of _____ sources.
_____ Information from the sources has been integrated to show my understanding of the topic.
_____ The paper meets the required length of at least _____ words/pages.
_____ It has a proper title page.
_____ It has an outline page that begins with a statement of my thesis or it has an abstract.
_____ The introduction clearly states my thesis.
_____ I have used separate paragraphs to develop the ideas in my argument.
_____ I have put most of the information into my own words.
_____ Quotation marks have been used around any words, phrases, or sentences that are copied exactly from a source.
_____ All quotations are documented.
_____ Paraphrases of facts and opinions from sources are documented.
_____ Documentation follows the NOTE or PARENTHESIS (circle one) form.

1. This paper is *completely* or *essentially* (circle one) my own work.
2. I wish to acknowledge help from the following people. (Explain who helped you do what: proofreading, typing, finding sources, etc.).

Signed _____

Date _____

CHAPTER 10

Sample Research Papers

ILLUSTRATION OF THE NOTE SYSTEM

Center information
on the page:
   title
   author's name
   instructor's name
   course
   date

Redress: From the Congressional Floor to the Hearts of the

Japanese Americans

by

Kevin M. Uriu

Dr. Ellen Strenski

English 100W

4 August 1988

No page number
on title page

Kevin has provided a topic outline rather than a sentence outline. Note the parallel structure.

                              Outline

Thesis: The main reason for the delay in getting redress was the
       complexity of the issue, caused by the different attitudes of the
       three generations of Japanese Americans involved.

Introduction
    A. Congressman Mineta's typical wartime experience
    B. Recent legislation to compensate internees
    C. Purpose of paper: to explore disagreements about redress in
       order to explain why redress has taken so long (over 40 years)
I. General responses of the three Japanese American generations
    A. Issei (first generation)
    B. Nisei (second generation)
    C. Sansei (third generation)
II. Commission on Wartime Relocation and Internment of Citizens
III. Arguments for and against monetary redress
    A. General criticism: no possible price tag
    B. General support
        1. Symbolic
        2. Preventive
    C. Hayakawa's specific criticisms
        1. Redress unnecessary: higher Japanese American income
        2. Redress irrelevant: Issei not consulted
        3. Internment good for Japanese Americans
IV. Deeper impact of redress on all Americans: constitutional issues
V. Reasons for the Japanese Americans' long silence
    A. Preoccupation with day-to-day practical matters
    B. Pain of reopening wounds
    C. Isolation
Conclusion: The Japanese Americans' complex feelings, tied to the three
generations' different experiences of relocation, prevented the redress
movement from gaining initial momentum and a single voice.

The outline section has no page numbers. Outline symbols track the order of ideas.

Redress: From the Congressional Floor to the Hearts
of the Japanese Americans

> I looked at Santa Clara's streets from the train over the subway. I thought this might be the last look at my loved home city. My heart almost broke, and suddenly hot tears came pouring out, and the whole family cried out, could not stop, until we were out of our loved county.[1]

These are not the laments of a victim of the Nazi Third Reich. Shockingly, they are the words of a United States Congressman, California Representative Norman Y. Mineta. He is referring to the forced evacuation of 120,000 Japanese Americans, 70,000 of whom were American citizens, during World War II. Beginning in 1942, these people, most of whom lived along the West Coast, were rounded up at short notice and, taking only what they could carry, they were shipped off under armed guard to inland internment camps. Mineta is describing to Congress the ordeal his family experienced during that time. He explains:

> We lost our homes, we lost our businesses, we lost our farms, but worst of all, we lost our most basic human rights. Our own government had branded us with the unwarranted stigma of disloyalty which clings to us still to this day.[2]

Mineta was just one of many Americans urging Congress to acknowledge the government's mistake and give restitution to those interned. As a result, recent congressional legislation acknowledged the unconstitutionality of the internment, officially apologized to those

---

[1] Normal Y. Mineta, ''Excerpts from Rep. Mineta's Statement,'' <u>Wall Street Journal</u>, 18 September 1987, sec. A, p. 3.

[2] Ibid., 3-4.

Subsequent pages of the paper are numbered top right.	2

interned, provided a fund to educate the public, and allotted $1.2 billion to be given to the surviving internees, $20,000 to each.[3]

This issue, called redress, has been a very heated issue. Although redress is a victory that directly affects all Japanese Americans, they have responded very differently to it. Most Japanese Americans seem to support redress in some form, but many still disagree on the route taken. My goal is to explore these current disagreements in order to explain why the Japanese Americans remained silent for so long and why it has taken over 40 years to get redress. It seems that the main reason was the complexity of the issue, caused by the very different attitudes of the three generations of Japanese Americans involved.

Kevin explains his purpose ("my goal...") as a way of introducing his thesis ("the main reason...").

For years, many Japanese Americans would not even speak of internment, let alone demand redress. The Issei (first generation immigrants, born in Japan, and the special target of the internment effort) were not American citizens. As Mike Masaoka, a Nisei (second generation Japanese American) and spokesman for the Japanese American Citizens League (JACL), pointed out in a congressional hearing in 1955, "unlike the Germans, or any other nationality group . . . our alien parents could not become citizens of the United States."[4] This prohibition against citizenship lasted until 1952. Not until then could the Issei become American citizens. So it is not hard to understand why the Issei were reluctant to press claims on the basis of the American Constitution

Notice how Kevin provides information about the people he quotes. He tells us that Mineta is a Congressman and Masaoka is a spokesman for the JACL. This information helps us judge their authority and credibility.

---

[3] Due in part to the testimony of Mineta and Senator Spark M. Matsunaga, the House of Representatives passed H. R. 442 on 17 September 1987, and the Senate passed S. 1009 on 20 April 1988.

[4] Congress, House of Representatives, Committee on the Judiciary, <u>Hearings on the Janpanese-American Evacuation Claims</u>, 84th Cong., 1st sess., 25 September 1955, 19.

which had deliberately excluded them as members. As for the Nisei, their American-born children, who were the majority of those interned, one of them explains,

> rejected as inferior Americans by our own country . . . we were neither totally American nor totally Japanese, but a unique fusion of the two. Small wonder that many of us felt insecure and ambivalent and retreated into our own special subculture where we were fully accepted.[5]

But as time progressed, the young Sansei (the third generation Japanese Americans) became curious and began asking about their parents' experiences during the war.[6] A movement took shape, and redress lobbyists began making slow progress in Congress. Then in 1980 the Commission on Wartime Relocation and Internment of Civilians was formed to investigate the evacuation. The commission interviewed many internees who, for the first time since the internment, "released the unforgotten frustration and humiliation in torrents of emotional testimony."[7] The Japanese Americans finally began opening up as they realized that redress was no longer just a vain hope. The fight for redress became a community effort, no longer the hopeless struggle of a radical few. Nevertheless, the debate continued through most of the Eighties.

The issue of monetary compensation accounts for the majority of arguments over redress. Some believe that one cannot put a price tag on the suffering and injustice, and doing so would only degrade the monstrosity of the act. For example, Eunice Sato spoke out, saying,

---

[5] Yoshiko Uchida, <u>Desert Exile. The Uprooting of a Japanese American Family</u> (Seattle and London: University of Washington Press, 1982), 45.

[6] Miyeko Uriu, interview by author, Los Angeles CA, 27 July 1988.

[7] Mike Masaoka with Bill Hosokawa, <u>They Call Me Moses Masaoka: An American Saga</u> (New York: William Morrow and Co., 1987), 324.

4

''I think it is demeaning to think that you can pay [us] off with dollars.'' She added, ''Any sum of money won't erase the fact that [the internment] took place. . . . [Our] civil liberty cannot be bought at any price, even the $20,000.''[8] Another internee agreed, ''I cannot sell my freedom, my rights for that kind of money.''[9] Others believe that a demand for monetary compensation would only cheapen the literally ''priceless sacrifice of freedom''[10] Japanese Americans were forced to make.

Although some individuals like these have spoken out against monetary redress, the results of a 1978 JACL survey showed strong general support for it from the beginning. ''Of 3,904 respondents, 94 percent was in favor of reparation from the Federal Government as redress for the evacuation and imprisonment.''[11] The JACL survey certainly was not scientific or conclusive, but it does demonstrate that a substantial number of Japanese Americans have indeed supported monetary redress.

One supporter of redress, Jerry Enomoto, quite convincingly counters the arguments against reparations: ''There is nothing cheap or dirty about money. What people sometimes do for it may be. The $20,000 is symbolic payment for what happened.''[12] Representative

---

[8] Eunice Sato, quoted in Glenn Bunting, ''Some Japanese-Americans Hit Internee Redress,'' <u>Los Angeles Times</u>, 4 July 1987, sec. I, p. 3.

[9] Ibid.

[10] Masaoka, 321.

[11] ''What the Surveys Show,'' <u>Pacific Citizen</u>, 20 January 1978, p. 4.

[12] Jerry Enomoto, ''Monetary Payment a Necessity,'' <u>Pacific Citizen</u>, 21 August 1987, p. 3.

Robert T. Matsui agrees, stressing that "it isn't the $20,000 that is so important. . . . the crucial point is the symbolic acknowledgment that justice must be done."[13] The JACL argues that "restitution does not put a price tag on freedom or justice. The issue is not to recover what cannot be recovered." The JACL adds, "the issue is to acknowledge the mistake by providing proper redress for the victims of the injustice, and thereby make such injustices less likely to recur."[14] According to spokesman Mike Masaoka, "Monetary compensation for damages is the 'American way'. . . . Apologies are easy to make, but the real impact of this historical tragedy," Masaoka insists, "will not be felt unless substantial money is involved."[15] Masaoka continues both lines of thinking, saying that

> monetary restitution may well establish a beneficial and precautionary precedent for the future by requiring justifications for arbitrary actions and making the price for such transgressions so expensive and costly that no official or agency can afford to be stampeded as they were in our case in 1942 to authorize the deprivations of our rights, privileges, and immunities as citizens. . . . If money talks, and I think it does, we should make the price of racial discrimination, prejudice, and bigotry so high none can afford to indulge in it.[16]

Nonetheless, many people still argued against monetary compensation, Senator Samuel I. Hayakawa's being the most prominent voice. Hayakawa's opinions infuriated many, if not most of the Japanese community, who delighted in pointing out that Hayakawa had been born

---

[13] Quoted in Paul Houston, "Japanese Americans Ask Reparations," Los Angeles Times, 29 April 1988, sec. I, p. 1.

[14] Bill Hosokawa, JACL: In Quest of Justice (New York: William Morrow and Co., 1982), 347.

[15] Masaoka, 325.

[16] Ibid., 326.

in Canada, he had spent the war in Chicago, and had not suffered incarceration by either his native or his adopted country.[17] One of Hayakawa's infuriating opinions is that, because the average income of Japanese Americans is higher than that of Anglo Americans, the Japanese Americans do not need the money.[18] Jerry Enomoto counters that argument with a very good analogy. Pointing out that not all surviving internees are rich, ''or even well off,'' he explains that

> Just as recent studies have shown that Japanese Americans are not all geniuses, there are former internees who could use the $20,000. Are we too proud to acknowledge that?[19]

Furthermore, others have brought up the fact that there are very wealthy whites, as well as wealthy Japanese Americans, and very poor Japanese Americans, as well as poor whites. So why should the poor lose this opportunity simply because of an average figure?

A second Hayakawa criticism of the redress fight is that the lobbyists did not consult the Issei (Issei are the older, first-generation Japanese Americans). He argued that

> the campaign for redress was conducted almost completely by American born, English-speaking, Japanese Americans [the Nisei, or second-generation, and the Sansei, or third-generation], not the older immigrant Japanese Americans.... The Nisei and Sansei are not the whole Japanese American community.... It would never have occurred to the Issei to ask for money for redress. Most of them were grateful for the relocation, which kept them from danger in the event of an invasion by the military on the American mainland.[20]

---

[17] Roger Daniels, Sandra C. Taylor, and Harry H. L. Kitano, eds., *Japanese Americans: From Relocation to Redress* (Salt Lake City: University of Utah Press, 1986), 189.

[18] George Johnston, ''Redress Will 'Reflect Unfavorably' Says S. I. Hayakawa,'' *Pacific Citizen*, 6 May 1988, p. 7.

[19] Enomoto, 3.

[20] Johnston, 8.

Allowing that the Nisei and Sansei are not the whole Japanese American community, the <u>Pacific Citizen</u> points out that the

> Issei, through no fault of their own, were citizens of a nation at war with the United States: Nisei and Sansei were American citizens deprived of Constitutional rights and imprisoned wrongfully by their own government.[21]

Redress legislation addresses this lawful wrong, as well as the moral wrong of incarceration based on race. The <u>Pacific Citizen</u> also points out that, of those questioned in the JACL survey already mentioned, 92% had experienced the evacuation. ''Therefore, the statement that reparation is being asked mostly by Sansei and others who had not known the agonies of evacuation is not a true statement.''[22]

Hayakawa's third suggestion, that the experience was good for those interned,[23] stirred up a great deal of emotion in the Japanese American community. A letter of Phil Shigekuni to the editor of the <u>Los Angeles Times</u> expresses the community's outrage well.

> When we were herded off to the internment camps we were told that the government really had our best interests at heart; we were being put away to protect us from a hostile American public. . . . The original ''protection'' line has since been revealed as outright deception used to justify an illegal act. . . .
> Seeking redress of grievances from my government is a right accorded to me by the First Amendment to the Constitution. It strikes me as blatantly contradictory that a congressman would suggest that I relinquish my right. . . .
> What occurred in 1942 to Japanese Americans struck a blow to the very foundation on which this nation exists, its Constitution. Seen in this light, redress legislation becomes not merely a matter of compensating a wronged group of people, but more importantly, it would affirm to America and the rest of the world that the Constitution has validity for all Americans, at war and at peace.[24]

---

[21] ''Editorial,'' <u>Pacific Citizen</u>, 13 May 1988, p. 4.

[22] ''What the Surveys Show,'' 4.

[23] Houston, 1.

[24] Phil Shigekuni, ''Letter to the Editor,'' <u>Los Angeles Times</u>, 27 September 1987, sec. V, p. 2.

The ellipsis (three periods plus a period to indicate the end of the sentence) replaces some omitted words in the quotation.

Transitional expressions like "therefore" do not always have to begin sentences. An effective stylistic alternative is to place them within a sentence where a natural pause would occur.

8

The impact of redress, therefore, has struck much deeper than merely paying off the Japanese American internees. To oppose redress would not only have denied Japanese Americans the justice due them, it would have denied America the chance to confirm the principles upon which it is based.

> One tenet of our judicial system is that bygones are not bygones, but that once approved in courts, they are precedents. The incarceration of a group of people based on country of origin is not a good precedent. . . . The separate but equal laws [set a precedent that] stood for nearly a century, but this did not make them moral or just. . . . We value our Constitutional rights so much, we let known criminals go free rather than set a precedent of abridgement of those rights. . . . So let us set a new precedent: that all people, regardless of race, color, creed, or religion have equal protection under the law, at all times. This is not a new concept, but is a fundamental precept of our country.[25]

The people opposing redress ignored this extremely important constitutional issue entirely. They based their arguments on either the amount of money given or the ''pride'' of the Japanese Americans. They claimed to represent a ''silent majority'' of Japanese Americans who did not support the redress lobbyists.[26]

The transitional expression "Yet" logically links this paragraph's topic sentence to the preceding paragraph.

The rhetorical question ("Why after all,....?") effectively introduces the paragraph's main point (reasons for silence).

Yet, this silence can have several other meanings. Silence about redress did not necessarily mean opposition to it. It could have meant tacit approval. Why, after all, were so many Japanese Americans silent at the end of the war? On a practical level, those interned were ''too preoccupied with the routine matters of establishing families and careers to do much about demanding recompense for their distressing experience.''[27] Emotionally, the internment was a devastating

---

[25] Harry G. Watson, ''Letter to the Editor,'' <u>Pacific Citizen</u>, 20 May 1988, p. 5.

[26] Bunting.

[27] Hosokawa, 343-4.

experience that victims buried deep down inside. Reopening the old wounds would have been much too painful.[28] For example, Representative Robert T. Matsui ''compared the difficulty many Issei and Nisei face in talking about their internment experience with the mental ordeal of a rape victim.''[29] It was questions (by the younger Sansei and the Commission on Wartime Relocation and Internment of Civilians), and a real possibility for action (redress legislation), that finally broke much of this silence.

It seems, then, that these complex feelings about the relocation experience prevented the redress movement from gaining initial momentum and a single voice. The Issei were not even American citizens until 1952. Although they were hurt by the American government and legal system, they were at the same time cut off from it. Their American-born children, the Nisei, were ''insecure and ambivalent.''[30] The title of Bill Hosokawa's book, <u>Nisei: The Quiet Americans</u>, describes them appropriately. Their grandchildren, the Sansei, were curious about the relocation experience, yet they, too, were cut off in several ways. Few of them speak Japanese, and because they lived through the Vietnam War and other episodes involving civil rights, they tended to see the experience from a legal and constitutional point of view as a violation of personal freedom. Accordingly, the argument for redress has reflected these different responses. The redress movement mixes a bit

---

[28] Uriu.

[29] Laurie Mochidome, ''L.A. Program Commemorates Redress Efforts,'' <u>Pacific Citizen</u>, 26 February 1988, p. 1.

[30] Uchida, 45.

of realism: Restitution must be paid for the wrongs done, and must serve as an example for future governments; and a bit of idealism: Redress legislation cannot erase the pain or replace what was lost. Although we can never heal the wounds suffered by 120,000 Japanese Americans, the silence has finally been broken, and a 40 year old wound to the Constitution has been healed.

Works Cited

Bunting, Glenn. "Some Japanese-Americans Hit Internee Redress." *Los Angeles Times*, 4 July 1987, sec. I, p. 3.

Daniels, Roger, Sandra C. Taylor, and Harry H. L. Kitano, eds. *Japanese Americans: From Relocation to Redress*. Salt Lake City: University of Utah Press, 1986.

"Editorial." *Pacific Citizen*, 13 May, 1988, p. 1.

Enomoto, Jerry. "Monetary Payment a Necessity." *Pacific Citizen*, 21 August 1987, p. 3.

Hosokawa, Bill. *JACL: In Quest of Justice*. New York: William Morrow and Co., 1982.

--------. *Nisei: The Quiet Americans*. New York: William Morrow and Co., 1969.

Houston, Paul. "Japanese Americans Ask Reparations." *Los Angeles Times*, 29 April 1988, sec. I, p. 1.

Johnston, George. "Redress Will 'Reflect Unfavorably' Says S. I. Hayakawa." *Pacific Citizen*, 6 May 1988, p. 7.

Masaoka, Mike with Bill Hosokawa. *They Call Me Moses Masaoka: An American Saga*. New York: William Morrow and Co., 1987.

Mineta, Norman Y. "Excerpts from Rep. Mineta's Statement." *Wall Street Journal*, 18 September 1987, sec. A, pp. 3-4.

Mochidome, Laurie. "L.A. Program Commemorates Redress Efforts." *Pacific Citizen*, 26 February 1988, p. 1.

Shigekuni, Phil. "Letter to the Editor." *Los Angeles Times*, 27 September 1987, sec. V, p. 2.

U. S. Congress. House of Representatives. Committee on the Judiciary. *Hearings on the Japanese-American Evacuation Claims*. 84th Cong., 1st Sess., 25 September 1955.

Uchida, Yoshiko. *Desert Exile. The Uprooting of a Japanese American Family*. Seattle and London: University of Washington Press, 1982.

Uriu, Miyeko. Interview by author. Los Angeles CA. 27 July 1988.

Watson, Harry G. "Letter to the Editor." *Pacific Citizen*, 20 May 1988, p. 5.

"What the Surveys Show." *Pacific Citizen*, 20 January 1978, p. 4.

ILLUSTRATION OF THE PARENTHESIS SYSTEM (MLA STYLE)

MLA Guidelines do not require a separate title page or outline, but your instructor may. The outline for this paper can be found in Chapter 7, p. 192.

Double-space entire paper.

Brandy Graves

Professor Manfred

English 111

3 April 1990

Center title.

Breakfast Cereal: Fact and Fantasy

Breakfast cereals present a myriad of choices and a multitude of claims to promote good health, but is there a ''grain'' of truth to their promises? Apparently consumers think so because the industry has yearly sales approaching 6.6 billion dollars (Freundlich and Cantrell 114). Mesmerized by boasts of improved health and fitness, consumers have paid little attention to the facts. Tony the Tiger may think cereals are ''G-G-Great!'' but as one TV commercial inadvertently hints, the promises are empty. When the character asks, ''What are you eating?'' the reply is telling: ''Nut-N-Honey.'' As these examples suggest, breakfast cereals offer entertaining advertising, but the claims for their health benefits have been exaggerated.

Authors and page number are cited for paraphrase of a specific fact.

Thesis statement is given prominence by placing it at the end of the introductory paragraph.

Indent all paragraphs 5 spaces.

Cereal products sound marvelous in the ads, but much of their natural mineral and vitamin power is lost in the processing. Although manufacturers add nutritional supplements to their products, the additions have little relevance to the consumer's needs (''Cereal: Breakfast Food'' 638). For example, a cereal box may boast that the product is fortified with vitamin C, but this is a relatively cheap vitamin that is added to many foods. According to Beth Newton, who teaches nutrition, the public may be getting more vitamin C than it needs, but losing out

Use short form title when no author is given.

Parentheses normally come at the end of the sentence.

[in text documentation go to p. 286 for reference]

on the variety of vitamins and trace elements that are part of a sound diet. Furthermore, the other additions made by the manufacturers are not quite as beneficial: sodium, sugar, and some saturated fats like coconut oil. Trying to figure out what is really in a box of cereal can be difficult. As John Carey points out, the government requires ''ingredients to be itemized in descending order by weight'' (133), but there is a bewildering array of sweeteners. In addition to sugar, there is corn syrup, maltodextrin, and aspartame. Under scrutiny, labels on cereal boxes reveal calorie counts that are often off by 20% (''Cereal: Breakfast Food'' 639).

Given the shaky nutritional claims of breakfast cereals, the real story of the industry's success lies in marketing. Since its birth circa 1878 with J.H. Kellogg's concoction of wheat flour, cornmeal, and oatmeal which he called ''Granula,'' the industry has promoted a link with good health (Green 305). Kellogg, a feverous health promoter, used cereal as a varietal in diet at his sanitarium in Battle Creek, Michigan (Samuelson 49). A patient at the sanitarium, a Mr. Charles W. Post, found cereal's potential so impressive that in 1898 he introduced ''Grape-Nuts'' to the market (Green 312).

Advertising claims and boasts followed quickly as a growing number of brands professed their power to promote good health. Green illustrates the assortment of health promises made in the early days. In 1924 Kellogg's claimed that two tablespoons daily of ''All-Bran'' would offer permanent relief from the most chronic cases of constipation, and in 1927 Post ''Bran Flakes'' pictured a woman with the caption ''could be beautiful'' but she was ''never quite up to par . . . she lacked natural bulk'' (312). Post went so far as to claim that ''Grape-Nuts'' contained ''natural phosphate of potash . . . used by the system in rebuilding and repairing the brain and the nerve centers'' (311).

Gradually the cereal industry moderated its claims, and the rule of thumb became to avoid remedial boasts. This calm lasted until 1984 when the National Cancer Institute announced ''a high-fiber, low-fat diet may reduce the risk of some types of cancer'' (Samuelson 49). The rallying word was fiber, and with it came a new market potential for bran. Fiber refers to the walls of the plant cell which have an exterior coating of bran. Astute marketers at Kellogg Company adopted the NCI findings in their advertising for ''All-Bran'' cereal. Soon health claims mushroomed, and products containing corn, wheat, oat, rice or barley bran flooded the market. Today, at least twenty-five varieties of bran/fiber cereals fill the supermarket shelves (''Cereal: Breakfast Food'' 646).

Although grain cereals provide fiber, their promise to reduce cancer may ring hollow. The actual fiber content of many cereals is less than two grams per one ounce serving, and ensuing research studies contradict one another (''Cereal: Breakfast Food'' 642). Research on fiber and its attributes is not definitive, according to Dr. David Klurfeld, professor at Wistor Institute.

> You can say fiber is certainly good in preventing constipation and diverticular disease, but most people are making claims that go beyond that. Fiber does play a role in preventing colon cancer, but which types of fiber and the amount necessary, I don't know (qtd. in Schnorbus 93).

> The ellipsis indicates that the original sentence did not stop here.

> The wording of the topic sentence ("A second major health claim...") signals the start of another major point.

> Use author's full name the first time; thereafter use last name only.

Understanding the link between fiber and cancer is complicated by the possibility that certain fibers or too much of any fiber may increase the risk of cancer. Victor Herbert, Professor of Medicine at Mt. Sinai School of Medicine, states ''cancer might result from too much or too little fiber'' (''The Fiber Furor'' 642). He prefers a diet offering a variety of fiber types. Dr. Klurfeld adds a note of warning when he states ''corn bran may provide more fiber than wheat bran; however, corn bran may increase chances of colon cancer . . . '' (qtd. in Schnorbus 93).

A second major health claim made by cereal manufacturers was that cholesterol could be reduced. Cholesterol has been implicated in heart disease, and the public has become increasingly concerned with finding foods that would help to reduce cholesterol levels. Cereal promoters latched on to the results of one study that espoused the benefit of oat bran. According to that study, eating a minimum of 39 grams of oat bran per day would result in a small reduction in cholesterol. However, as Marian Burros points out, no one specified how small the reduction was or stressed that the 39 grams had to be consumed daily to achieve the reduction (''Oat Bran May Be'' C4).

The health juggernaut sputtered when the <u>New England Journal of Medicine</u> reported a recent study which concluded that oat bran did not significantly reduce cholesterol levels any more successfully than other grains (''Hold the Oat Bran'' 80). Findings indicate that drops in cholesterol seem related to people eating grain or bran and having less room for high cholesterol foods. In other words, cutting out high cholesterol foods leads to the reduction, not eating bran.

As the hunt for the ultimate health cereal continued, Kellogg's introduced ''Ken Mei Rice Bran.'' Knowing the fickleness of the consumer, Kellogg's set out to promote the ''age'' of rice bran. They also tapped into the aura of success that surrounds the Japanese by choosing a name that in Japanese means wisdom or prudence (''Obstacles Mount'' 58). Unfortunately, research on rice bran was disappointing. The University of Texas Health Science Center, after a fifteen week review on rice bran, concluded that there were no attributable reductions in cholesterol from rice bran (''Obstacles Mount'' 58).

> *Topic sentence provides transition between discussion of bran and new ingredient*

Bran was not the only cereal ingredient that was touted for its beneficial effects. General Mills placed ''Benefit'' on the shelves, promising consumers reduced cholesterol, thanks to psyllium. A by-product of the seeds of the Fleawart, psyllium is also a staple in numerous laxatives. Laxative manufacturers, including Proctor and Gamble and Ciba-Geigy, have been prohibited by the Food and Drug Administration (FDA) from claiming that their laxatives reduced cholesterol (Freeman 3). Both manufacturers then questioned the FDA as to why General Mills was allowed to make comparable claims.

> *Mention of author early in paragraph clarifies that information in the following sentences came from this source.*

Not to be outdone, Kellogg's entered the foray with ''Heartwise,'' featuring a double whammy: psyllium and oat bran in the same box! Kellogg budgeted some 40 million dollars to a ''Heartwise'' campaign designed to raise the consumers' awareness of good health principles (''Cereal: Breakfast Food'' 646). However, ''Heartwise'' and ''Benefit'' are under scrutiny of the FDA, and a number of state attorney generals have promised legal action if medicinal claims persist.

Meanwhile, the laxative manufacturers have learned from the cereal makers that clever advertising pays off. Toufexis explains how Proctor and Gamble, the producer of the laxative Metamucil, cunningly circumvented the FDA's ruling on psyllium. Ads profess that soluble fiber can make a ''difference in your health,'' but do not claim to produce good health. Ads also tout Metamucil as an excellent source of ''remarkable health fiber'' and point out that its fiber content is eight times more concentrated than oat bran. The ads for Metamucil state that it is fat free, sugar free, and contains only five calories per spoonful. An assessment of these ads is offered by Michael Jacobsen, spokesperson for the Center for Science in Public Interest: ''The words may be honest, but the implication may exaggerate the benefit'' (qtd. in Toufexis 66).

> Use of running acknowledgment highlights the credentials of the source.

General Mills ceased production of ''Benefit'' cereal, citing weak sales and a backlash from adverse publicity generated by the FDA's investigation into overzealous health boasts. Another, and perhaps more compelling, reason for the product's demise was that the consumers said the cereal just didn't taste good (''Cereal With Psyllium'' 20).

The FDA deserves considerable blame for the chaotic food market. Their regulations did not stipulate how much substantiation was required of a manufacturer before making health boasts. Furthermore, the difference between a health statement and a health claim was a grey area (''Sensible Start For Heartwise'' 54). That grey area allowed advertisers the latitude to design misleading appeals to the consumer's desire for a healthful diet. Recently, guidelines have been proposed which state that health promises must be based on the totality of publicly available evidence. A significant agreement must exist among qualified experts that the statement is supported by such evidence ("Obstacles Mount" 58).

Meanwhile the consumer continues to shop the cereal aisles looking for the best health products possible. The experts say the jury is still out, that current research cannot substantiate or refute all that is claimed by manufacturers. The soundest advice seems to be to concentrate on a variety of fiber sources. Cereals are not the only source of fibers. In fact, fruits, vegetables, whole grains, dried peas, beans, and lentils offer fiber, plus proteins, vitamins, and minerals with less fat and cholesterol than anything Kellogg's, Post, or General Mills currently has on the shelf. The old maxim sounds trite, yet the advice rings true: moderation, variety, and balance in one's diet helps promote the best health possible.

Works Cited

Burros, Marian. "Oat Bran May Be on the Label, but How Much Is in the Box?" The New York Times 22 March 1989: C4.

---. "Eating Well." The New York Times 19 July 1989: C10.

Carey, John. "Now I've Read the Label, What's in the Package?" Business Week 9 Oct. 1989: 133.

"Cereal With Psyllium No Benefit to the Bottom Line." The Day 5 Jan. 1990: 20.

"Cereal: Breakfast Food or Nutritional Supplement." Consumer Reports Oct. 1989: 638-646.

Freeman, Laurie. "Metamucil Eyes New Claim: P&G Cites Cholesterol Study." Advertising Age 15 Feb. 1988: 3.

Freundlich, Naomi, and Wanda Cantrell. "Great American Health Pitch." Business Week 9 Oct. 1989: 114-122.

Green, Harvey. Fit For America: Health, Fitness, Sport, and American Society. New York: Pantheon, 1986.

"Hold the Oat Bran." Time 29 Jan. 1990: 80.

Newton, Beth. Personal interview. 12 Feb. 1990.

"Obstacles Mount for Healthy Foods." Advertising Age 29 Jan. 1990: 1, 58.

Samuelson, Robert. "The Great Cereal Wars." Newsweek 7 Sept. 1987: 49.

Schnorbus, Paula. "Brantastic." Marketing and Media Decisions Apr. 1987: 93.

"Sensible Start For Heartwise." Advertising Age 11 Sept. 1989: 54.

"The Fiber Furor." Consumer Reports Oct. 1986: 640-642.

Toufexis, Anastasia. "Battle for the Food Blurbs." Time 11 Sept. 1989: 66.

ILLUSTRATION OF THE PARENTHESIS SYSTEM (APA STYLE)

Running head and page number are flush right.

Hypnosis

1

Title of paper, author, course, and date are centered on page.

Double-space

Hypnosis: What's in a Name?

Sylvia Jefferson

Psychology 240

15 November 1984

Identification of the running head is flush left.

Running Head: Hypnosis

Abstract

An analysis of the research on the essence of hypnosis suggests that the debate between state and non-state theorists is a problem of terminology, stemming from different orientations. Barber's research demonstrates that a special hypnotic state cannot be identified on the basis of physiological changes. Furthermore, he shows that most of the traits associated with the hypnotic state can be produced through a process of involved imagining. Barber is criticized for arguing against a position never espoused by state researchers, for paying insufficient attention to the subjective experience of hypnotism, and for flaws in his research design. Edmonston argues that hypnosis is basically a state of relaxation; however, he is unable to fit alert hypnosis into his model. The debate over terminology has practical implications because hypnosis has long been recognized as a powerful and potentially dangerous procedure.

Hypnosis: What's in a Name?

When Anton Mesmer, the father of modern hypnotism, treated his patients, they spontaneously fell into fits from which they awoke cured. Later practitioners discovered that the hypnotized person was capable of extraordinary feats: clairvoyance, physical endurance, supression of pain, age regression, and amnesia. Today the fits are gone, along with many other claims for dramatic changes. In fact, recent research leads us to wonder if the term hypnosis is an accurate label for the various traits that have been associated with it. In searching for the essence of hypnosis, researchers may have uncovered several altered states of consciousness. Given this possibility, the current difference of opinion between those who view hypnosis as a special trance state and those who see it simply as a set of easily manipulated behaviors may be a problem with terminology.

Although the therapeutic use of trance states was common in many societies before the rise of empirical science, Anton Mesmer was the first to apply the principles of science to the investigation of trances (Shor, 1979). Reasoning from Newton's laws of gravity, Mesmer postulated a magnetic force that affected people, as well as objects. He tested his theory in 1774 by using magnets to treat some of his patients. Although he had not anticipated that his patients would fall into a seizure, he assimilated this behavior into a theory that illness resulted from an imbalance of fluids. Interested primarily in a theory of magnetism, Mesmer did not focus his attention on the state into which his patients fell while the cure was taking place.

Mesmer attracted the attention of the scientific community, most of it rather skeptical of his theories. A committee, which included Benjamin Franklin, conducted a study of Mesmer's claims, and concluded that although the remarkable recoveries seemed authentic, the cause was not physical (magnetism) but due to ''mere imagination.'' Interest in the therapeutic use of Mesmer's technique spread despite the committee's conclusions. As the practice spread, reports on the experience began to change. For instance, the Marquis de Puysegur, writing in 1784, stated that the seizure or crisis was not necessary to the cure. Instead he emphasized the sleeplike trance, the hypersuggestibility, and subsequent amnesia (Shor, 1979). Gradually the analogy with sleep led James Braid in 1840 to rename the phenomenon ''hypnosis,'' derived from the Greek word meaning sleep. Braid was very careful to limit the use of the term to cases where the patient appeared to be asleep and later could not recall what had happened except during a subsequent induction (Edmonston, 1981). Since Braid's time the essence of hypnosis has continued to interest researchers, but there is still disagreement over this most basic issue.

> Identifies the current debate

Traditionally the debate has centered on whether hypnosis is a special trance state or a more ordinary set of behaviors that can be elicited through various means. The most recent assault on the equation between hypnosis and trance has been conducted on two fronts. T. X. Barber and his associates have argued that hypnosis is no more exotic than the state of mind we achieve when we allow ourselves to empathize with the actors during a play. They suggest that the term ''involved imagining'' is a less confusing term than hypnosis. A different view is proposed by W. E. Edmonston, who links hypnosis with relaxation and urges that we adopt the term ''anesis'' to describe this passive, receptive state.

Barber's 1979 article pulls together data that prove that the physical traits associated with the hypnotic state are fairly ordinary. For example, the stage hypnotist's feat of suggesting extreme rigidity and thereby turning the participant into a ''human plank'' is not all that difficult. Many nonhypnotized subjects in an experiment were able to achieve the same degree of body rigidity. Barber also explains away most of the other remarkable physical traits associated in the past with hypnotism: skin blisters, temporary deafness, removal of warts, and supression of pain. Summing up, Barber asserts that no physiological indicators have been found that distinguish the hypnotic state. Certain physiological changes, such as raising the skin temperature, can be achieved not only with hypnosis but with ''vividly imagining a sensation'' (p. 259).

Barber's personal experience has led him to conclude that the hypnotic state consists primarily of focusing one's attention and suspending negative thoughts. He claims that he has been able to experience all the typical hypnotic behaviors without the benefit of another person to induct him into a trance. In a 1965 experiment he tested the hypothesis that the hypnotic induction was not necessary to produce the cluster of behaviors that are associated with hypnosis. He compared a group of hypnotized subjects with a control group and with a group who had been given task-motivational instructions. All subjects were asked to respond to suggestions ranging from locked hands to amnesia. The success rate on each of the suggestions ranged in the conotrol group from 13% to 48%, in the task-motivational group from 39% to 81%, and in the hypnotized group 29% to 74%. In other words, suggestibility, which has been considered an essential part of the hypnotic state, can be achieved through directions given to subjects who are fully awake.

> Analysis of commentary on Barber

In reporting his research, Barber depicted his theory as a revolutionary new paradigm which would be met with hostile criticism from those who had a vested interest in the special-state theory of hypnotism. However, most of the contemporary researchers have used terms like "trance state" very tentatively and have admitted that there is no current theory that satisfactorily explains hypnosis (Orne, 1957). Their goal has been to determine whether there is an essential component of hypnosis that cannot be accounted for in terms of the sociocultural context (Orne, 1959).

> Contrast of Barber's research with research by "state theorists"

Barber's research has focused primarily on the observable behavior of the hypnotic subject, and until recently, has eliminated the inner experience of hypnotism as an area of inquiry. His skepticism about subjective reports stemmed from a series of experiments that he conducted between 1965 and 1969 which demonstrated that a subject's report on his inner experience varied with the definition of the situation, the subject's expectations, and the way in which the questions were presented to the subject (Spanos, 1979). State theorists, on the other hand, have concentrated on the inner experience of hypnosis because efforts to develop objective tests of the hypnotic state proved fruitless (Orne, 1959). Rather than concluding that hypnosis was not a trance state, as Barber did, they turned their attention inward, recognizing that context, expectations, and the wording of questions could affect the outcome of subjective reports (Tellegen, 1970).

Supporters of Barber's theory have tried to dismiss subjective reports as scientifically unacceptable, comparing them to reports of spirit possessions (Spanos, 1970). This comparison, however, ignores the fact that psychologists for years have accepted subjective testimony of depression and anxiety as evidence that those states exist. Furthermore, psychologists differentiate between fear and anger, although there is no way to distinguish between these states on the basis of psychological effects (Orne, 1967).

The keystone of Barber's theory, his comparison of hypnosis with task-motivational instructions, has generated a number of exchanges between researchers. Hilgard and Tart (1966) criticized Barber's design and ran a corrected version of the experiment in which the same subject was tested on different days. However, the validity of their research was questioned by Spanos (1970) who pointed out that a subject's experience with one type of suggestibility could affect performance with another type.

A follow-up on Barber's research was conducted in 1967 by Edmonston and Robertson (cited in Hilgard, 1973) who pretested subjects for suggestibility and then matched a task-motivational group with a hypnotic

Hypnosis

8

group. Their results showed that hypnosis produced greater suggestibility than task-motivational instructions. Hilgard (1973) replicated the Barber experiment but corrected the directions to the subjects to encourage honesty in reporting. His results showed that hypnosis produced greater visual hallucinations than did task-motivational instructions. Hilgard concedes, however, that these gains are small and that for some types of suggestion, such as pain reduction, task-motivational instructions may work as well as hypnosis.

Contrasting arguments

For Barber and Spanos (1974) the difference between hypnosis and involved imagining is not great enough to justify the construct of a special trance state, a construct which they think should be abandoned because of the ''many misleading implications that have accumulated during the past 200 years'' (p. 506). The special-state theorists counter this line of thinking by arguing that hypnosis is not synonymous with suggestibility. Hilgard (1973) summarizes research that shows important differences between forms of suggestibility. He specifically mentions the work of Hull, Furneaux, and Stukat which showed a distinction between hypnotizability and forms of social suggestibility, such as conformity and gullibility. He cites additional research by Burns and Hammer in 1970 and by Moore in 1964 which showed that there is no correlation between social suggestibility and hypnotizability. Hypnotic suggestibility is also distinct from that induced by placebos, according to other research cited by Hilgard.

Summary of another theory

The search for the essence of hypnosis has led Edmonston (1981) to a different equation. He argues that if we examine the inner experience of hypnosis rather than the uses made of this state, such as increased suggestibility, we will see that relaxation is the essential characteristic. He supports this equation by citing the 1967 study by Evans which showed that subjects who were given relaxation instructions exhibited the same traits usually associated with hypnosis. Edmonston also cites a study by Coleman in 1977 which compared a relaxation group and a hypnotic group against two control groups. On tests of suggestibility the subjects in both the relaxation group and the hypnotic group had higher scores than subjects in the two control groups. Furthermore, the suggestibility scores of the hypnosis group and the relaxation group did not differ from one another. Edmonston also points out that the therapeutic results of hypnosis, meditation, and desensitization therapy rely on the common ingredient of relaxation. In his historical review of the literature of hypnosis, he notes that the link between hypnosis and a sleeplike state goes all the way back to the Egyptians.

Analysis of the theory

The major problem with Edmonston's theory is that it does not account for ''alert hypnosis,'' a state that has been identified by Hilgard. Alert hypnosis produced all the characteristics of hypnosis except the resemblance to sleep. Edmonston suggests that alert hypnosis is a state different from traditional hypnosis. Moreover, he believes that certain traits elicited from only a small number of deeply hypnotizable subjects, such as disassociation, may indicate still another state that is different from traditional hypnosis.

Summary of what research shows

At the moment we are left with at least four possible positions regarding the essence of hypnosis: hypnosis is sufficiently different from our waking consciousness to constitute a special kind of trance state; hypnosis is significantly different from ordinary consciousness because we are more relaxed and therefore more open to suggestions; hypnosis is not sufficiently different from ordinary consciousness to be considered a special trance state; the term hypnosis has been used to refer to a variety of related but not identical experiences. There is the additional complication that the experience of hypnosis may have changed over time as the expectations about it and the setting for the research have shifted.

<small>Synthesis of theories</small>

Both the state and the non-state theorists now seem to agree that many of the traits previously associated with hypnosis can be elicited through other means, such as relaxation and involved imagining. At issue is whether we should use the term hypnosis to refer to that mental state which can be achieved through a variety of procedures or whether the term hypnosis should be reserved for deeper trancelike states. State theorists still cling to the small differences between hypnotically induced experiences and those achieved through other means. They are interested in mapping the continuum of consciousness and, therefore, want to distinguish between the experience of being entranced by a play or day-dreaming and that of light hypnosis. The non-state proponents seem to be more interested in behavior and, therefore, want to know whether the same therapeutic results can be achieved with procedures other than the standard hypnotic induction. State theorists suggest that if the same results can be achieved, then it is because the procedure has induced a hypnotic state, even if the instructions did not mention hypnosis (Fromm, 1979).

> Conclusion states implications/ significance of the issue.

There are practical implications to this seemingly esoteric debate. For instance, professional and governmental guidelines recognize the potential for misuse of hypnosis. The government requires that special steps be followed in experiments on hypnosis, and professional societies prohibit the training of lay people as hypnotists. One potential problem is that a person can sidestep these guidelines by renaming the process. Likewise, if a client objects to therapy which involves hypnosis, but agrees to relaxation procedures that create the same level of suggestibility as hypnosis, this raises another ethical problem. In light of these clinical problems, it is important that research continue into the nature of hypnosis.

References

Barber, T. X. (1965). Measuring ''hypnotic-like'' suggestibility with and without ''hypnotic induction''; psychometric properties, norms, and variables influencing response to the Barber Suggestibility Scale (BSS). Psychological Reports, 16, 809-844.

Barber, T. X. (1979). Suggested (hypnotic) behavior: The trance paradigm versus an alternative paradigm. In E. Fromm (Ed.), Hypnosis: Developments in research and new perspectives. Hawthorne, NY: Aldine.

Edmonston, W. E. (1981). Hypnosis: Modern verification of an old equation. New York: Wiley.

Edmonston, W. E., and Robertson, T. G. (1967). A comparison of the effects of task motivational and hypnotic induction instructions on responsiveness to hypnotic suggestibility scales. American Journal of Clinical Hypnosis, 9, 184-187.

Fromm, E. (1979). The nature of hypnosis and other altered states of consciousness on ego psychological theory. In E. Fromm (Ed.), Hypnosis: developments in research and new perspectives (pp. 27-39). Hawthorne, NY: Aldine.

Hilgard, E. R. (1973). The domain of hypnosis: With some comments on alternative paradigms. American Psychologist, 28, 972-981.

Hilgard, E. R. (1979). Divided consciousness in hypnosis: The implications of the hidden observer. In E. Fromm (Ed.), Hypnosis: Developments in research and new perspectives (pp. 97-121). Hawthorne, NY: Aldine.

Hilgard, E. R., and Tart, C. T. (1966). Responsiveness to suggestions following waking and imagining instructions and following induction of hypnosis. Journal of Abnormal Psychology, 71, 196-208.

Orne, M. T. (1959). The nature of hypnosis: Artifact and essence. Journal of Abnormal and Social Psychology, 58, 277-299.

Orne, M. T. (1967). What must a satisfactory theory of hypnosis explain? International Journal of Psychiatry, 3, 206-211.

Shor, R. E. (1979). Fundamental problems in hypnosis research as viewed from a historic perspective. In E. Fromm (Ed.), Hypnosis: Developments in research and new perspectives (pp. 9-17). Hawthorne, NY: Aldine.

Spanos, N. P. (1970). Barber's reconceptualization of hypnosis: An evaluation of criticisms. Journal of Experimental Research in Personality, 4, 241-258.

Spanos, N. P., and Barber, T. X. (1974). Toward a convergence in hypnosis research. American Psychologist, 29, 500-511.

Tellegen, A. (1970). Some comments on ''Barber's reconceptualization of hypnosis.'' Journal of Experimental Research in Personality, 4, 259-267.

Anthology: A Conversation about Our Use and Abuse of Animals

INTRODUCTION

The following readings illustrate a range of attitudes about our relationship with animals. We eat them; we wear their skins for clothes; we share our houses with some of them whom we treat like family members; we perform scientific experiments on them; we collect and protect some of them in zoos; we train some of them to perform for us in amusement parks or to compete for, and with, us in various sports. Animals are important parts of our lives.

In this collection of readings you will hear a group of people discuss our use and abuse of animals. They include professors of political science and anthropology, a journalist, a magazine editor, a novelist, a medical physician, a zoo administrator, and the scientific director of the Humane Society. Taken together, these readings are a conversation, blending different voices, beliefs, and points of view. We invite you to join these people by thinking and writing about some of the same ideas.

These readings are talking points and also information. As in any conversation, you can listen for a while, develop your own opinion on the topic under discussion, and then join in. What do you think about these issues? Who do you agree with? Who do you think is wrong? Where exactly do you stand?

Even more important, **why** do you hold your opinion(s)? What are your reasons? What is your evidence? This collection includes enough information—examples, statistics, historical background, and authoritative opinion—to support almost any position on this topic, at least in a short paper. Remember that a thesis is an informed opinion; a research paper supports that opinion with the borrowed evidence that informs it.

Joining the Conversation

Here is a choice of possible questions to address in a short research paper. Read the following selections, take notes, and use this borrowed information to support your own opinion. Write on one of the following topics:

1. If you are a carnivore, explain and justify that position.
2. If you are a carnivore *and* a pet owner or "animal lover," justify and explain that position.
3. If you are not a carnivore, do you use or wear products that involve pain or death to animals? Explain and justify.
4. Explain and support your position on animal experimentation. For what purposes? What limits, if any, would you impose, and why?
5. Argue in favor of zoos, or argue against. Support your position. Do not argue both sides.
6. Argue for or against cruelty to animals in situations in which animals are trained, say, for work in circuses. Support and explain your stand.
7. Choose one of these readings and argue against it, using information from some of the other readings to help you back up your own criticism.
8. Animal rights activists sometimes attack animal experimentors as "speciesists" (like racists or sexists). Explain what they mean by "speciesism" and either support their attack or criticize it.
9. Consider the use of animals in sport, for example, greyhound racing or cockfighting. Argue for or against its legality.
10. ALF (Animal Liberation Front) is a militant group that has broken into labs, "rescued" the lab animals, and caused millions of dollars of damage, particularly to university labs. The FBI considers the ALF one of the most dangerous terrorist organizations in the nation. Are ALF members justified in these terrorist acts? Ever? Why, or why not?
11. Mankind is often thought to be superior to the animals, and it is this superiority which entitles mankind to use (and abuse) the animals for its own purpose(s). Examine this notion of human superiority and assess it. Is it accurate? Is it adequate? What else is involved in mankind's relationship with animals?
12. Choose any aspect of our relationship with animals and write an argumentative paper, taking a position and defending it (that means you may argue *against* a position so long as you back it up.)

CONTENTS OF THE ANTHOLOGY

_____ **A Conversation about Our Use and Abuse of Animals**

1. "Why Worry about the Animals?" Jean Bethke Elshtain, *The Progressive*
2. "Animal Rights," Molly O'Neill, *New London Day*
3. "Am I Blue? . . ." Alice Walker, *Living by the Word*
4. "What's Wrong with Animal Rights?" Barbara Grizzuti Harrison, *Mademoiselle*
5. "At Issue: Does Conservation Justify Keeping Animals in Zoos?" *Editorial Research Reports*
6. "The Facts about Animal Research," Robert J. White, *Reader's Digest*
7. "Better Health Care Doesn't Justify Animal Research," Kenneth L. Feder and Michael Alan Park, *Hartford Courant*

WHY WORRY ABOUT THE ANIMALS?

Jean Bethke Elshtain

These things are happening or have happened recently:

> The wings of seventy-four mallard ducks are snapped to see whether crippled birds can survive in the wild. (They can't.)
>
> Infant monkeys are deafened to study their social behavior, or turned into amphetamine addicts to see what happens to their stress level.
>
> Monkeys are separated from their mothers, kept in isolation, addicted to drugs, and induced to commit "aggressive" acts.
>
> Pigs are blowtorched and observed to see how they respond to third-degree burns. No pain-killers are used.
>
> Monkeys are immersed in water and vibrated to cause brain damage.
>
> For thirteen years, baboons have their brains bashed at the University of Pennsylvania as research assistants laugh at signs of the animals' distress.
>
> Monkeys are dipped in boiling water; other animals are shot in the face with high-powered rifles.

The list of cruelties committed in the name of "science" or "research" could be expanded endlessly. "Fully 80 per cent of the experiments involving rhesus monkeys are either unnecessary, represent useless duplication of previous work, or could utilize nonanimal alternatives," says John E. McArdle, a biologist and specialist in primates at Illinois Wesleyan University.

Growing awareness of animal abuse is helping to build an increasingly militant animal-welfare movement in this country and abroad—a movement that is beginning to have an impact on public policy. Secretary of Health and Human Services Frederick Goodwin complained recently that complying with new Federal regulations on the use—or abuse—of animals will drain off some 17 per cent of the research funds appropriated to the National Institutes of Health. (It is cheaper to purchase, use, and destroy animals than to retool for alternative procedures.) One of the institutes, the National Institute of Mental Health, spends about $30 million a year on research that involves pain and suffering for animals.

The new animal-welfare activists are drawing attention in part because of the tactics they espouse. Many preach and practice civil disobedience,

---

Jean Bethke Elshtain is the Centennial Professor of Political Science at Vanderbilt University and a member of *The Progressive*'s Editorial Advisory Board.
Reprinted by permission from *The Progressive*, 409 E. Main Street, Madison, WI 53703.

violating laws against, say, breaking and entering. Some have been known to resort to violence against property and—on a few occasions—against humans.

Some individuals and groups have always fretted about human responsibility toward nonhuman creatures. In the ancient world, the historian Plutarch and the philosopher Porphyry were among those who insisted that human excellence embodied a refusal to inflict unnecessary suffering on all other creatures, human and nonhuman.

But with the emergence of the Western rationalist tradition, animals lost the philosophic struggle. Two of that tradition's great exponents, René Descartes and Immanuel Kant, dismissed out of hand the moral worth of animals. Descartes's view, which has brought comfort to every human who decides to confine, poison, cripple, infect, or dismember animals in the interest of human knowledge, was the more extreme: He held that animals are simply machines, devoid of consciousness or feeling. Kant, more sophisticated in his ethical reasoning, knew that animals could suffer but denied that they were self-conscious. Therefore, he argued, they could aptly serve as means to human ends.

To make sure that human sensibilities would not be troubled by the groans, cries, and yelps of suffering animals—which might lead some to suspect that animals not only bleed but feel pain—researchers have for a century subjected dogs and other animals to an operation called a centriculocordectomy, which destroys their vocal chords.

Still, there have long been groups that placed the suffering of animals within the bounds of human concern. In the Nineteenth and early Twentieth Centuries, such reform movements as women's suffrage and abolitionism made common cause with societies for the prevention of cruelty to animals. On one occasion in 1907, British suffragettes, trade-unionists, and their animal-welfare allies battled London University medical students in a riot triggered by the vivisection of a dog.

Traditionally, such concern has been charitable and, frequently, highly sentimental. Those who perpetrated the worst abuses against animals were denounced for their "beastly" behavior—the farmer who beat or starved his horse; the householder who chained and kicked his dog; the aristocratic hunter who, with his guests, slew birds by the thousands in a single day on his private game preserve.

For the most part, however, animals have been viewed, even by those with "humane" concerns, as means to human ends. The charitable impulse, therefore, had a rather condescending, patronizing air: Alas, the poor creatures deserve our pity.

The new animal-welfare movement incorporates those historic concerns but steers them in new directions. Philosophically, animal-rights activists seek to close the gap between "human" and "beast," challenging the entire Western rationalist tradition which holds that the ability to reason abstractly is *the* defining human attribute. (In that tradition, women were often located on a scale somewhere between "man" and "beast," being deemed human but not quite rational.)

Politically, the new abolitionists, as many animal-welfare activists call themselves, eschew sentimentalism in favor of a tough-minded, insistent claim that animals, too, have rights, and that violating those rights constitutes oppression. It follows that animals must be liberated—and since they cannot liberate themselves in the face of overwhelming human hegemony, they require the help of liberators much as slaves did in the last century.

Thus, the rise of vocal movements for animal well-being has strong historic antecedents. What is remarkable about the current proliferation of efforts is their scope and diversity. Some proclaim animal "rights." Others speak of animal "welfare" or "protection." Still others find the term "equality" most apt, arguing that we should have "equal concern" for the needs of all sentient creatures.

When so many issues clamor for our attention, when so many problems demand our best attempts at fair-minded solution, why animals, why now? There is no simple explanation for the explosion of concern, but it is clearly linked to themes of peace and justice. Perhaps it can be summed up this way: Those who are troubled by the question of who is or is not within the circle of moral concern; those who are made queasy by our use and abuse of living beings for our own ends; those whose dreams of a better world are animated by some notion of a peaceable kingdom, *should* consider our relationship with the creatures that inhabit our planet with us—the creatures that have helped sustain us and that may share a similar fate with us unless we find ways to deflect if not altogether end the destruction of our earthly habitat.

Dozens of organizations have sprung up, operating alongside—and sometimes in conflict with—such older mainline outfits as the Humane Society, the Anti-Vivisection League, and the World Wildlife Fund. Among the new groups are People for the Ethical Treatment of Animals (PETA), Trans-Species Unlimited, In Defense of Animals, the Gorilla Foundation, Primarily Primates, Humane Farming Association, Farm Animal Reform, Alliance for Animals, Citizens to End Animal Suffering and Exploitation (CEASE), Whale Adoption Project, Digit Fund—the list goes on and on.

Some organizations focus on the plight of animals on factory farms, especially the condition of anemic, imprisoned veal calves kept in darkness and unable to turn around until they are killed at fourteen weeks. Others are primarily concerned with conditions in the wild, where the habitat of the panda, among others, is being destroyed or where great and wonderful creatures like the black rhinoceros and the African elephant or magnificent cats like the snow leopard or the Siberian tiger are marching toward extinction, victims of greedy buyers of illegal tusks or pelts.

Another group of activists clusters around the use of animals in such profitable pursuits as greyhound racing, where dogs by the hundreds are destroyed once they cease "earning their keep," or in tourist attractions where such wonderfully intelligent social beings as the orca and the dolphin are turned into circus freaks for profit. In the wild, orcas can live for up to 100 years; in captivity, the average, sadly misnamed "killer whale" lasts about five.

Those wonderful chimpanzees that have been taught to speak to us through sign-language also arouse concern. If the funding ends or a researcher loses interest, they are sometimes killed, sometimes turned over to the less-than-tender mercies of laboratory researchers to be addicted to cocaine, infected with a virus, or subjected to some other terrible fate. Eugene Linden describes, in his study *Silent Partners,* chimps desperately trying to convey their pain and fear and sadness to uncomprehending experimenters.

Use of animals in war research is an industry in itself, though one usually shielded from public view. Monkeys are the most likely subjects of experiments designed to measure the effects of neutron-bomb radiation and the toxicity of chemical-warfare agents. Beginning in 1957, monkeys were placed at varying distances from ground zero during atomic testing; those that didn't die immediately were encaged so that the "progress" of their various cancers might be noted.

Radiation experiments on primates continue. Monkeys' eyes are irradiated, and the animals are subjected to shocks of up to 1,200 volts. Junior researchers are assigned the "death watch," and what they see are primates so distressed that they claw at themselves and even bite hunks from their own arms or legs in a futile attempt to stem the pain. At a Government proving ground in Aberdeen, Maryland, monkeys are exposed to chemical-warfare agents.

Dolphins, animals of exquisite intelligence, have been trained by the military in such scenarios as injecting carbon dioxide cartridges into Vietnamese divers and planting and removing mines. The Navy announced in April 1989 that it would continue its $30 million clandestine program, expanded in the Reagan years, to put dolphins to military use. The aim, *The New York Times* reported, is to use dolphins captured in the Gulf of Mexico to guard the Trident Nuclear Submarine Base at Bangor, Washington.

Several years ago, when I was writing a book on women and war, I came across references to the use of dogs in Vietnam. When I called the Pentagon and was put through to the chief of military history, Southeast Asia Branch, he told me that no books existed on the subject, but he did send me an excerpt from the *Vietnam War Almanac* that stated the U.S. military "made extensive use of dogs for a variety of duties in Vietnam, including scouting, mine detecting, tracking, sentry duty, flushing out tunnels, and drug detecting." Evidently, many of these dogs were killed rather than returned home, since it was feared their military training ill-suited them for civilian life.

Much better known, because of an increasingly successful animal-rights campaign, is the use of animals to test such household products as furniture polish and such cosmetics as shampoo and lipstick.

For years, industry has determined the toxicity of floor wax and detergents by injecting various substances into the stomachs of beagles, rabbits, and calves, producing vomiting, convulsions, respiratory illness, and paralysis. The so-called LD (lethal dose) 50 test ends only when half the animals in a test group have died. No anesthesia or pain killers are administered.

Dr. Andrew Rowan, assistant dean of the Tufts University School of Medicine, has offered persuasive evidence that such testing methods are crude and inaccurate measures of a product's safety. For one thing, a number of potentially significant variables, including the stress of laboratory living, are not taken into account, thus tainting any comparison of the effect of a given substance on human consumers.

The LD50 is notoriously unreproducible; the method for rating irritation is extremely subjective; and interspecies variations make test results highly suspect when applied to the human organism.

Most notorious of the "tests" deployed by the multibillion-dollar cosmetics industry is the Draize, which has been used since the 1940s to measure the potential irritative effects of products. Rabbits—used because their eyes do not produce tears and, therefore, cannot cleanse themselves—are placed into stocks and their eyes are filled with foreign substances. When a rabbit's eyes ulcerate—again, no pain killers are used—the cosmetics testers (who are usually not trained laboratory researchers) report a result. To call this procedure "scientific" is to demean authentic science.

Curiously, neither the LD50 test nor the Draize are required by law. They continue in use because manufacturers want to avoid alarming consumers by placing warning labels on products. More accurate methods available include computer simulations to measure toxicity, cell-culture systems, and organ-culture tests that use chicken-egg membranes.

The disdainful response by corporate America to animal-protection concerns seems, at least in this area, to be undergoing a slow shift toward new laboratory techniques that abandon wasteful, crude, and cruel animal testing. Several large cosmetics manufacturers, including Revlon, have only recently announced that they will phase out animal testing, confirming the claim of animal-welfare groups that the tests are unnecessary.

Among the nastier issues in the forefront of the "animal wars" is the controversy over hunting and trapping.

It's estimated that about seventeen million fur-bearing animals (plus "trash" animals—including pets—the trapper doesn't want) are mangled each year in steel-jaw leg-hold traps that tear an animal's flesh and break its bones. Many die of shock or starvation before the trapper returns. Some animals chew off part of a limb in order to escape. More than sixty countries now ban the leg-hold trap, requiring the use of less painful and damaging devices.

Protests against the manufacture, sale, and wearing of fur coats have been aggressively—and successfully—mounted in Western Europe. In Holland, fur sales have dropped 80 per cent in the last few years. Radical groups in Sweden have broken into fur farms to release minks and foxes. An effort to shame women who wear fur has had enormous impact in Great Britain.

Similar campaigns have been mounted in the United States, but the fur industry is waging a well-financed counterattack in this country. Curiously, the industry's efforts have been tacitly supported by some rights-absolutists within feminism who see wearing a fur coat as a woman's right. It's difficult to think of a greater *reductio ad absurdum* of the notion of "freedom of choice," but it seems to appeal to certain adherents of upwardly mobile, choice-obsessed political orthodoxy.

Hunting may be the final frontier for animal-welfare groups. Because hunting is tied to the right to bear arms, any criticism of hunting is construed as an attack on constitutional freedoms by hunting and gun organizations, including the powerful and effective National Rifle Association. A bumper sticker I saw on a pickup truck in Northampton, Massachusetts, may tell the tale: My wife, yes. My dog, maybe. But my gun, never.

For some animal protectionists, the case against hunting is open and shut. They argue that the vast majority of the estimated 170 million animals shot to death in any given year are killed for blood sport, not for food, and that the offspring of these slaughtered creatures are left to die of exposure or starvation. Defenders of blood sports see them as a skill and a tradition, a lingering relic of America's great frontier past. Others—from Nineteenth Century feminists to the Norman Mailer of *Why Are We in Vietnam?* —link the national mania for hunting with a deeper thirst for violence.

I am not convinced there is an inherent connection between animal killing and a more general lust for violence, but some disquieting evidence is beginning to accumulate. Battered and abused women in rural areas often testify, for example, that their spouses also abused animals, especially cows, by stabbing them with pitchforks, twisting their ears, kicking them, or, in one reported incident, using a board with a nail in it to beat a cow to death.

But even people who recoil from hunting and other abuses of animals often find it difficult to condemn such experiments as those cited at the beginning of this article, which are, after all, conducted to serve "science" and, perhaps, to alleviate human pain and suffering. Sorting out this issue is no easy task if one is neither an absolute prohibitionist nor a relentless defender of the scientific establishment. When gross abuses come to light, they are often reported in ways that allow and encourage us to distance ourselves from emotional and ethical involvement. Thus the case of the baboons whose brains were bashed in at the University of Pennsylvania prompted *The New York Times* to editorialize, on July 31, 1985, that the animals "seemed" to be suffering. They *were* suffering, and thousands of animals suffer every day.

Reasonable people should be able to agree on this: that alternatives to research that involves animal suffering must be vigorously sought; that there is no excuse for such conditions as dogs lying with open incisions, their entrails exposed, or monkeys with untreated, protruding broken bones, exposed muscle tissue, and infected wounds, living in grossly unsanitary conditions amidst feces and rotting food; that quick euthanasia should be administered to a suffering animal after the conclusion of a pain-inducing procedure; that pre- and postsurgical care must be provided for animals; that research should not be needlessly duplicated, thereby wasting animal lives, desensitizing generations of researchers, and flushing tax dollars down the drain.

What stands in the way of change? Old habits, bad science, unreflective cruelty, profit, and, in some cases, a genuine fear that animal-welfare groups want to stop all research dead in its tracks. "Scientists fear shackles on research," intones one report. But why are scientists so reluctant to promote such research alternatives as modeling, in-vitro techniques, and the use of lower organisms? Because they fear that the public may gain wider knowledge of what goes on behind the laboratory door. Surely those using animals should be able to explain themselves and to justify their expenditure of the lives, bodies, and minds of other creatures.

There is, to be sure, no justification for the harassment and terror tactics used by some animal-welfare groups. But the scientist who is offended when an animal-welfare proponent asks, "How would you feel if someone treated your child the way you treat laboratory animals?" should ponder one of the great ironies in the continuing debate: Research on animals is justified on grounds that they are "so like us."

I *do* appreciate the ethical dilemma here. As a former victim of polio, I have thought long and hard for years about animal research and human welfare. This is where I come down, at least for now:

First, most human suffering in this world cannot be ameliorated in any way by animal experimentation. Laboratory infliction of suffering on animals will not keep people healthy in Asia, Africa, and Latin America. As philosopher Peter Singer has argued, we already know how to cure what ails people in desperate poverty; they need "adequate nutrition, sanitation, and health care. It has been estimated that 250,000 children die each week around the world, and that one quarter of these deaths are by dehydration due to diarrhea. A simple treatment, already known and needing no animal experimentation, could prevent the deaths of these children."

Second, it is not clear that a cure for terrible and thus far incurable diseases such as AIDS is best promoted with animal experimentation. Some American experts on AIDS admit that French scientists are making more rapid progress toward a vaccine because they are working directly with human volunteers, a course of action Larry Kramer, a gay activist, has urged upon American scientists. Americans have been trying since 1984 to infect chimpanzees with AIDS, but after the expenditure of millions of dollars, AIDS has not been induced in any nonhuman animal. Why continue down this obviously flawed route?

Third, we could surely agree that a new lipstick color, or an even more dazzling floor wax, should never be promoted for profit over the wounded bodies of animals. The vast majority of creatures tortured and killed each year suffer for *nonmedical* reasons. Once this abuse is eliminated, the really hard cases having to do with human medical advance and welfare can be debated, item by item.

Finally, what is at stake is the exhaustion of the Eighteenth Century model of humanity's relationship to nature, which had, in the words of philosopher Mary Midgley, "built into it a bold, contemptuous rejection of the nonhuman world."

Confronted as we are with genetic engineering and a new eugenics, with the transformation of farms where animals ranged freely into giant factories where animals are processed and produced like objects, with callous behavior on a scale never before imagined under the rubric of "science," we can and must do better than to dismiss those who care as irrational and emotional animal-lovers who are thinking with their hearts (not surprisingly, their ranks are heavily filled with women), and who are out to put a stop to the forward march of rationalism and science.

We humans do not deserve peace of mind on this issue. Our sleep should be troubled and our days riddled with ethical difficulties as we come to realize the terrible toll one definition of "progress" has taken on our fellow creatures.

We must consider our meat-eating habits as well. Meat-eating is one of the most volatile, because most personal, of all animal-welfare questions. Meat-eaters do not consider themselves immoral, though hard-core vegetarians find meat-eating repugnant—the consumption of corpses. Such feminist theorists as Carol Adams insist that there is a connection between the butchering of animals and the historic maltreatment of women. Certainly, there is a politics of meat that belongs on the agenda along with other animal-welfare issues.

I, for one, do not believe humans and animals have identical rights. But I do believe that creatures who can reason in their own ways, who can suffer, who are mortal beings like ourselves, have a value and dignity we must take into account. Animals are not simply a means to our ends.

When I was sixteen years old, I journeyed on a yellow school bus from La Porte, Colorado, to Fairbanks, Iowa, on a 4-H Club "exchange trip." On the itinerary was a visit to a meat-packing plant in Des Moines. As vivid as the day I witnessed it is the scene I replay of men in blood-drenched coats "bleeding" pigs strung up by their heels on a slowly moving conveyor belt. The pigs—bright and sensitive creatures, as any person who has ever met one knows—were screaming in terror before the sharp, thin blade entered their jugular veins. They continued to struggle and squeal until they writhed and fell silent.

The men in the slaughter room wore boots. The floor was awash in blood. I was horrified. But I told myself this was something I should remember. For a few months I refused to eat pork. But then I fell back into old habits—this was Colorado farm country in the late 1950s, after all.

But at one point, a few years ago, that scene and those cries of terror returned. This time I decided I would not forget, even though I knew my peace of mind would forever be disturbed.

ANIMAL RIGHTS

Molly O'Neill

The steam from four outdoor lobster pots rose toward the blue sky and danced like happy ghosts in a balsam-scented breeze over Mount Desert Island, Me. It was a perfect Maine day. A lobster kind of day. And a line of station wagons and campers, sports cars and Jeeps pulled into the Bar Harbor Snack Bar.

The crunch of gravel under tires, the distant surf, the lip-smacking clamor of lunch orders was punctuated by the splash of live lobsters being tossed into the vats of boiling sea water and by the thumping staccato of the lobsters flailing inside the pots.

"This is starting to gross me out," murmured Larraine Brown, a 40-year-old radio producer at WERU in nearby Blue Hill who had stopped by for lunch.

She might as well have screamed "JAWS!" The crowd of vacationers did double takes. The splash-thump swelled like a dirge. "I'm sorry," Ms. Brown said to the 14 people around the pots. She had ordered a two-pounder, but the sound of her lunch cooking changed her appetite.

She is not alone.

The wellspring of humane sentiment tapped by recent anti-fur campaigns is trickling toward America's dinner tables.

In grocery stores, restaurants and national advertising campaigns, animal rights advocates—some concerned with the quality of animal life, others defending the sanctity of animal life—are confronting consumers.

Consumers are beginning to listen, especially as nutritional studies undermine the rationale that humans require a meat-based diet to be healthy.

And now, even moderate organizations like the American Society for the Prevention of Cruelty to Animals have begun to take a hard stand against raising animals for the table.

"The term 'meat' is a kinder label than 'dead animal,'" said Dr. John F. Kullberg, president of the ASPCA. After touring farms, Kullberg concluded, "Factory farm animals are treated more like machine parts on an assembly line than sentient creatures who feel and suffer pain."

And the issue is moving beyond images of cuddly lambs and sad-eyed calves. Today, animal rights advocates are not just asking whether raising

Reprinted from *New York Times*. Copyright © 1990 New York Times Company. Reprinted by permission.

animals for the table is torture, but whether cooks themselves are executioners. Consider the lobster.

On to New Horizons

"Lobster is the litmus test," said Daniel Mason, a spokesman for People for the Ethical Treatment of Animals, a group that has campaigned against the use of animals for fur coats and laboratory tests and next month will begin a $650,000 drive against eating meat.

In an urban society, preparing a lobster is one of the few times that a cook witnesses the transition from "animal" to "food," and confronts the possibility of inflicting pain. And cooks are increasingly squeamish.

Across the nation, lobster sales have remained constant at 40 million pounds for the past decade. But vendors notice that customers are increasingly concerned about cruelty to lobsters.

"More and more people want a very detailed explanation of how to cook the lobster painlessly," said Paul Burnish, a spokesman for Kroger, the chain of 1,200 supermarkets based in Cincinnati.

Most experts recommend boiling. Dr. Robert Bayer, who has studied lobster for 15 years at the University of Maine, agrees. Boiling is quick and a lobster's sensitivity to pain is difficult to gauge, he said.

"They don't really have a brain and they have a decentralized nervous system like a large insect," he said. That lobsters twitch when tossed into boiling water could indeed be an "involuntary response," Bayer said.

Nevertheless, around the pots at the Bar Harbor Snack Bar recently, the twitching sounds made the lunch crowd uncomfortable.

Ms. Brown lost her apetite, Elisa Launder, of nearby Hulls Cove, said that while she has been catching, cooking and eating lobster for nearly 70 years, "now I'd rather have somebody else do the dirty work; it started to bother me."

Formerly Focused on Veal

Until recently, most anti-meat advocates have focused on veal. Over the last five years, the Humane Farming Association in San Francisco has spearheaded a national veal boycott. Its advertising pictured a calf said to be chained in a 22-inch crate and administered a diet intended to keep it anemic, making the meat look like the pale, milk-fed veal that epicureans prize.

Since the campaign started, national veal sales have fallen an average of 15 percent a year, the largest drop of any federally inspected meat, said Alice Burroughs, a statistical assistant with the National Agricultural Statistics Service in Washington.

"Factory-farmed veal is about as socially acceptable as fur coats these days," said Jasper White, an owner of Restaurant Jasper in Boston. Along with an increasing number of chefs, he buys veal from a small farm where calves are raised under more humane conditions.

But humane farming skirts the issue for advocates who believe in the sanctity of animal life. "We don't want bigger cages or cleaner cages; we want empty cages," said Robin Walker, coordinator of PETA's campaign for vegetarianism.

The campaign will include ads featurng "dead pigs and butchers with blood-splattered aprons," Ms. Walker said. The campaign slogan is, "If you knew how your dinner was made, you'd lose your lunch."

"Americans must confront reality and make ethical decisions," said John Robbins, whose book "Diet for a New America," (Stillpoint Publishing, 1987) is the bible of the anti-meat campaign. Like most advocates, he is opposed to eating any flesh.

"Don't eat anything that has a face," he said. "Don't eat anything that has sexual urges, that has a mother and father or that tries to run away from you."

Robbins believes that a confluence of recent trends strengthens the case for vegetarianism. Public concern for residual antibiotics in meat, the health risks of a meat-dependent diet and the environmental impact of factory farming may have weakened the "sacred cow of meat-eating in America," he said.

"We can use these issues to address the speciesism and cruelty involved in killing animals for the table," he said.

"Speciesism," said Peter Singer, author of "Animal Liberation," (Avon Books, 1975) "is the presumption that humans are superior to other sentient creatures and therefore entitled to eat them." Those who believe in the sanctity of animal life say speciesism is tantamount to racism or sexism.

To a traditional meat-and-potatoes person, such thinking is un-American. "The vegetarian is at odds with our way of life," said Kendal Frazier, spokesman for the American Cattleman's Association in Englewood, Colo.

"Should I stop swatting flies?" Julia Child said. "Should I invite mice into my kitchen and serve them lunch? This speciesism is specious."

White of Restaurant Jasper asked, "Where do you draw the line?"

Gilbert Le Coze, the chef and an owner of Le Bernardin, the seafood restaurant in Manhattan, asked the same question and then answered: "I am human. I eat meat."

Even so, Le Coze said, sometimes when he lowers a lobster in a pot of boiling court-bouillon he thinks: "Poor guy. I hope it doesn't hurt."

Mrs. Child believes that such sentimentality shows that "Americans have gotten so far from the farm and food production that they have lost all perspective."

Or perhaps anti-meat advocates have tweaked the American conscience. This summer, PETA representatives are demonstrating at 4-H events and state fairs "to support the children who feel bad about killing their pets," Ms. Walker said.

The organization is also touring with Paul McCartney, a vegetarian, to distribute anti-meat materials at his concerts. The country singer K.D. Lang has made an anti-meat commercial. Ms. Walker said Madonna and Michael Jackson also support the anti-meat campaign.

In 1988, People for the Ethical Treatment of Animals sponsored its first act of "lobster liberation," raising money to buy all the lobsters that were in the tank of a Maryland restaurant, fly them to Maine and free them. Members of the group have repeated the action in retail stores and restaurants, Mason said.

With other animals, the issue can be diffused into concern for the quality of animal life. But lobsters, which roam freely and are trapped painlessly, pose a difficult mealtime conundrum. In confrontations with shopper and restaurant diners, animal rights advocates effectively frame the question.

"We let them know that lobsters have feelings," Mason said. "Lobsters live for up to 200 years in established communities and mate very lovingly for life."

While the image of the cooperative, faithful lobster resonates as deeply as the pictures of cuddly animals in fur traps, PETA's lobster image differs from the traditional view of lobsters as predators who prey on crabs, snails, mussels and even each other. But the "nice-guy" lobster is also based, at least in part, on scientific observation.

For 20 years Dr. Jelle Atema, a professor with the Boston University Marine Program at Woods Hole, Mass., has studied lobsters.

Using scuba gear, a flashlight and a waterproof notebook, he swims along the ocean floor, studying groupings of 20 to 30 lobsters that he calls "villages."

His tests have established that a wounded lobster emits a chemical that "serves as a feeding signal," but otherwise the crustaceans are not cannibals. Another chemical emission, a pheromone secretion by the female, begins "a tender, two-week mating ritual," he said.

"Lobsters are remarkable, sophisticated creatures," Dr. Atema said. They are not, however, monogamous, they do not tend their young, they do not settle for more than a year and they are not likely to live more than 80 years, he said.

Atema has found no effective way of determining a lobster's capacity to experience pain. But he continues to skirt the ocean floor and study the denizens of the deep.

"I spend most nights with the lobster. I respect them," he said. "I only eat them boiled."

Am I Blue? . . .

Alice Walker

For about three years my companion and I rented a small house in the country that stood on the edge of a large meadow that appeared to run from the end of our deck straight into the mountains. The mountains, however, were quite far away, and between us and them there was, in fact, a town. It was one of the many pleasant aspects of the house that you never really were aware of this. It was a house of many windows, low, wide, nearly floor to ceiling in the living room, which faced the meadow, and it was from one of these that I first saw our closest neighbor, a large white horse, cropping grass, flipping its mane, and ambling about—not over the entire meadow, which stretched well out of sight of the house, but over the five or so fenced-in acres that were next to the 20-odd that we had rented. I soon learned that the horse, whose name was Blue, belonged to a man who lived in another town, but was boarded by our neighbors next door. Occasionally, one of the children, usually a stocky teenager, but sometimes a much younger girl or boy, could be seen riding Blue. They would appear in the meadow, climb up on his back, ride furiously for 10 or 15 minutes, then get off, slap Blue on the flanks, and not be seen again for a month or more.

There were many apple trees in our yard, and one by the fence that Blue could almost reach. We were soon in the habit of feeding him apples, which he relished, especially because by the middle of summer the meadow grasses—so green and succulent since January—had dried out from lack of rain, and Blue stumbled about munching the dried stalks half-heartedly. Sometimes he would stand very still just by the apple tree, and when one of us came out he would whinny, snort loudly, or stamp the ground. This meant, of course, I want an apple.

It was quite wonderful to pick a few apples, or collect those that had fallen to the ground overnight, and patiently hold them, one by one, up to his large, toothy mouth. I remained as thrilled as a child by his flexible dark lips, huge, cube-like teeth that crunched the apples, core and all, with such finality, and his high, broad-breasted enormity; beside which I felt small indeed. When I was a child, I used to ride horses, and was especially friendly with one named Nan until one day I was riding and my brother deliberately spooked her and I was thrown, head first, against the trunk of a tree. When I came to, I was in bed and my mother was bending

Reprinted from *Living by the Word.* Copyright © 1988 by Harcourt, Brace, Jovanovich.

worriedly over me; we silently agreed that perhaps horseback riding was not the safest sport for me. Since then I have walked, and prefer walking to horseback riding—but I had forgotten the depth of feeling one could see in horses' eyes.

I was therefore unprepared for the expression in Blue's. Blue was lonely. Blue was horribly lonely and bored. I was not shocked that this should be the case; five acres to tramp by yourself, endlessly, even in the most beautiful of meadows, cannot provide many interesting events. No, I was shocked that I had forgotten that human animals and non-human animals can communicate quite well; if we are brought up around animals as children we take this for granted. By the time we are adults we no longer remember. However, the animals have not changed. It is their nature to express themselves. And they do. And, generally speaking, they are ignored.

After giving Blue the apples, I would wander to the back of the house, aware that he was observing me. Were more apples not forthcoming then? Was that to be his sole entertainment for the day? My partner's small son had decided he wanted to learn how to piece a quilt; we worked in silence on our respective squares as I thought . . .

Well, about slavery: about white children, who were raised by black people, who knew their first all-accepting love from black women, and then, when they were 12 or so, were told that they must "forget" the deep levels of communication between themselves and "mammy" that they knew. Later they would be able to relate quite calmly, "My old mammy was sold to another good family." "My old mammy was _____." Fill in the blank. Many more years later the same person would say: "I can't understand these Negroes, these blacks. What do they want? They're so different from us."

And about the Indians, considered to be "like animals" by the "settlers" (a very benign euphemism for what the settlers actually were), who did not understand their description as a compliment.

And about the thousands of American men who marry Japanese, Korean, Filipina, and other non-English-speaking women and of how happy they report they are, "blissfully," until their brides learn to speak English, at which point the marriages tend to fall apart. What then did the men see, when they looked into the eyes of the women they married, before they could speak English? Apparently only their own reflections.

I thought of society's impatience with the young. "Why are they playing the music so loud?" Perhaps the children have listened to much of the music of oppressed people their parents danced to before they were born, with its passionate but soft cries for acceptance and love, and they have wondered why their parents failed to hear.

I do not know how long Blue had inhabited his five beautiful, boring acres before we moved into our house; a year after we had arrived he was still there.

But then, in our second year at the house, something happened in Blue's life. One morning looking out the window at the fog that lay like a ribbon over the meadow, I saw another horse, a brown one, at the other end of Blue's field. Blue appeared to be afraid of it, and for several days made no attempt to go near. We went away for a week. When we returned, Blue had decided to make friends and the two horses ambled or galloped along together, and Blue did not come nearly as often to the fence underneath the apple tree.

When he did, bringing his new friend with him, there was a different look in his eyes. A look of independence, of self-possession, of inalienable horseness. His friend eventually became pregnant. For months and months there was, it seemed to me, a mutual feeling between me and the horses—of justice, of peace. I fed apples to them both. The look in Blue's eyes was one of unabashed "this is itness."

It did not, however, last forever. One day, after a visit to the city, I went out to give Blue some apples. He stood waiting, or so I thought, though not beneath the tree. When I shook the tree and jumped back from the shower of apples, he made no move. I carried some over to him. He managed to half-crunch one. The rest he let fall to the ground. I dreaded looking into his eyes—because I had of course noticed that Brown, his partner, had gone—but I did look. If I had been born into slavery, and my partner had been sold or killed, my eyes would have looked like that. The children next door had explained that Blue's partner had been "put with him" (the same expression that old people in the South used when speaking of an ancestor during slavery who had been impregnated by her owner) so that they could mate and she conceive. Since that was accomplished, she had been taken back by her owner, who lived somewhere else.

Will she be back? I asked.

They didn't know.

Blue was like a crazed person. Blue *was*, to me, a crazed person. He galloped furiously, as if he were being ridden, around and around his five beautiful acres. He whinnied until he couldn't. He tore at the ground with his hooves. He butted himself against his single shade tree. He looked always and always toward the road down which his partner had gone. And then, occasionally when he came up for apples, or I took apples to him, he looked at me. It was a look so piercing, so full of grief, a look so human, I almost laughed (I felt too sad to cry) to think there are people who do not know that animals suffer. People like me who have forgotten, and daily forget, all that animals try to tell us. "Everything you do to us will happen to you; we are your teachers, as you are ours." There are those who never once have even considered animals' rights: those who have been taught that animals actually want to be used and abused by us, just as small children "love" to be frightened, or women "love" to be mutilated and raped. . . . They are the great-grandchildren of those people who honestly thought, because someone taught them this: "Women can't think," and "niggers can't faint." But most disturbing of all, in Blue's large brown eyes was a new look, more painful than the look of despair: the look of disgust with human beings, with life; the look of hatred. And it was odd what the look of hatred did. It gave him, for the first time, the look of a beast. And what that meant was that he had put up a barrier within to protect himself from further violence; all the apples in the world wouldn't change that fact.

And so Blue remained, a beautiful part of our landscape, very peaceful to look at from the window, white against the grass. Once a friend came to visit and said, looking out on the soothing view: "And it *would* have to be a *white* horse; the very image of freedom." And I thought, yes, the animals are forced to become for us merely "images" of what they once so beautifully expressed. And we are used to drinking milk from containers showing "contented" cows, whose real lives we want to hear nothing about, eating eggs and drumsticks from "happy" hens, and munching hamburgers advertised by bulls of integrity who seem to command their fate.

As we talked of freedom and justice one day for all, we sat down to steaks. I am eating misery, I thought, as I took the first bite. And spit it out.

WHAT'S WRONG WITH ANIMAL RIGHTS?

Barbara Grizzuti Harrison

Vivisection, when I was in junior high school, was a frequent topic of formal debate, the occasion for rhetorical flourishes, for indulged and cultivated hamminess (no pun intended). But never did I think that animal rights would one day be something around which large numbers of people might rally and protest. That day has come . . . with, if not a vengeance, a passion.

It's estimated that 10 million people now belong to animal-rights groups. Of course, there are trends in everything, including causes, but it's reasonable to assume that the accelerated concern for animals is not unrelated to our heightened concerns about the neglected and abused planet. If apparently commonsensical people are ready to declare that trees cry when they are cut down, we can't be surprised when animal lovers go cuckoo over the use of cats, say, for lab experiments on barbiturate addiction.

The absolutist position on the issue is articulated by Gary Francione, a professor at the University of Pennsylvania Law School who litigates animal-rights cases. He contends that humans who deny animals their "rights" are "speciesists" (as in racists or sexists), no better than slaveholders, and that animal rights "will emerge as *the* civil rights movement of the twenty-first century." If the abrogation of the "rights" of one sewer rat could rid the entire world of cancer, says Francione, its "rights" would have, nevertheless, to be honored. No experimenting; no cure.

By what criteria do animals have "rights"? Ingrid E. Newkirk, national director of People for the Ethical Treatment of Animals, would grant entitlement—to life and to pain-free life—to "all those with faces. If you can look into the eyes of another and that other looks back," she says, "that's one measure." Newkirk would regard humans as "just another animal in the pack."

I think this verges on lunacy.

Civilized people can agree not to perform unnecessary or repetitive tests on animals and not to inflict gratuitous pain. To most of us, for example, forcing open the eyes of rabbits to test mascara is as loathsome as it is unnecessary (and, indeed, many cosmetic companies now perform a skin-patch test that obviates the need for rabbits). But we can make a hierarchy of needs: While it may seem frivolous to kill animals to find a cure for baldness or zits, it is not frivolous—it is incumbent upon us—to

Reprinted from *Mademoiselle* Magazine. Copyright © July 1989 by Barbara Grizzuti Harrison. Reprinted by permission.

find a cure for AIDS, cancer, Alzheimer's; and if that requires the sacrifice of laboratory animals, so be it. There is, not so incidentally, diabetes in my family—and there are members of my family who were able to live because of insulin, which was derived, initially, from the pancreas of pigs.

And, as one ethicist has said, you can teach a human being to care about a pig, but you can't teach a pig to care about a human being—i.e., humans and animals are (isn't it crazy to have to say this?) not entitled to the same rights, in part because there is no reciprocity of feelings. (Have you ever seen a rat smile?)

What is "good" for animals is not necessarily good for humans, and vice versa. Suppose a sewer rat were found to have bubonic plague. Suppose a human being—Mother Teresa, or Tina Turner, or your brother, or Ivan Boesky, or Solzhenitsyn, or the newspaper delivery boy—were found to have bubonic plague. What would you do? I'll save you the trouble of answering. You'd kill the rat; you'd quarantine the human being. Anybody who says otherwise is living in gaga land.

AT ISSUE: DOES CONSERVATION JUSTIFY KEEPING ANIMALS IN ZOOS?

Yes

Yes, says William G. Conrad, director of the New York Zoological Society. "With the advent of an age wherein man is finally being forced to become concerned with the health of his environment, zoo roles in education, conservation, research and recreation are assuming far greater breadth and significance. . . . Until recently, the number of kinds of animals a zoo exhibited determined its status in the world zoo hierarchy. . . . Today, the 'species race' has been abandoned. The quality of a zoo's exhibits and other educational offerings, its propagation results, and its research and conservation programs are the measure of its standing.

"Currently, zoos are in the throes of a remarkable expansion in capabilities and programs. New techniques in veterinary care, new understandings of animal behavior and ecology and a new technology of zoological park exhibition have coincided with an emerging generation of visitors who seem to have a more sophisticated and compelling interest in wild creatures. . . . A zoo can function directly to broaden its visitors' base of environmental and scientific literacy. . . . Broadly, zoo education reveals the interrelationship of animal societies and, ultimately, of animals and man.

"Conservation has become one of the most compelling purposes of zoos. . . . Zoo-based education and wildlife promotion programs can be a natural foundation for nurturing a responsible attitude toward wildlife and wild places—the development of a conservation ethic.

"Remaining wildlife populations may become so small or fragmented that breeding is prevented or that minor environmental fluctuations could result in their extinction. Where wild populations and their habitat cannot be saved, manipulative approaches developed through research in captivity and even captive propagation become last resorts as parks are fenced and, inevitably, become more zoo-like. . . . It is just possible that some of these creatures may be reintroduced to nature, even a reconstituted nature, if zoos can sustain them for yet a while.

"However, the captive propagation of vanishing species must be recognized as a treatment for the symptoms of extinction, not as a cure for the disease. While zoos are growing increasingly skillful in reproducing rare wild animals, their contribution towards conservation may have a more lasting effect through exciting the interest and concern of human beings in their environment and in the creatures with which they share it."

Reprinted from *Editorial Research Reports.* Copyright © 1987 Congressional Quarterly, Inc.

No

No, says Michael W. Fox, scientific director of the Humane Society of the United States. "The best of zoos claim to be advanced in conservation, in research into wildlife diseases, surgery and reproduction, and in educating the public. But could they not just as well, if not better, educate the public with documentary films? A polar bear or a fish in a zoo or aquarium does not—and cannot—show people the chemical and radiation pollution in their bodies.... Instead, many zoos thoroughly miseducate; they exhibit unhealthy, neurotic animals that in no way represent the true, full range of behavior of the species.... But what zoo explains to its visitors that 'amusing antics' [of animals] are abnormal and symptoms of suffering?... The upshot is that zoos are too... sanitized and beautified to be authentic reflections of the wild.

"Zoos are becoming facsimiles—or perhaps caricatures—of how animals once were in their natural habitat. And too often, these are high-tech facsimiles that do not enhance the animals' welfare and are a waste of good resources.

"As to the claim that the best zoos are helping save species... by breeding them in captivity, it may be best to let these animals become extinct if there is no place for them in the wild.... To put animals on exhibit as 'specimens' and 'social groups' torn from the very fabric of the ecosystems and bio-fields in which they evolved... is a violation of the biological and spiritual unity of all life.

"Even if zoos enhance endangered species' welfare and encourage reproduction, where are their offspring to go? To other zoo collections—or worse, to a 'game ranch' where, for a fee, hunters can bag a trophy animal from Africa or South America without having to leave the United States....

"Are zoos a necessary evil? Wildlife's last refuge? Considering the rate of destruction of animals and habitat around the world, sometimes I think so. I respect the many people who are dedicated to good zoo management, research, species preservation and veterinary medicine. But all this dedication can be seriously misplaced if we lose sight of the fact that the problems of zoo animals and the crisis of wildlife's threatened annihilation are primarily man-made and need a political, not a technocratic, solution. Building better zoos at the expense of efforts to conserve nature, be it at the local, national or international level, is wrong. If the right policies toward nature were pursued, we should need no zoos at all."

THE FACTS ABOUT ANIMAL RESEARCH

Robert J. White

Four years ago I was part of a surgical team trying to remove a malignant tumor from the brain of a nine-year-old girl. The operation failed because we could not stem the hemorrhaging in the brain tissue. We were unable to separate the little girl from the cancer that was slowly killing her. To buy time, we put her on a program of radiation.

Concurrently we were experimenting in our brain-research laboratory with a new high-precision laser scalpel. Working with monkeys and dogs that had been humanely treated and properly anesthetized, we perfected our operating technique. Then, in July 1985, my associate, pediatric neurosurgeon Matt Likavec, and I used the laser to remove all of that little girl's tumor. Now 13, she is healthy, happy, and looking forward to a full life. The animal experiments had enabled us to cure a child we could not help 15 months earlier.

There is virtually no major treatment or surgical procedure in modern medicine that could have been developed without animal research. Work with dogs and other animals led to the discovery of insulin and the control of diabetes, to open-heart surgery, the cardiac pacemaker and the whole area of organ transplantation. Polio, which once killed some 30,000 people annually and crippled thousands of children, has been almost totally eradicated in the United States by preventive vaccines perfected on monkeys. By working with animals, researchers have raised the cure rate for children afflicted with acute lymphocytic leukemia from four percent in 1965 to 70 percent today.

Animal research has vanquished smallpox and enabled us to immunize our children against mumps, measles, rubella and diphtheria, and to defend them against infections by means of an arsenal of medical "magic bullets" called antibiotics.

Animals, too, have profited from this research. Many a family pet has had cataracts removed, has undergone open-heart surgery or wears a pacemaker, and many animals have benefited from vaccines for rabies, distemper, anthrax, tetanus and feline leukemia.

Robert J. White, M.D., Ph.D., is director of Neurological Surgery at Cleveland Metropolitan General Hospital and professor of neurosurgery at Case Western Reserve University Medical School.
Reprinted from *Reader's Digest*, March 1988, pp. 127–132. Copyright © 1988 Reader's Digest.

Regulatory Straitjacket

The dramatic medical strides of the past 50 years far exceed the progress in all of previous history. Unhappily, the next 50 years may not see comparable accomplishments. We owe this cloudy outlook to a radical element within the animal-rights movement, spearheaded by People for the Ethical Treatment of Animals (PETA) and other anti-vivisectionist groups, whose leaders insist that *all* research involving animals must cease. These extremists are applying pressure at every level of government, trying to fashion a regulatory straitjacket that is sure to slow medical progress.

Rep. Robert Mrazek (D., N.Y.) and Sen. Wendell Ford (D., Ky.) have introduced companion bills in Congress that would effectively prohibit the sale of pound animals for any medical research funded by the National Institutes of Health (NIH). Twelve states already have banned such sales, and five more have similar legislation under active consideration.

In addition, Rep. Charles Rose (D., N.C.) has introduced a bill that would, in effect, give animals "standing" in court. Should the bill pass, anyone who decides that an animal has been misused in an animal-research facility could file suit in the animal's behalf against the government. Thus, misguided radicals could choke our courts with nuisance suits.

Economic Realities

It is not hard to understand why opponents of research with animals have received such a sympathetic response. The idea conjures up images of experiments on beloved family pets. But the fact is that over 90 percent of the more than 20 million animals used annually in medical research are mice, rats and other rodents. A small percentage are farm animals and monkeys, and less than one percent are dogs and cats.

About 200,000 dogs and cats are abandoned *each week* in the United States. These are animals that people have left to roam the streets, forage in garbage dumps and run wild. After a waiting period in the pound, during which time any pet picked up accidentally may be claimed by its owner or adopted, the animals are put to death. It is only after this waiting period has expired that medical researchers purchase a few already doomed animals—in 1986, for example, less than two percent of them. That same year, about one-tenth of our dog and cat populations—some ten million animals—were destroyed.

Researchers obtain animals from pounds because the cost for each is usually $15 or less, while animals bred by commercial suppliers for research purposes cost several hundred dollars. If medical centers are prohibited from purchasing pound animals, many researchers will not be able to afford to continue their work.

This is nowhere more evident than in Massachusetts, one of the world's most productive medical-research centers and the first state to ban totally the sale of pound animals for medical-research purposes. The high cost of commercially supplied dogs has forced noted Harvard Medical School physiologist Dr. A. Clifford Barger to cut back on work aimed at finding cures for hypertension and coronary-artery disease. "The dog is essential to the study of such diseases," says Dr. Barger. "In the end, it's the public that is going to suffer."

In the November 1986 issue of The Washingtonian magazine, Katie McCabe recounted another aspect of the Massachusetts pound law: at Massachusetts General Hospital "cost factors have forced Dr. Willard Daggett to limit his cardiovascular studies to the rat heart, which severely limits the research questions that can be explored and applied to human cardiac patients."

Additionally, regulations governing the way we care for research animals have already increased costs substantially, and animal-rights activists continue to make new proposals to drive costs higher. "It has even been proposed that dogs used in research have individual, isolated runs so they can defecate in privacy," says Dr. Mark Ravitch, surgeon-in-chief-emeritus at the University of Pittsburgh's Montefiore Hospital. "All of this has little to do with dog welfare, and everything to do with raising the price of medical research."

Shackled Experiments

The public should have confidence that the animals used in our medical-research laboratories are well treated. Every federally funded facility has an "institutional animal-care-and-use committee," one of whose functions is to ascertain that animals are being cared for properly. The committee must include a medical-research scientist, a nonscientist, someone not affiliated with the institution, and a veterinarian. Additional monitoring is provided by federal agents.

I certainly have no objection to these safeguards. Government-funded projects involve many thousands of scientists in some 800 institutions, and the probability that there won't be some carelessness is zero. But all good researchers insist that animals be treated humanely—not only out of compassion but also because valid work depends on clean, healthy research subjects that are not victims of physical or emotional stress.

Charles McCarthy, Director of NIH's Office for Protection from Research Risks, says: "We have had a half-dozen abuse cases since 1981. Either animals have not been properly cared for—usually over a long weekend—or an attendant has not conscientiously provided an animal with adequate anesthetics. But we have *never* run into a sadist who got his kicks inflicting pain on animals."

My main objection is to regulations requiring animal-care-and-use committees to pass on all research proposals involving animals. While experiments begin with specific goals, a scientist never knows at the outset where the research will lead. Yet he may not deviate from the original plan—in order to pursue an unexpected opportunity—without first filling out costly, time-consuming paper work to obtain committee approval. New regulations governing the use of animals have already increased the financial burden on the nation's 127 medical schools by many millions of dollars annually. "But the real cost is that there will be less research," says Carol Scheman of the Association of American Universities, "and when research is slowed, people die."

Damaging Setbacks

Public-opinion polls have shown that nearly 80 percent of us approve of the use of animals in medical experimentation. I am convinced that most Americans are unaware of the devastating effect animal-rights extremists are having on such research. Frankie L. Trull, president of the Foundation for Biomedical Research, says, "People don't realize that they are being steamrollered. They may not recognize what is happening until a lot of damage has been done."

The damage is already considerable. For example, Stanford University's proposal to build a state-of-the-art animal laboratory and a new biology building met with opposition from the Palo Alto Humane Society. First objecting to the lab, partly out of concern for the well-being of Stanford's animals, the Society later joined in an appeal to delay construction of the biology building on the basis of possible environmental damage. These delays will cost Stanford some $2 million.

What are the human stakes? Stanford University scientists have already developed a permanent cure for diabetes in mice. It isn't known yet whether this will lead to a permanent cure for human diabetes, but there is a strong basis for optimism. If this dream is to be realized, research must proceed with more mice, then with larger animals.

Animal-rights activists like to claim that work accomplished with animals can be done by other means, that we can unlock medical mysteries with computers and with cell cultures grown in test tubes. But, as yet, there is no computer that can even come close to matching the nervous system that tells a mouse how to move a leg or a monkey a finger.

How can researchers using cell cultures, which do not have bones, develop a treatment for arthritis or other bone diseases? How can cell cultures help us to perfect the surgical techniques used in organ transplantation? For the foreseeable future the answers to such questions can be found only by scientists working with living species.

Intimidation Tactics

Not content to impose their views through lawful means, fringe elements of the animal-rights movement have resorted to terrorist activity. Last April, intruders who left behind graffiti and vandalized university vehicles set afire an unfinished veterinary diagnostic laboratory at the University of California's Davis campus, causing damage estimated at $3.5 million. A few months later a group calling itself "The Band of Mercy" took 28 cats from a Department of Agriculture research center in Beltsville, Md.

Eleven of these cats had been infected with a parasite, Toxoplasm gondii, which infects pregnant women and causes some 2000 birth defects annually in the United States. The incident severely hampered the work of researchers who were investigating the effects of the parasite in animals as a potential source for infection in not only pregnant women but also victims of AIDS and other diseases that weaken the immune system.

The international Animal Liberation Front (ALF) was identified by California's attorney general, John Van De Kamp, as among the state's three most active terrorist organizations during 1985. In a foray into the City of Hope National Medical Center in Duarte, the ALF did sufficient damage to set back a cancer research project by two years. At a University of California at Riverside research facility, the ALF destroyed $683,500 worth of equipment and records, painted walls with slogans and turned loose 467 animals, including a monkey involved in a program to improve the lives of blind children. By last September, animal-rights groups throughout the country had perpetrated 26 such serious crimes at medical-research facilities over a two-year period.

We are a people who love animals, but we must be realistic. Through the ages we have harvested animals for food, clothing, shelter, and in this century alone medical scientists working with animals have played a major role in increasing our average life-span from 50 to 75 years. What a tragic disservice to ourselves and future generations if we allow the animal-rights extremists to quell this marvelous momentum!

What to do? First, an important don't: Don't be misled by emotional and false propaganda. The animals in our reputable research laboratories are *not* being wantonly tortured by sadistic scientists. Such reports should not be taken seriously.

Do let your representatives in Congress know:

- That you oppose the so-called pet-protection bills. The Mrazek bill is H.R. 778; the Ford bill is S. 1457. It makes no sense to require scientists to pay exorbitant prices to commercial suppliers for animals while countless millions are put to death in pounds.
- That you oppose legislation permitting animal-rights nuisance suits aimed at stopping research.
- That you oppose the bureaucratic regulations that already have added far too much to the cost of medical research.

Do we want to wipe out leukemia? Alzheimer's? AIDS? Diabetes? Do we want better vaccines, more effective treatments and cures for high blood pressure, coronary-artery disease, stroke and myriad other ills? All of these things and more are possible within the next 25 years, some of them sooner, because of the work medical scientists are now doing with animals. But they can't be accomplished if we surrender to the mindless emotionalism and intimidation of the animal-rights fanatics. The choice is ours.

BETTER HEALTH CARE DOESN'T JUSTIFY ANIMAL RESEARCH

Kenneth L. Feder and Michael Alan Park

Last month animal-rights protesters challenged medical students at Yale University over the use of animals in medical research. As the confrontation made clear, the issue has neither faded away nor been resolved.

Proponents of the practice usually cite the importance of animal research to the level of medical care Americans now enjoy. They claim that animal-rights activists take this medical care for granted and fail to show compassion for human suffering.

But this position ignores the morality of the issue. It accepts the philosophy that the end—in this case, better human health—justifies the means—the infliction of suffering and premature death on animals.

Few of us, upon reflection, would subscribe to such a philosophy. Is it enough, to justify experiments on living organisms, to show that they have proved successful and useful? Of course not.

Controversy recently erupted when it was discovered that some scientists were using data derived from Nazi experiments in hypothermia. Human subjects—prisoners in concentration camps—were immersed in cold water to study their various reactions as they suffered and died. Such cruelty is horrifying. But it turns out that these experiments could provide useful data to help save people with hypothermia. While some have questioned the morality of even looking at the Nazi data, certainly no one would justify the experiments themselves.

Of course the data might be useful, but the means to them are immoral. If most people had had a choice, they would have preferred to do without the information rather than acquire it in such a fashion.

So the mere fact that past experiments on animals have produced important data misses the point. The question remains whether it is moral now to continue to put animals through painful and frightening procedures and even to kill them for the sake of human health.

Or, as is often the case, to satisfy human curiosity. Among pointless recent experiments are those that subjected animals to extreme heat until they died, that deprived animals important nutrients until they starved to

---

Kenneth L. Feder is an associate professor, and Michael Alan Park a professor of anthropology at Central Connecticut State University.
Reprinted from *The Hartford Courant.* Copyright © 1989 The Harford Courant. Reprinted by permission.

death, and that forced monkeys to use narcotics until they behaved abnormally or died.

One factor to consider is just how accurate animal models are for human medical research in the first place. Species of animals differ in their anatomy and physiology. Thus, illness and health are relative terms that make sense only with regard to a particular organism. There are very few diseases you can catch from your dog or vice versa, for example.

Animal research may not always be the best method and may, in some instances, mislead. Thalidomide, not a life-saving drug to begin with, proved perfectly safe when tested on some half-dozen animal species. The response in humans proved disastrous. Insulin and penicillin, on the other hand, are harmful to some non-human species, and might have been rejected for human use if animal tests were the sole basis for research.

One solution, of course, is to use species as close to humans as possible. Indeed, any experiment that provides useful data does so because the species used as a model shares with humans relevant features of nervous, circulatory and digestive systems, and even features of brains and behavior. The irony, of course, is that the more similar we believe an animal species is to us, the more morally questionable some research becomes.

Chimpanzees, for example, share with humans 99 percent of their genetic material. Chimps, therefore, are an excellent model for research into human disease and psychology. They are now being used, in fact, for AIDS research. But isn't that extent of similarity troubling? How much more similar than 99 percent would they have to be before those who support medical experiments on them find such experimentation objectionable? Ninety-nine and a half percent? Ninety-nine point nine percent?

The argument that human intelligence is qualitatively different from animal intelligence, and that intelligence is therefore the key criterion for differentiating and ranking species, is also untenable. A normal adult chimpanzee is far more intelligent than a human in a coma, or a person severely brain-damaged or retarded. Yet no moral person would consider inflicting the kind of pain on such humans that we regularly inflict on our closest non-human relatives—even though the humans would provide ideal experimental models.

Those of us working to put an end to the suffering of animals, in part by trying to eliminate their use in medical research, could hardly fail to show compassion for humans; at the very least we must consider that humans are animals, too. Nor do we take medical care for granted. More than most people, perhaps, we appreciate that much of the medical care we enjoy rests on the bodies and minds of countless animals—human and non-human—who suffered in the past.

Our position is a simple one: We can no longer morally afford to separate ourselves from the rest of the living world, of which we are an inextricable part and from which we are not all that different.

Index

Abbreviations
  in documentation, 248
  in periodical indexes, 38
Abstracts, 42–43, 88, 127
  APA style using, 254
  illustration of, 288, 218
  preparing, 218, 254
Acknowledgment of sources.
    See Sources, acknowledging
Active reading, 77–78
  illustrated, 79–83
Alternating pattern for comparing and
    contrasting, 143
American Psychological Association
    system. *See* APA system
"Am I Blue? . . ." (Walker), 316–319
Analogies, 156, 207
Analysis, 16
"Animal Rights" (O'Neill), 312–315
Annotated bibliography, 49–50
APA system, 234–235
  formatting a final draft, 253–254
  illustration of, 287–299
  models of documentation, 236–246
  typing guidelines, 254–255
Appendix, 251, 252, 255
Architecture reference books, 29
Argument, 146–154
  body of, 150
  checklist for, 151
  conclusion of, 150
  counter arguments, 149
  definition of, 146–147
  developing, 148–149
  introduction to, 149–150
  sample argumentative paper, 151–154
  steps in writing, 148–151
  support points for, 148–149
Articles
  annotated bibliographies for, 49
  bibliography card for, 243
  documentation for, 243
  sample note cards for, 180–186
Art reference books, 28
Assessing sources, 47–48, 154
"At Issue: Does Conservation Justify
    Keeping Animals in Zoos?"
    322–323
Audience, analysis of, 139, 148,
    190–191, 205–206, 223
Author cards, 34–35
Authors
  credentials of, 47
  documentation for, 236–248
  finding information about, 28

"Better Health Care Doesn't Justify
    Animal Research" (Feder and
    Park), 329–330
Bias, 48
Bibliographies. *See also*
    Documentation
  annotated, 49–50
  references, 233
  refining, 48
  works cited, 233
Bibliography cards, 24
  for articles, 42
  for books, 36
  for encyclopedias, 25–26
Bioethics reference books, 29
Biography reference books, 46

Block pattern for comparing and contrasting, 143
Block quotation, 243
Book reviews
  documentation for, 241–242
  guides for, 48
Books
  annotated bibliographies for, 49–50
  bibliography cards for, 36
  documentation for, 237–242
  locating, 34–36
  review of (see Book reviews)
Brackets for adding information to text, 25
Brotman, Barbara, 5–7

Call numbers, 34, 36
Capitalization
  of major words in titles, 222
  of titles of articles, 42
  of titles of books, 36
"Can We Buy Our Way Out of Overpopulation?" (Gardner), 166–167
Card catalogs, 34–35
Checklist
  for argumentative paper, 151
  for comparison/contrast paper, 143
  for reaction paper, 159–160
  for summary, 131
  final, 263
Circular reasoning, 158
Colons
  to introduce a quotation, 213
  in magazine numbers, 38
  outside quotation marks, 213
Comparative models, documentation, 236–248, 257–258
Comparing and contrasting
  alternating pattern, 143
  block pattern, 143
  for critical reading, 92–93
  sample comparison/contrast paper, 144–146
  for writing assignments, 142–146
Computer applications
  commercial databases, 46–47
  computerized indexes, 40–41
  on-line systems in library, 34–35
  use in documentation, 236
Conclusions
  of papers, 221–222
  unwarranted, 156–158
Contrasting and comparing. See Comparing and contrasting

Critical thinking
  comparing/contrasting, 92–93
  evaluating, 93–96
  paraphrasing, 86–88
  summarizing, 88–91
Current issues and popular culture reference books, 29

Dictionaries, 27
Documentation. See also Note system for sources; Parenthesis system for sources; Running acknowledgments
  note system, 249–251
  number system, 255–257
  overview of methods, 233–236
  parenthesis system, 251–255
  purpose of, 231
  use of computers in, 236
  weaving in, 214–215
  what needs documenting, 232–233
Drafts, 205–206
  rough, 223–225
Drama reference books, 29

Economics reference books, 29
Editing, 223
Editorial Research Reports, 45
Education reference books, 29
Ellipsis for omitting words in quotations, 177–178, 212
Elshtain, Jean Bethke, 304–311
Encyclopedia of Associations, 68
Encyclopedias
  bibliography cards for, 25–26
  documentation for, 244–245
  reasons for using, 27
  specialized, 28–33
Environment reference books, 29
Errors, logical, 155–158
Essays, 207
  documentation for, 241
Evaluating, 93–96
  illustrated, 95–96, 168–171
Evidence, 147, 155–156
Expressions, transitional, 215–218

Facts, 94–95, 110
"Facts about Animal Research, The" (White), 324–328
Facts on File, 45
Fallacies, 156–158
Feder, Kenneth L., 329–330

INDEX   333

Films
  documentation for, 246
  reference books on, 29
Firsthand information, benefits of, 65–66
Foreign relations reference books, 29
Format, two basic, 3
Formatting
  APA system, 253–254
  MLA system, 251–252
  note system, 249–250
Gallup Poll Reports, 45
Gardner, Marilyn, 166–167
Generalizations, 155, 208
Government publications, documentation for, 242
Guide to Reference Books (Sheehy), 30–33

Harrison, Barbara Grizzuti, 320–321
Hidden premise, 157–158
"High-Tech House Arrest" (Peck), 133–137
History reference books, 29
Hyphens in bibliographies, 250, 278, 286

Ibid., 234
Indexes
  computerized, 40–41
  one-step, 37–38
  periodical, 37–41
  two-step, 42–43
Information
  recording, with note cards, 173–188
  sources of, in libraries, 46
  telephoning for, 67
  writing letters for, 67–69
Interlibrary loan, 45–46
Interviews
  arranging, 69–70
  conducting, 69–70
  documentation for, 245
Introductions to papers, 149–150, 219–221
Isolated examples, 155
"It's (Yawn) the Natural Thing to Do" (Brotman), 5–7

Journals. *See* Articles

Labels, subject, 174–175
Lamm, Kathryn, 18
LC (Library of Congress) classification, 33–34
Lectures, documentation for, 245

Lehmann, Heinz E., 8, 51
Letters, writing, for information, 67–69
Librarians, 30
Libraries
  information sources in, 46
  using, 23
Library of Congress (LC) classification, 33–34
Library of Congress Subject Headings, 33–34
Literature reference books, 29
Logic, 146–160

Magazine articles. *See* Articles
Microfiches, 34
Million Dollar Directory, 68
Minorities and ethnic groups reference books, 30–33
MLA system
  formatting a final draft, 251–252
  illustration of, 279–286
  models of documentation, 236–248
  typing guidelines, 252
Models, comparative, use in documentation, 236–248
Modern Language Association style. *See* MLA system
Moine, Donald J., 79–83, 90–91
Music reference books, 30

National Directory of Addresses and Telephone Numbers, 68
Newspapers, 44
  documentation for, 244
New York Times, The, 44
"Nonbearing Account, A" (Perrin), 161–163
Note cards, 173. *See also* Notes; Note system for sources
  appearance of, 174–175
  for an article, 180–186
  comments on, 176
  for direct quotations, 177
  grouping, 189–190
  improving, 186–188
  necessity of, 173–174
  outlines from, 188–193
  for paraphrasing, 177
  quotations on, 177
  recording information with, 177
  revising, 186–188
  sample, 175, 179–186

INDEX

Note system for sources, 233–234
  illustration of, 266–278
  typing guidelines for, 249–251
Notes. *See also* Note cards
  sorting and organizing, 189–191
  taking, 173
Number system variation of
  parenthesis system for sources,
  235–236, 255–258

O'Neill, Molly, 312–315
Opinions, 94–95, 110
  evaluating, 94–95
  surveying, 71
Outlines
  making, 191
  mechanics for, 128, 191–192
  from note cards, 188–191
  parallelism in, 192
  provisional, 188–189
  rearranging parts of, 224–225
  for research papers, 188–193
  sample, 192–193, 265
  sentence, 128–129, 192
  short topic, 139, 193–194
  in writing summaries, 128–129, 139

Page/pages, abbreviations for, 248
Painting reference books, 30
Pamphlets, documentation for, 242
Papers
  argumentative (*see* Argument)
  conclusions for, 221–222
  introductions to, 149–150, 219–221
  reaction (*see* Reaction papers)
  readability of, 223
  titles of, 222
Paragraphs, 206–209
  typical, 208
Parallelism in outlines, 192
Paraphrasing, 86–88, 130–131
  note cards for, 177
  with running acknowledgments, 209–210, 212–213
Parenthesis system for sources, 233–235
  APA system variation of (*see* APA system)
  MLA system variation of (*see* MLA system)
  Number system variation of (*see* Number system)
Park, Michael Alan, 329–330
Peck, Keenen, 133–137

Performance, live, documentation for, 246
Periodicals. *See* Articles
Perrin, Noel, 161–163
Philosophy reference books, 30
Photography reference books, 30
Plagiarism, 178–179
Poems, documentation for, 241
Post-reading, 85–86
Precis, 127
Premises, hidden, 157–158
Pre-reading, 75–76
Programs, radio or television, documentation for, 247
Proposal, 107, 114–115
Psychology reference books, 30
Public meetings or events, 69
Punctuation, of quotations, 213–214
Purpose in writing, 129–130, 139

Question marks, quotation marks and, 213
Questionnaires, 71
Questions
  asking, 15
  kinds of, in interviews, 70
  kinds of, to avoid, 18
  objective and unbiased, 18
  research, developing, 15–18
  trigger, 112–115
Quotation marks
  in avoiding plagiarism, 177
  double, 213
  double quotes, quotes inside, 213
  punctuation inside and outside, 213
  single, 213
  for subjects in encyclopedias, 25
  for titles of articles, 42
Quotations
  block form, 214
  changes in, 177, 212
  identifying, in parenthesis system for sources, 233–235
  long, placing, 214
  on note cards, 179–180
  omitting words in, 177–178
  punctuating, 213–214
  review of, 177
  with running acknowledgments, 209, 212
  using, 138

Reaction papers, 154–171
  sample, 168–171
  writing, 154–160

INDEX

Readability of papers, 223
Readers' Guide to Periodical Literature, The, 15, 37–39
Reading
  active, 77–85
  critical, 75–96
  post-reading, 85–86
  pre-reading, 75–76
  techniques for difficult material, 83–85
Reasoning, 155–158
Records, documentation for, 246
References
  APA system for, 155
  illustration of, 298–299
  in number system, 256–257
Reference works, 26–33
  specialized, 28–33
Reports, 2, 13
Reviews of books. *See* Book reviews
Revising, 223–235
Roman numerals, 191
Rosenberger, Jack, 181–186
Running acknowledgments, 209–213
  phrases to use, 210
  placing, in a sentence, 211

Sample papers
  argumentative, 151–154
  comparison/contrast, 144–146
  proposal, 115–117
  reaction paper, 168–171
  research paper, note system, 266–278
  research paper, parenthesis system (APA), 287–299
  research paper, parenthesis system (MLA), 279–286
  statement of intent, 112–114
  summary, 140–141
Schedule, 13–14
Science reference books, 30
Semicolons outside quotation marks, 213
Sentences, 207
  acknowledging sources in, 213
  complete, for thesis, 110–111
  thesis (*see* Thesis statements)
  topic, 207–208
Sheehy, Eugene P., 30–33
Sources, 1
  academic reputation of, 47–48
  acknowledging, 209–213
  acknowledging, phrases in, 210
  acknowledging in sentences, 211
  documenting, 231–258
  incorporating and, 209–213
  note system (*see* Note system for sources)
  parenthesis system for (*see* Parenthesis system for sources)
Statement of intent, 107, 111–114
Strategy
  for reading difficult material, 83–85
  for reading in general, 75–76
  for research, 46
Style, sense of, 205–206
Subject cards, 34
Subject headings (LC), 33–34
Subject labels, 174–175
Suggestions for possible topics, 14–18
Summaries, 127–131
  checklist for, 131
  sample, 140–141
  writing, 128–131
Summarizing, 88–90
  illustrated, 90–91
Support points for arguments, 148–149
Surveys of opinions, 71

Telephoning for information, 67
"Tell Us How You Feel about This Issue" (*Glamour*), 72
10,000 Ideas for Term Papers, Projects, and Reports (Lamm), 18
Theology and religion reference books, 30
Theses, 2, 14
Thesis
  complete sentence for, 110, 129
  defined, 77, 108–109
  provisional outline and, 188
  strategies for developing a tentative, 109
Thesis statements, 207
  guidelines for, 110–111
  negative, 168
  positive, 168
Title cards, 34
Titles
  of articles, 42
  of magazines, underlining, 42
  of papers, 222
Topics
  to avoid, 18
  identifying, suggestions for, 14–18
Topic sentences, 207–208
"To Trust, Perchance to Buy" (Moine), 79–83, 90–91

Transitions, providing, 215–218
Translations of books, documentation for, 240
Typing guidelines
　for APA system, 254–255
　for MLA system, 252
　for note system, 250–251

Underlining
　names of encyclopedias, 25
　titles of books, 36
　titles of magazines, 42

Vocabulary, 83–84
Volume numbers, colons in, 38

Walker, Alice, 316–319
"What's Wrong with Animal Rights?" (Grizzuti), 320–321
White, Robert J., 324–328
Who's Who, 68
"Whose Life Is It, Anyway?" (Rosenberger), 181–186
"Why Worry about the Animals?" (Elshtain), 304–311
Women's studies reference books, 30
Words
　choice of, 205–206
　omitting, in quotations, 177–178, 212

"Yawning: A Homeostatic Reflect and Its Psychological Significance" (Lehmann), 8, 51

Zoology reference books, 30